You're Golden, Charlie Brown

You're Golden, Charlie Brown

Charles M. Schulz

Ballantine Books
New York

A Ballantine Books Trade Paperback Original

Published in the United States by Ballantine Books,
an imprint of Random House, a division
of Penguin Random House LLC, New York.

BALLANTINE and the HOUSE colophon are registered trademarks
of Penguin Random House LLC.

The comic strips in this book were originally published in newspapers worldwide.

ISBN 978-0-8041-7949-2
eBook ISBN 978-0-8041-7950-8

Printed in the United States of America on acid-free paper

www.ballantinebooks.com

2 4 6 8 9 7 5 3 1

Book design by Donna Sinisgalli

You're Golden, Charlie Brown

I HATE THIS YEAR!
© 1986 Peanuts Worldwide LLC. Dist. by Universal Uclick
EVERYONE SAID THINGS WOULD BE BETTER, BUT THEY'RE NOT!
www.snoopy.com
I DON'T THINK THIS IS A NEW YEAR AT ALL...
I THINK WE'VE BEEN STUCK WITH A USED YEAR!!
1-2
SCHULZ

WHAT GRADE DID YOU GET ON YOUR BOOK REPORT, CHARLIE BROWN?
www.snoopy.com
"D MINUS"! THAT'S AS LOW AS YOU CAN GET WITHOUT FAILING!
1-3
© 1965 Peanuts Worldwide LLC, Dist. by Universal Uclick
THE TEACHER SAID IT LOOKED LIKE THE SORT OF REPORT THAT WAS WRITTEN AFTER MIDNIGHT ON THE LAST DAY OF CHRISTMAS VACATION
WHAT COULD I SAY? I CONGRATULATED HER ON HER REMARKABLE PERCEPTIVITY!
SCHULZ

www.snoopy.com
ALL RIGHT! CUT IT OUT!
© 1986 Peanuts Worldwide LLC, Dist. by Universal Uclick
I ALWAYS THOUGHT MAKING SNOWMEN WAS SUPPOSED TO BE FUN..
1-9
SCHULZ

1-10
www.snoopy.com
© 1966 Peanuts Worldwide LLC, Dist. by Universal Uclick
SCHULZ

HA! YOU MISSED AGAIN!
YOU GUYS AREN'T ORGANIZED! YOU HAVE NO TEAMWORK!
YOU'LL NEVER HIT ME BECAUSE YOU CAN'T ALL THROW TOGETHER!
1-11
www.snoopy.com
© 1966 Peanuts Worldwide LLC, Dist. by Universal Uclick
SCHULZ

WELL, DON'T JUST STAND THERE... GO GET A SHOVEL, AND HELP ME!
1-18
www.snoopy.com
© 1966 Peanuts Worldwide LLC, Dist. by Universal Uclick
SCHULZ

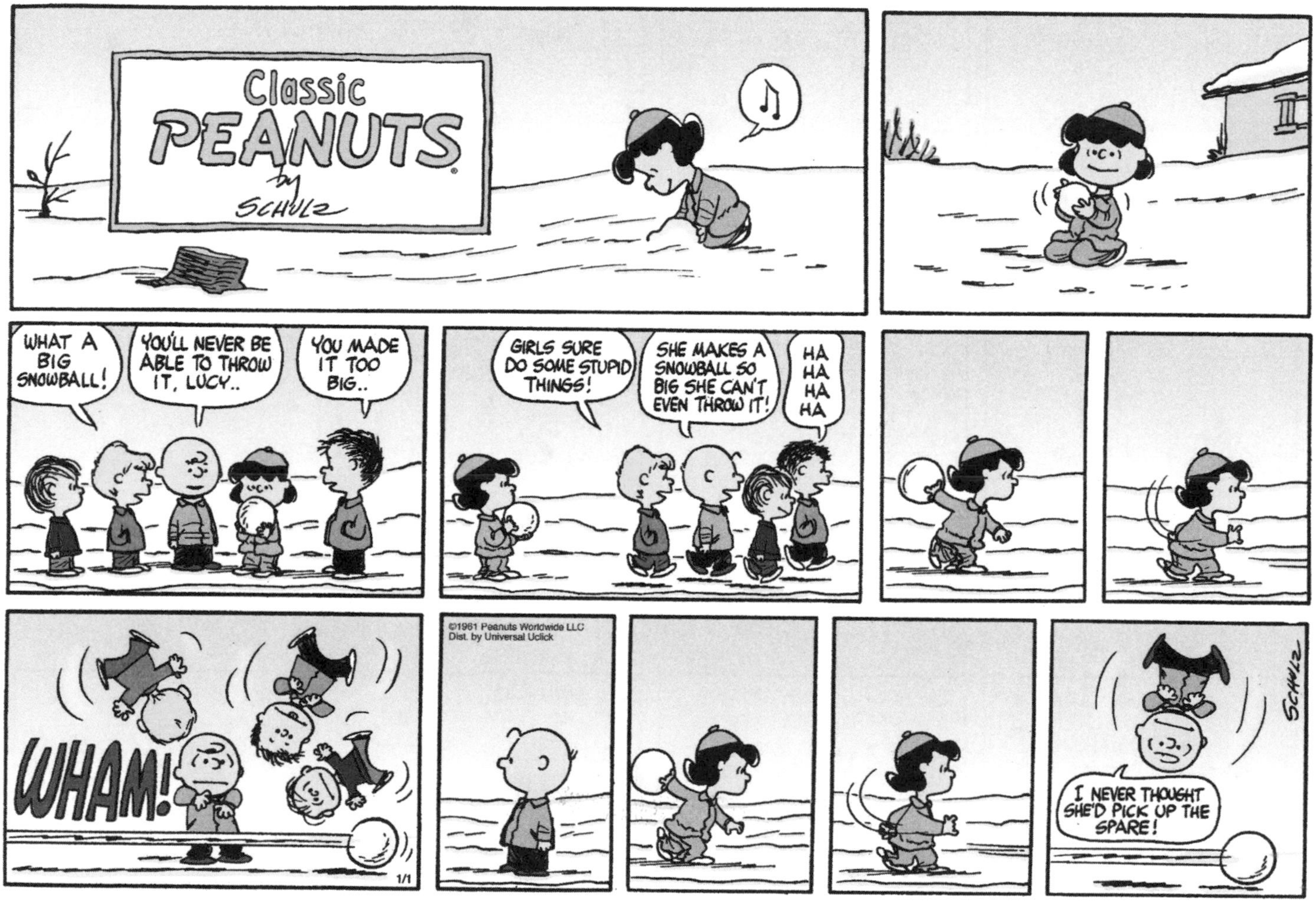
Classic PEANUTS by SCHULZ
♫
WHAT A BIG SNOWBALL!
YOU'LL NEVER BE ABLE TO THROW IT, LUCY..
YOU MADE IT TOO BIG..
GIRLS SURE DO SOME STUPID THINGS!
SHE MAKES A SNOWBALL SO BIG SHE CAN'T EVEN THROW IT!
HA HA HA HA
WHAM!
1/1
©1961 Peanuts Worldwide LLC
Dist. by Universal Uclick
I NEVER THOUGHT SHE'D PICK UP THE SPARE!
SCHULZ

SHOVEL YOUR WALK ?
YOU MEAN FOR MONEY?
YES, I DON'T HAVE ANY USE FOR BEADS!
SLAM!
I GUESS A GOOD BUSINESSMAN CAN'T AFFORD TO BE SARCASTIC...
1-15
www.snoopy.com
© 1966 Peanuts Worldwide LLC. Dist. by Universal Uclick
SCHULZ

SHOVEL YOUR WALK ?
ARE YOU TRYING TO TAKE ADVANTAGE OF OUR MISFORTUNE? OUR SIDEWALK IS COVERED WITH SNOW THROUGH NO FAULT OF OURS, AND YOU WANT TO PROFIT BY THIS TERRIBLE MISFORTUNE?
I THINK THAT'S DISGRACEFUL, CHARLIE BROWN!
FROM NOW ON, EVERY TIME IT SNOWS, I'LL FEEL GUILTY!
1-16
www.snoopy.com
© 1966 Peanuts Worldwide LLC. Dist. by Universal Uclick
SCHULZ

ASK YOUR MOTHER IF SHE WANTS HER SIDEWALK SHOVELED
TELL HER I'LL DO IT FOR ONLY EIGHTY-FIVE DOLLARS!
SHE SAYS SHE'LL GIVE YOU FIFTY CENTS...
IT'S A DEAL!
I'M NOT MUCH FOR HAGGLING..
1-17
www.snoopy.com
© 1966 Peanuts Worldwide LLC. Dist. by Universal Uclick
SCHULZ

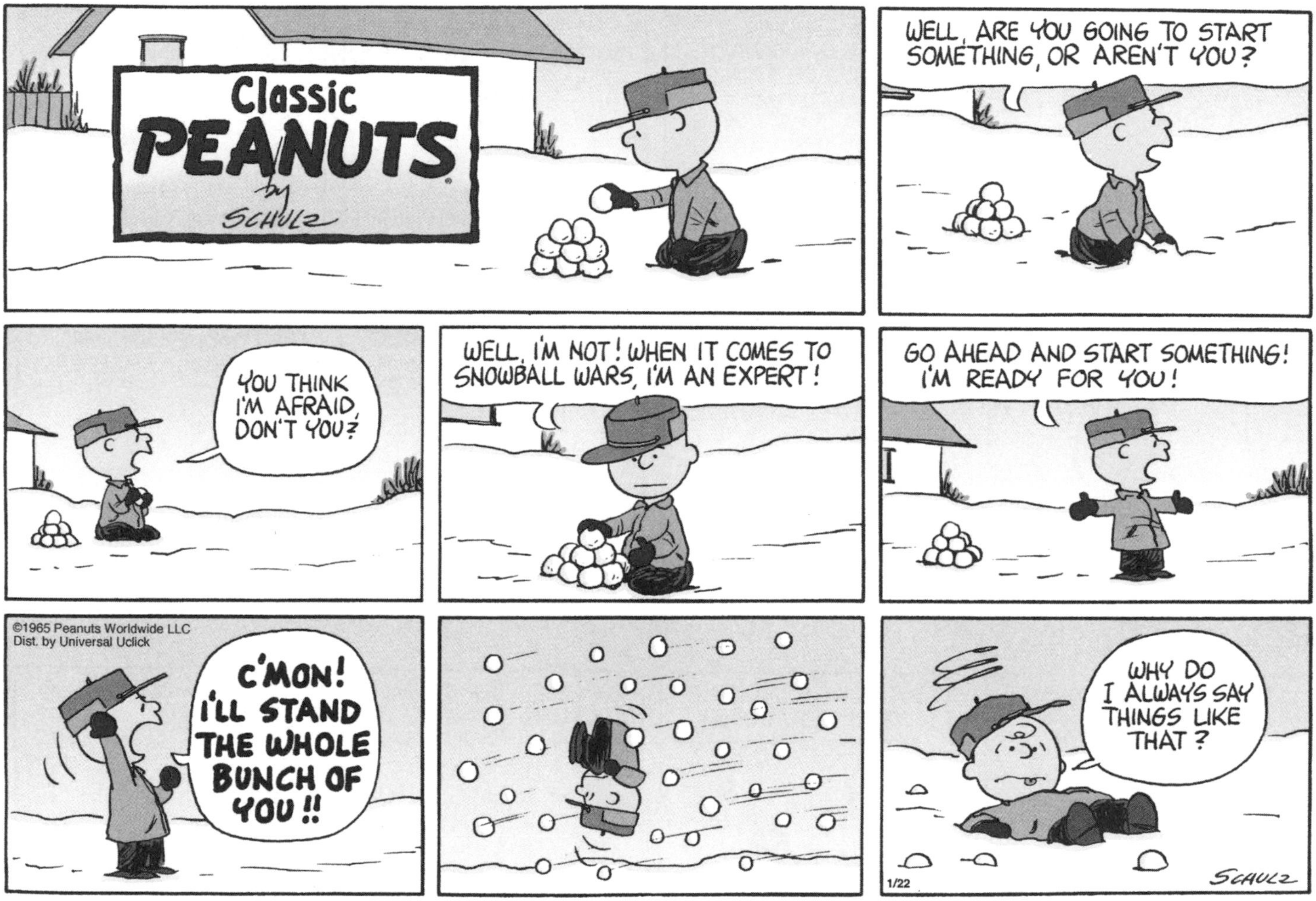
Classic PEANUTS by SCHULZ
WELL, ARE YOU GOING TO START SOMETHING, OR AREN'T YOU?
YOU THINK I'M AFRAID, DON'T YOU?
WELL, I'M NOT! WHEN IT COMES TO SNOWBALL WARS, I'M AN EXPERT!
GO AHEAD AND START SOMETHING! I'M READY FOR YOU!
©1965 Peanuts Worldwide LLC
Dist. by Universal Uclick
C'MON! I'LL STAND THE WHOLE BUNCH OF YOU!!
WHY DO I ALWAYS SAY THINGS LIKE THAT?
1/22
SCHULZ

MY POOR OL' PITCHER'S MOUND IS COVERED WITH SNOW..

STANDING HERE, A FLOOD OF MEMORIES COMES POURING OVER ME...SCENE AFTER SCENE FLASHES THROUGH MY MIND... ALL THE GAMES WE'VE PLAYED...

I CAN REMEMBER EVERY GAME... EVERY INNING...EVERY PITCH... EVERY STOLEN BASE...EVERY CATCH...EVERY HIT.....

1-19

I CAN EVEN REMEMBER THE DAY WE SCORED OUR RUN ...

© 1966 Peanuts Worldwide LLC, Dist. by Universal Uclick

SCHULZ

OUR TEACHER, MISS OTHMAR, STAYED HOME TODAY...

YESTERDAY, WE HAD TO BRING MILK MONEY ENVELOPES, CLASS PICTURE MONEY ENVELOPES, PTA MONEY ENVELOPES AND HOT DOG MONEY ENVELOPES...

1-17

THIRTY KIDS BRINGING FOUR ENVELOPES EACH MAKES ONE HUNDRED AND TWENTY ENVELOPES.. POOR MISS OTHMAR...

SHE CRACKED UP... SHE WENT "ENVELOPE HAPPY"!

SCHULZ

© 1965 Peanuts Worldwide LLC, Dist. by Universal Uclick

MISS OTHMAR CAME BACK TO SCHOOL TODAY, BUT SHE DIDN'T LAST VERY LONG..

SEVEN KIDS HAD ABSENCE EXCUSES IN ENVELOPES...

TWENTY-EIGHT OTHERS BROUGHT BACK VACCINATION NOTICES WHICH THEIR PARENTS HAD SIGNED..... POOR MISS OTHMAR...

1-19

THAT'S THE FIRST TIME I'VE EVER SEEN A TEACHER CRAWL RIGHT UP THE CHALKBOARD!

SCHULZ

© 1965 Peanuts Worldwide LLC, Dist. by Universal Uclick

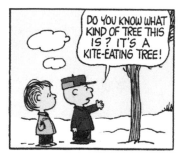

DO YOU KNOW WHAT KIND OF TREE THIS IS? IT'S A KITE-EATING TREE!
LAST YEAR IT ATE TWENTY-FOUR OF MY KITES! IT JUST REACHED OUT AND GRABBED THEM WITH ITS GREEDY BRANCHES, AND THEN IT STOOD THERE AND ATE THEM...
1-21
© 1967 Peanuts Worldwide LLC, Dist. by Universal Uclick
BE CAREFUL! DON'T GET TOO CLOSE!
www.snoopy.com
AFTER A LONG WINTER WITHOUT ANY KITES, IT CAN GET PRETTY MEAN!
SCHULZ

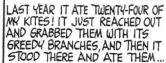

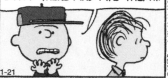

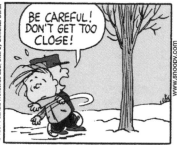

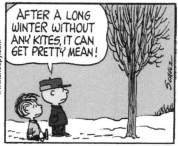

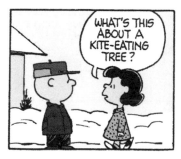

WHAT'S THIS ABOUT A KITE-EATING TREE?
HAVE YOU EVER SEEN A KITE IN A TREE? HAVE YOU NOTICED HOW IT HANGS THERE FOR WEEKS?
1-22
© 1967 Peanuts Worldwide LLC, Dist. by Universal Uclick
THEN, SUDDENLY, ONE DAY IT'S GONE!
www.snoopy.com
THIS TREE EATS KITES!!
SCHULZ

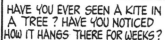

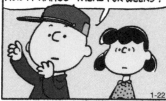

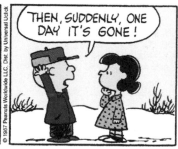

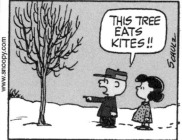

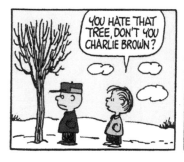

YOU HATE THAT TREE, DON'T YOU CHARLIE BROWN?
IT'S A KITE-EATING TREE, AND I HATE IT!
© 1967 Peanuts Worldwide LLC, Dist. by Universal Uclick
YOU KNOW WHY I HATE IT? BECAUSE IT'S GREEDY, THAT'S WHY! EVEN WHILE IT HAS A KITE IN ITS BRANCHES, IT'LL REACH OUT AND GRAB ANOTHER ONE! IT'S LIKE A LITTLE KID EATING FRENCH FRIES
1-23
www.snoopy.com
YOU DIRTY KITE-EATING TREE!
WHEN CHARLIE BROWN HATES SOMETHING, HE REALLY HATES IT!
SCHULZ

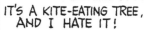

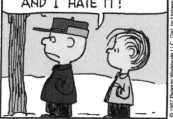

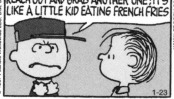

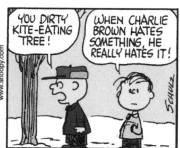

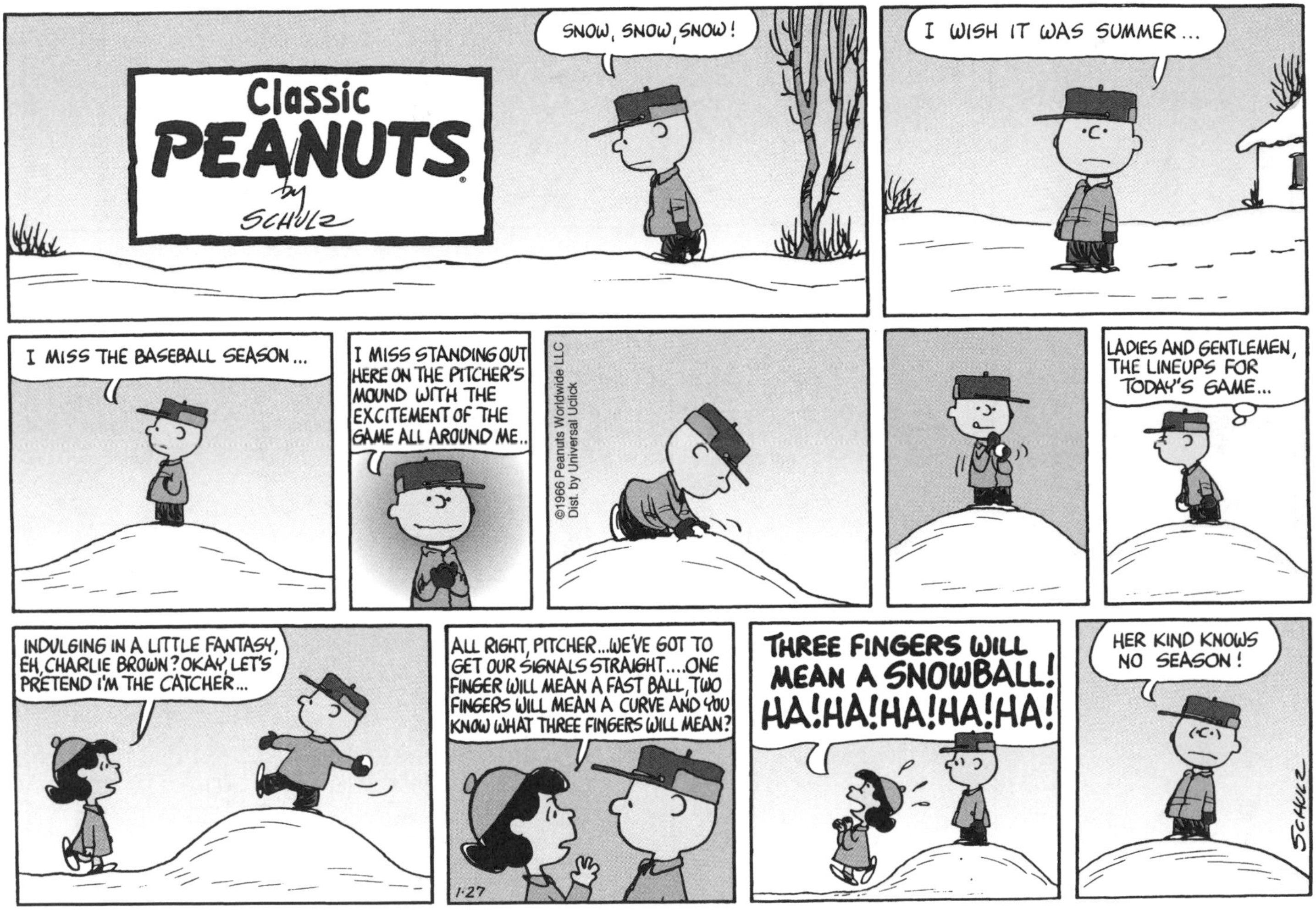
Classic PEANUTS by SCHULZ
SNOW, SNOW, SNOW!
I WISH IT WAS SUMMER...
I MISS THE BASEBALL SEASON...
I MISS STANDING OUT HERE ON THE PITCHER'S MOUND WITH THE EXCITEMENT OF THE GAME ALL AROUND ME..
©1966 Peanuts Worldwide LLC
Dist. by Universal Uclick
LADIES AND GENTLEMEN, THE LINEUPS FOR TODAY'S GAME...
INDULGING IN A LITTLE FANTASY, EH, CHARLIE BROWN? OKAY, LET'S PRETEND I'M THE CATCHER...
ALL RIGHT, PITCHER...WE'VE GOT TO GET OUR SIGNALS STRAIGHT....ONE FINGER WILL MEAN A FAST BALL, TWO FINGERS WILL MEAN A CURVE AND YOU KNOW WHAT THREE FINGERS WILL MEAN?
1·27
THREE FINGERS WILL MEAN A SNOWBALL! HA! HA! HA! HA! HA!
HER KIND KNOWS NO SEASON!
SCHULZ

A SPELLING BEE? THEY'RE GOING TO HAVE A CITY-WIDE SPELLING BEE?
www.snoopy.com
1-30
I SHOULD ENTER IT...THAT'S THE SORT OF THING I NEED TO DO TO GAIN CONFIDENCE AND SELF-ESTEEM...
I THINK I'LL RAISE MY HAND AND VOLUNTEER...IT'LL BE GOOD FOR ME...I THINK I'LL JUST RAISE MY HAND AND VOLUNTEER...
© 1966 Peanuts Worldwide LLC, Dist. by Universal Uclick
MY HAND WON'T GO UP...IT'S SMARTER THAN I AM!
SCHULZ

YOU? YOU'RE GOING TO ENTER THE CITY-WIDE SPELLING BEE? YOU?
www.snoopy.com
1-31
OH, BROTHER!
WELL, WHAT'S WRONG? WHAT'S WRONG WITH TRYING?!
I CAN TRY, CAN'T I? WHAT'S THE GOOD OF LIVING IF YOU DON'T TRY A FEW THINGS?
© 1966 Peanuts Worldwide LLC, Dist. by Universal Uclick
SPELL "ACETYLCHOLINESTERASE"
MAYBE I SHOULDN'T ENTER...
SCHULZ

YES, MA'AM... I'D LIKE TO BE IN THE SPELLING BEE...
www.snoopy.com
PSST...YOU'RE CRAZY...DON'T DO IT...YOU'LL JUST MAKE A FOOL OUT OF YOURSELF...
I WILL NOT!
2-1
© 1966 Peanuts Worldwide LLC, Dist. by Universal Uclick
EXCUSE ME, MA'AM...I WAS ANSWERING ONE OF MY MANY DETRACTORS...
SCHULZ

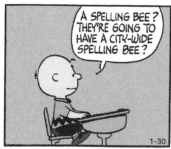

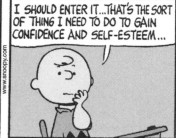

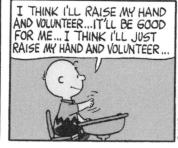

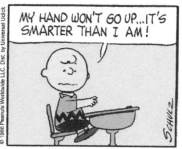

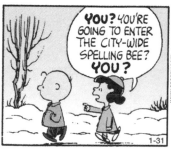

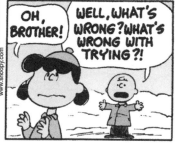

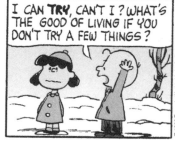

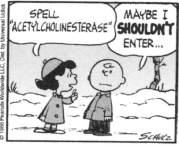

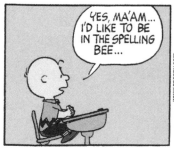

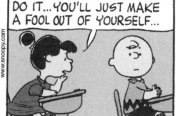

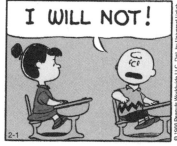

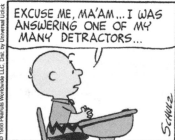

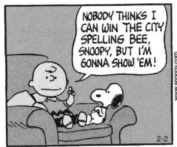

NOBODY THINKS I CAN WIN THE CITY SPELLING BEE, SNOOPY, BUT I'M GONNA SHOW 'EM!
2-2
www.snoopy.com
I NOT ONLY KNOW A LOT OF HARD WORDS, BUT I KNOW EVERY SPELLING RULE IN THE BOOK...
THE ONLY ONE I HAVE TROUBLE REMEMBERING IS, "I BEFORE E EXCEPT AFTER D".....OR IS IT, "E BEFORE I EXCEPT AFTER G"?
© 1966 Peanuts Worldwide LLC, Dist. by Universal Uclick
"I BEFORE B EXCEPT AFTER T"? "V BEFORE Z EXCEPT AFTER E"?
GOOD GRIEF!
SCHULZ

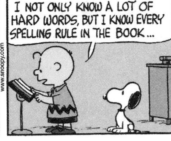

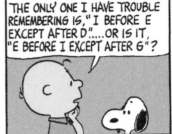

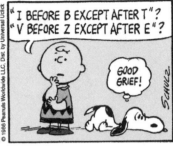

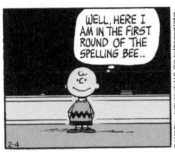

WELL, HERE I AM IN THE FIRST ROUND OF THE SPELLING BEE..
2-4
© 1966 Peanuts Worldwide LLC, Dist. by Universal Uclick
I'VE GOT TO STAY CALM AND NOT GET RATTLED...THIS IS MY BIG CHANCE TO PROVE TO EVERYONE THAT I CAN DO SOMETHING!
www.snoopy.com
I DON'T CARE IF I DON'T ACTUALLY WIN..ALL I WANT IS TO GET PAST THE FIRST FEW ROUNDS, AND MAKE A DECENT SHOWING...LET'S SEE NOW...HOW DOES THAT RULE GO?
"E BEFORE I EXCEPT AFTER G" NO, THAT'S NOT RIGHT.."I BEFORE G EXCEPT AFTER.." NO..."C BEFORE E EXCEPT...EXCEPT."...HMMM.....
SCHULZ

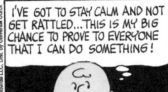

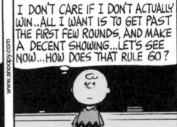

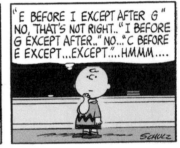

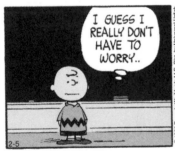

I GUESS I REALLY DON'T HAVE TO WORRY..
2-5
© 1966 Peanuts Worldwide LLC, Dist. by Universal Uclick
ALL THE WORDS IN THE FIRST ROUND OF A SPELLING BEE USUALLY ARE QUITE EASY... THAT KID SURE GOT AN EASY ONE...
www.snoopy.com
IN A WAY, I'D ALMOST LIKE TO START OFF WITH A HARD ONE.. YOU KNOW, TO KIND OF SHAKE UP THE OTHER KIDS...TO SORT OF LET THEM SEE WHO THEY'RE UP AGAINST
I FEEL STRANGELY CALM..
SCHULZ

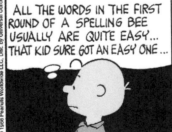

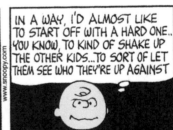

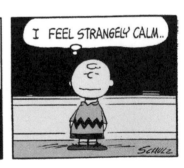

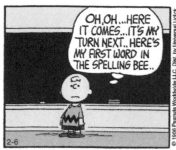

OH, OH...HERE IT COMES...IT'S MY TURN NEXT.. HERE'S MY FIRST WORD IN THE SPELLING BEE..
"MAZE"? YES, MA'AM... THAT'S AN EASY ONE...
M...A...Y...S....
AAUGH!
2-6
© 1956 Peanuts Worldwide LLC, Dist. by Universal Uclick
www.snoopy.com
SCHULZ

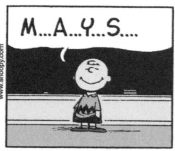

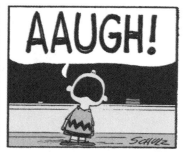

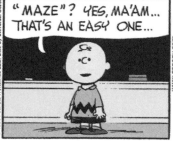

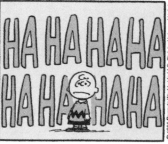

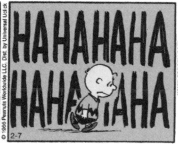

HA HA HA HA HA HA HA HA HA HA
HAHAHAHA HAHAHAHA
HAHAH
I TOLD YOU YOU'D MAKE A FOOL OUT OF YOURSELF..
A COMFORTING WORD FROM A FRIEND!
2-7
© 1956 Peanuts Worldwide LLC, Dist. by Universal Uclick
www.snoopy.com
SCHULZ

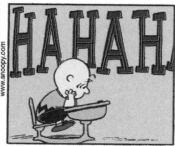

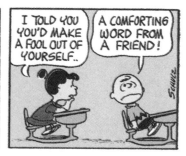

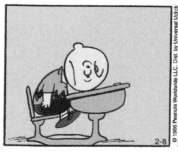

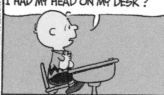

YES, MA'AM? ME? WHY DID I HAVE MY HEAD ON MY DESK? YOU DON'T KNOW? YOU'RE ASKING ME WHY I HAD MY HEAD ON MY DESK?
BECAUSE I BLEW THE STUPID SPELLING BEE, THAT'S WHY!!!
OH, GOOD GRIEF! NOW, I'VE DONE IT!
2-8
© 1956 Peanuts Worldwide LLC, Dist. by Universal Uclick
www.snoopy.com
SCHULZ

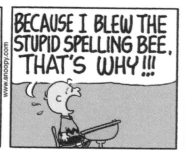

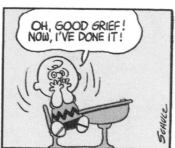

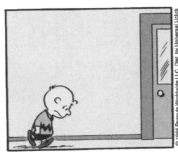

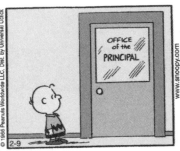

© 1966 Peanuts Worldwide LLC, Dist. by Universal Uclick
2-9
OFFICE of the PRINCIPAL
www.snoopy.com
"PLEAD MY CAUSE, O LORD, WITH THEM THAT STRIVE WITH ME: FIGHT AGAINST THEM THAT FIGHT AGAINST ME...DELIVER ME FROM THE HAND OF THEM THAT PERSECUTE ME.."
OFFICE of the PRINCIPAL
MY STOMACH HURTS!
OFFICE of the PRINCIPAL
SCHULZ

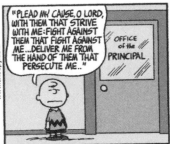

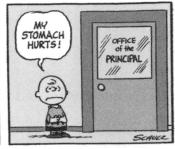

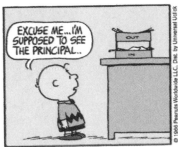

EXCUSE ME...I'M SUPPOSED TO SEE THE PRINCIPAL..
OUT
IN
© 1966 Peanuts Worldwide LLC, Dist. by Universal Uclick
2-11
WHAT ABOUT? WELL, MY TEACHER SENT ME IN...I GUESS I YELLED AT HER..
www.snoopy.com
I DIDN'T MEAN TO YELL AT HER..I WAS SORT OF UPSET AT THE TIME, AND...WELL...
NOW I'M SUPPOSED TO SEE THE PRINCIPAL..
SCHULZ

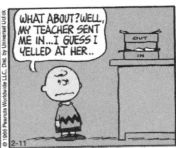

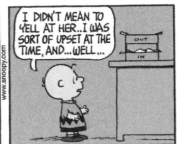

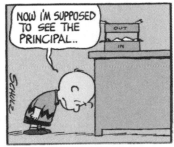

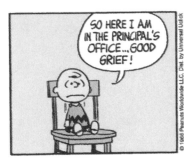

SO HERE I AM IN THE PRINCIPAL'S OFFICE...GOOD GRIEF!
© 1966 Peanuts Worldwide LLC, Dist. by Universal Uclick
2-12
THIS NEVER WOULD HAVE HAPPENED IF I HADN'T GOOFED UP THAT STUPID SPELLING BEE..
www.snoopy.com
WHEN THE TEACHER SAID FOR ME TO SPELL "MAZE," THE FIRST THING THAT CAME TO MY MIND WAS WILLIE MAYS....OH, WELL...
MAYBE SOMEDAY AFTER I'M GROWN UP, I'LL MEET WILLIE MAYS, AND I'LL TELL HIM WHAT HAPPENED, AND WE'LL HAVE A GOOD LAUGH TOGETHER
SCHULZ

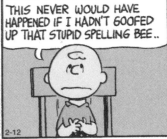

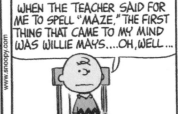

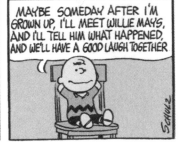

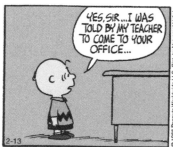

YES, SIR...I WAS TOLD BY MY TEACHER TO COME TO YOUR OFFICE...
2-13
© 1966 Peanuts Worldwide LLC. Dist. by Universal Uclick
NO, I'VE NEVER BEEN HERE BEFORE.. I'VE NEVER DONE ANYTHING REALLY WRONG BEFORE......
www.snoopy.com
YOU HAVE A NICE OFFICE..
HOW ARE YOU AND THE P.T.A. GETTING ALONG?
SCHULZ

WHAT DO I THINK MY FATHER WILL SAY?!
NO, SIR, I DON'T THINK IT WAS RIGHT TO YELL AT MRS. DONOVAN, MY TEACHER..
2-14
© 1966 Peanuts Worldwide LLC. Dist. by Universal Uclick
WELL, SIR, HE'S A VERY UNDERSTANDING PERSON...I REALLY THINK THAT WHEN I EXPLAIN THE WHOLE STORY, HE'LL UNDERSTAND...HE WON'T CONDEMN ME...
www.snoopy.com
HE'S LEARNED A LOT ABOUT PEOPLE IN HIS BARBER SHOP, AND HE KNOWS HOW THINGS SOMETIMES JUST SORT OF HAPPEN...SO I DON'T THINK HE'LL SAY MUCH...MOM IS THE SAME WAY...
I DO HAVE A FEW FRIENDS, HOWEVER, WHO MIGHT HAVE SOME THOUGHTS ON THE SUBJECT!
SCHULZ

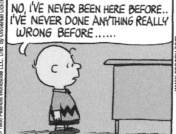

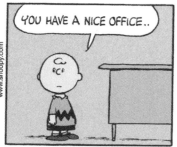

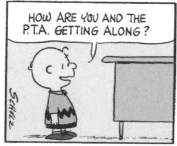

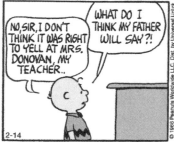

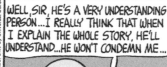

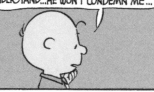

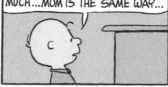

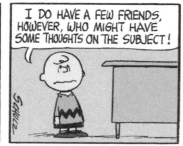

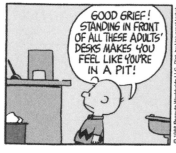

GOOD GRIEF! STANDING IN FRONT OF ALL THESE ADULTS' DESKS MAKES YOU FEEL LIKE YOU'RE IN A PIT!
© 1966 Peanuts Worldwide LLC. Dist. by Universal Uclick
MRS. DONOVAN, I WANT TO APOLOGIZE FOR YELLING AT YOU...IT WAS VERY RUDE OF ME, AND I'M SORRY...
2-15
www.snoopy.com
OH, INCIDENTALLY.... M...A...Z...E!
SCHULZ

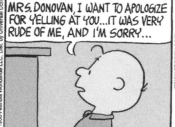

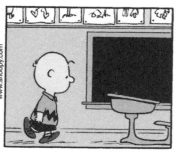

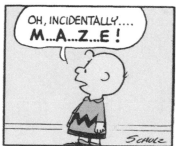

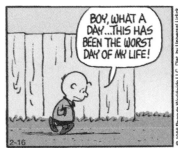

2-16
BOY, WHAT A DAY...THIS HAS BEEN THE WORST DAY OF MY LIFE!
© 1966 Peanuts Worldwide LLC. Dist. by Universal Uclick
I WOKE UP THIS MORNING LOOKING FORWARD TO THE SPELLING BEE, AND I END UP IN THE PRINCIPAL'S OFFICE.... GOOD GRIEF!
www.snoopy.com
ON A DAY LIKE THIS, A PERSON REALLY NEEDS HIS FAITHFUL DOG TO COME RUNNING OUT TO GREET HIM...
HERE'S THE WORLD WAR I PILOT IN HIS FIGHTER PLANE LOOKING FOR THE RED BARON!
SIGH
SCHULZ

1-26
LISTEN..
www.snoopy.com
DON'T YOU THINK SOME NICE MUSIC IN THE MORNING IS A GOOD WAY TO START THE DAY?
I NEVER WORRY ABOUT HOW I START THE DAY...
© 1966 Peanuts Worldwide LLC. Dist. by Universal Uclick
IT'S HOW IT ENDS UP THAT BOTHERS ME!
SCHULZ

SIGH
© 1967 Peanuts Worldwide LLC. Dist. by Universal Uclick
RE-LIVING PAST GLORIES, CHARLIE BROWN?
www.snoopy.com
YES, I'VE BEEN THINKING ABOUT THE DAY I THREW MY STRIKE!
1-31
SCHULZ

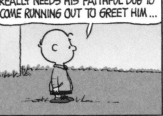

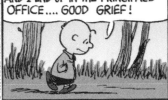

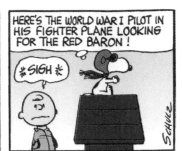

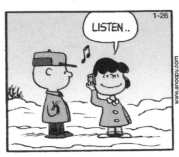

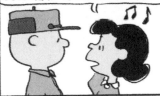

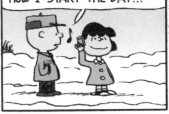

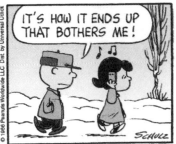

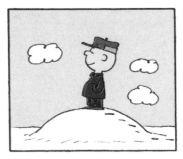

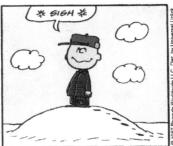

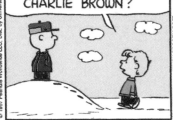

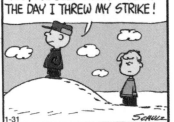

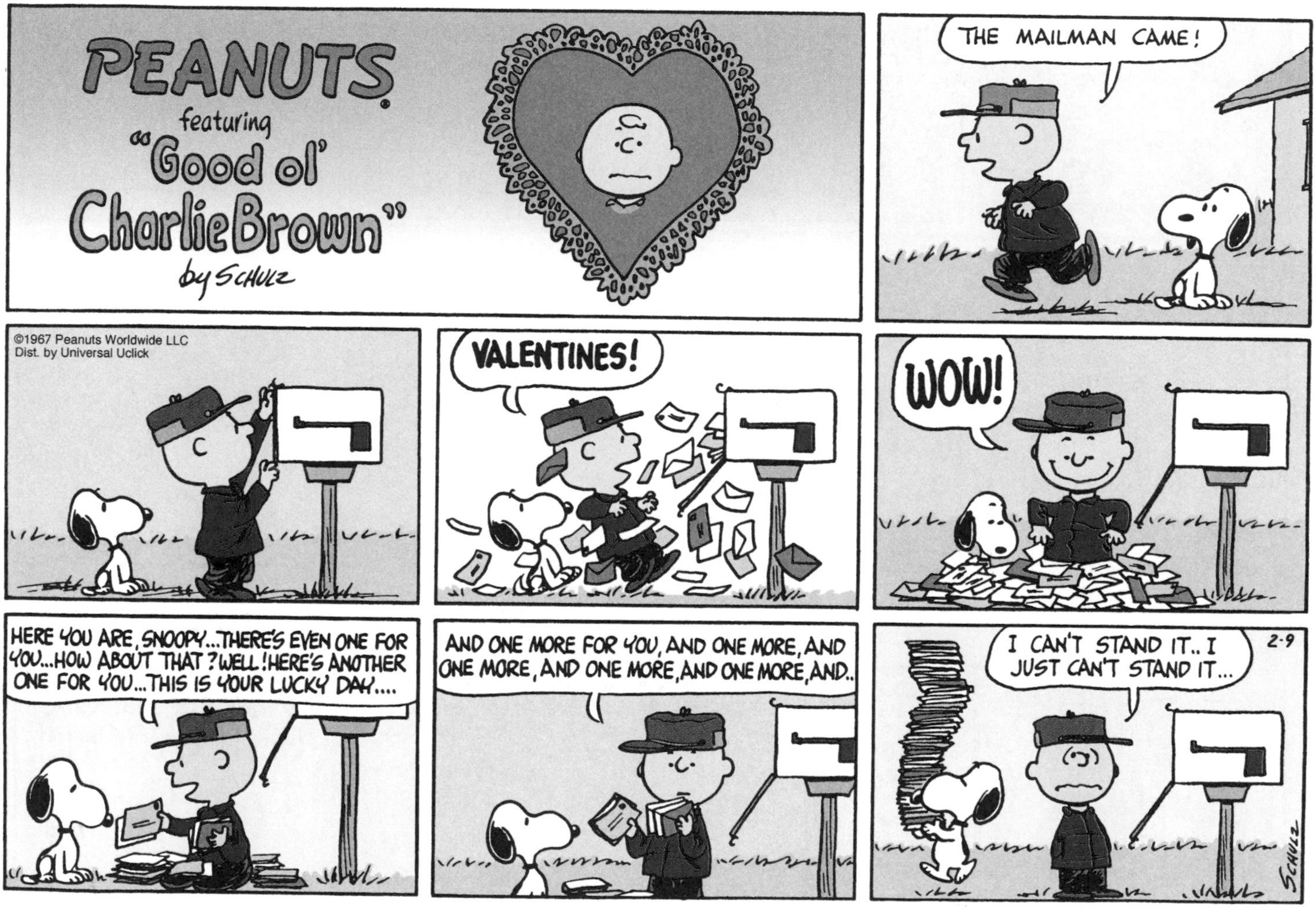
PEANUTS
featuring
"Good ol' Charlie Brown"
by SCHULZ
THE MAILMAN CAME!
©1967 Peanuts Worldwide LLC
Dist. by Universal Uclick
VALENTINES!
WOW!
HERE YOU ARE, SNOOPY...THERE'S EVEN ONE FOR YOU...HOW ABOUT THAT? WELL! HERE'S ANOTHER ONE FOR YOU...THIS IS YOUR LUCKY DAY....
AND ONE MORE FOR YOU, AND ONE MORE, AND ONE MORE, AND ONE MORE, AND ONE MORE, AND..
I CAN'T STAND IT.. I JUST CAN'T STAND IT...
2-9
SCHULZ

2-13
LOOK!
LOOK AT WHAT?
DON'T YOU KNOW WHAT THIS IS?
© 1967 Peanuts Worldwide LLC. Dist. by Universal Uclick
IT'S A CRAYON! I TOOK IT FROM SCHOOL... I'M NOT SUPPOSED TO HAVE IT! DON'T YOU UNDERSTAND?
www.snoopy.com
THEY'RE GOING TO KILL ME!!
SCHULZ

SO YOU TOOK A CRAYON FROM SCHOOL.. SO WHAT? TAKE IT BACK...
I CAN'T... I'VE BROKEN IT
WELL, CAN'T YOU EXPLAIN WHAT HAPPENED TO YOUR TEACHER? TELL HER THAT..
2-14
© 1967 Peanuts Worldwide LLC. Dist. by Universal Uclick
HER? HE'S NOT A HER! HE'S A HIM! HE'LL KILL ME! HE HATES KIDS WHO BREAK CRAYONS!
www.snoopy.com
AS SOON AS I SHOW HIM WHAT I'VE DONE, HE'LL GIVE ME A JUDO CHOP!
OH, GOOD GRIEF!
SCHULZ

ALL RIGHT, BIG BROTHER... HOW ARE YOU GOING TO HELP ME?
HELP YOU?
OF COURSE! MY TEACHER WILL KILL ME IF HE FINDS OUT I TOOK A CRAYON HOME! HE'S VERY STRICT ABOUT SUCH THINGS
2-15
© 1967 Peanuts Worldwide LLC. Dist. by Universal Uclick
NOW, WHY DON'T YOU BE A GOOD GUY AND GET ME OFF THE HOOK?
NO! IT'S YOUR PROBLEM! YOU SOLVE IT!
www.snoopy.com
I HATE YOUR GENERATION!!!
SCHULZ

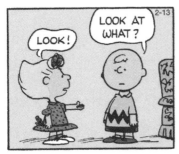

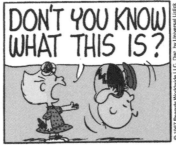

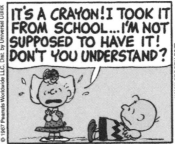

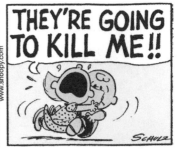

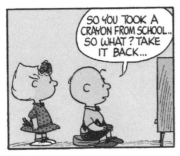

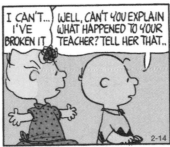

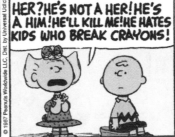

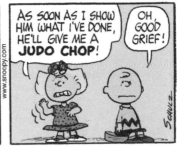

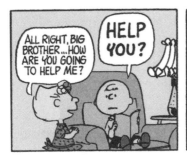

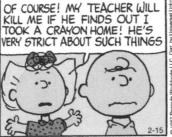

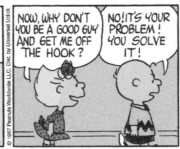

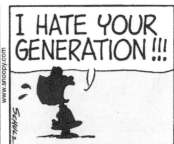

WELL, I SOLVED MY PROBLEM WITHOUT YOUR HELP, STUPID WISHY-WASHY, BIG BROTHER!
WHEN MY TEACHER ASKED ME IF I HAD TAKEN THAT CRAYON, I MERELY SAID, "NO!"
YOU MEAN YOU LIED?!
© 1967 Peanuts Worldwide LLC, Dist. by Universal Uclick
OF COURSE, I LIED! SO WHAT?
BUT THAT'S WRONG! IT'S WRONG TO LIE! IT'S ALWAYS WRONG TO LIE!
www.snoopy.com
DON'T GIVE ME ANY OF YOUR MIDDLE-CLASS MORALITY!
SCHULZ
2-17

PSYCHIATRIC HELP 5¢
THE DOCTOR IS IN
I'M HAVING TROUBLE WITH MY BABY SISTER..
SHE TOOK THIS CRAYON FROM SCHOOL, SEE, AND HER TEACHER SAID,"DID YOU TAKE A CRAYON HOME?" AND SALLY SAID,"NO, I DIDN'T TAKE A CRAYON HOME".....SHE LIED....WHAT DO YOU DO WITH A BABY SISTER WHO LIES?
2-18
© 1967 Peanuts Worldwide LLC, Dist. by Universal Uclick
THAT'S A GOOD QUESTION...NOW, I HAVE A QUESTION FOR YOU...
THE DOCTOR IS IN
www.snoopy.com
I'M THINKING OF RE-PAINTING THIS BOOTH...DO YOU THINK I SHOULD PAINT IT BLUE OR KIND OF A PALE GREEN?
SCHULZ
I CAN'T STAND IT!
THE DOCTOR

YOU'VE BEEN TELLING EVERYONE THAT I LIED TO MY TEACHER, HAVEN'T YOU?
DON'T YOU KNOW THAT PSYCHOLOGISTS SAY CHILDREN DON'T ALWAYS KNOW THAT THEY'RE LYING?! TO AN INNOCENT CHILD LIKE ME, IF A LIE WORKS, IT ISN'T A LIE! WHAT DO YOU THINK OF THAT?!
© 1967 Peanuts Worldwide LLC, Dist. by Universal Uclick
GEORGE WASHINGTON!!
2-19
www.snoopy.com
YOU'RE RIGHT! WHAA! I'LL NEVER LIE AGAIN!
I HATED TO DO IT, BUT SOME PROBLEMS CALL FOR DRASTIC ACTION...
SCHULZ

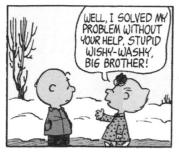

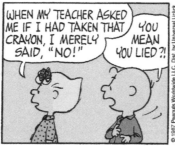

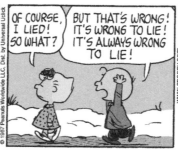

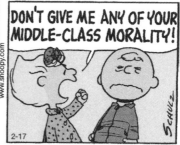

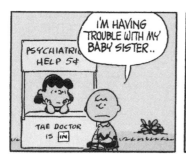

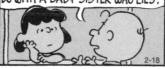

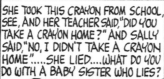

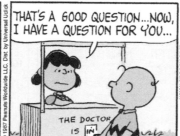

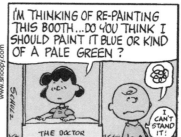

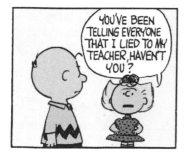

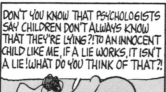

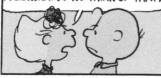

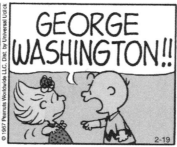

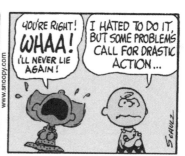

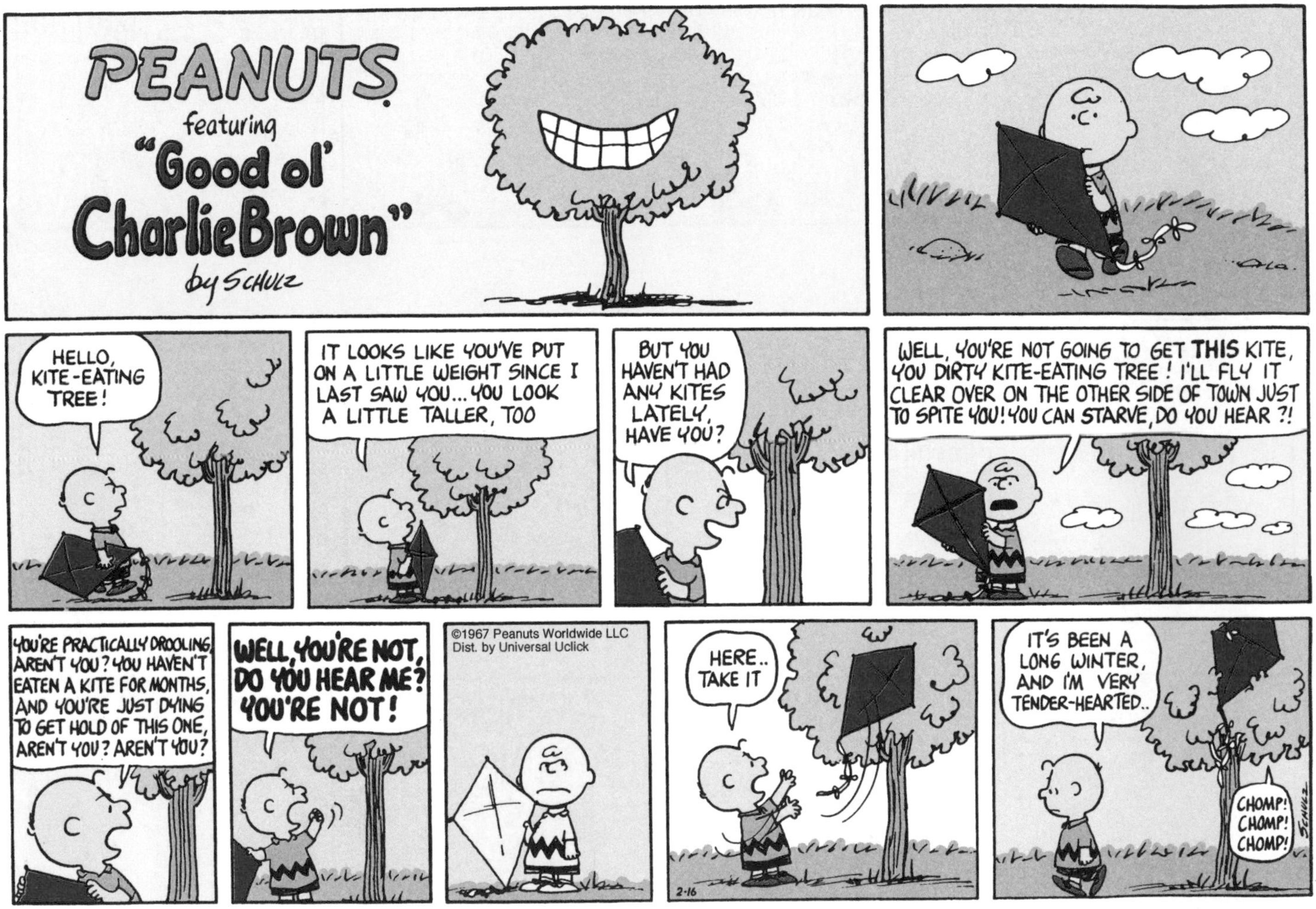
PEANUTS
featuring
"Good ol' CharlieBrown"
by SCHULZ
HELLO, KITE-EATING TREE!
IT LOOKS LIKE YOU'VE PUT ON A LITTLE WEIGHT SINCE I LAST SAW YOU... YOU LOOK A LITTLE TALLER, TOO
BUT YOU HAVEN'T HAD ANY KITES LATELY, HAVE YOU?
WELL, YOU'RE NOT GOING TO GET THIS KITE, YOU DIRTY KITE-EATING TREE! I'LL FLY IT CLEAR OVER ON THE OTHER SIDE OF TOWN JUST TO SPITE YOU! YOU CAN STARVE, DO YOU HEAR ?!
YOU'RE PRACTICALLY DROOLING, AREN'T YOU? YOU HAVEN'T EATEN A KITE FOR MONTHS, AND YOU'RE JUST DYING TO GET HOLD OF THIS ONE, AREN'T YOU? AREN'T YOU?
WELL, YOU'RE NOT, DO YOU HEAR ME? YOU'RE NOT!
©1967 Peanuts Worldwide LLC
Dist. by Universal Uclick
HERE.. TAKE IT
2-16
IT'S BEEN A LONG WINTER, AND I'M VERY TENDER-HEARTED..
CHOMP! CHOMP! CHOMP!
SCHULZ

YOU WANT TO "ARM WRESTLE" ME? YOU MUST BE CRAZY!
2-3
NOBODY BEATS OL' CHARLIE BROWN AT "ARM WRESTLING"!
OH?
© 1967 Peanuts Worldwide LLC. Dist. by Universal Uclick
WHAM!
www.snoopy.com
SHE DIDN'T BEAT MY ARM... SHE BEAT MY WHOLE BODY!
SCHULZ

..AND BESIDES, NEVER FORGET THAT BEAUTY IS ONLY SKIN DEEP!
© 1965 Peanuts Worldwide LLC. Dist. by Universal Uclick
I DENY THAT! MY BEAUTY IS NOT ONLY ON THE SURFACE, IT GOES DOWN DEEP...LAYER AFTER LAYER AFTER LAYER!
2-10
www.snoopy.com
YES, SIR!
I HAVE VERY THICK BEAUTY!
SCHULZ

I'M TIRED AND DISCOURAGED.. EVERYTHING SEEMS HOPELESS..
© 1965 Peanuts Worldwide LLC. Dist. by Universal Uclick
WHAT YOU NEED, CHARLIE BROWN, IS A VACATION
www.snoopy.com
THAT'S A GOOD IDEA...TELL THAT TO MY MOM, MY TEACHER, THE PRINCIPAL AND ALL EIGHT MEMBERS OF THE SCHOOL BOARD!
2-15
I NEVER CAN TELL WHEN HE'S BEING SARCASTIC..
SCHULZ

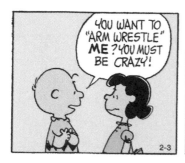

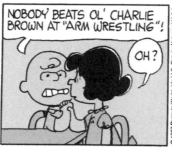

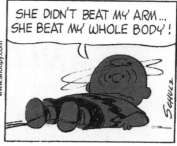

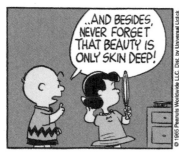

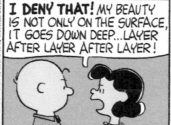

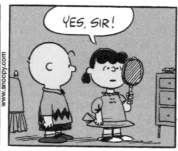

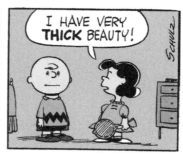

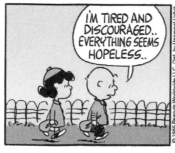

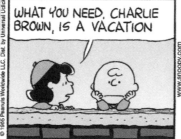

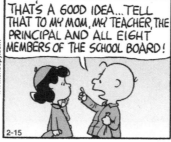

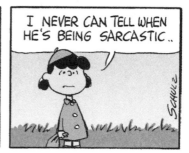

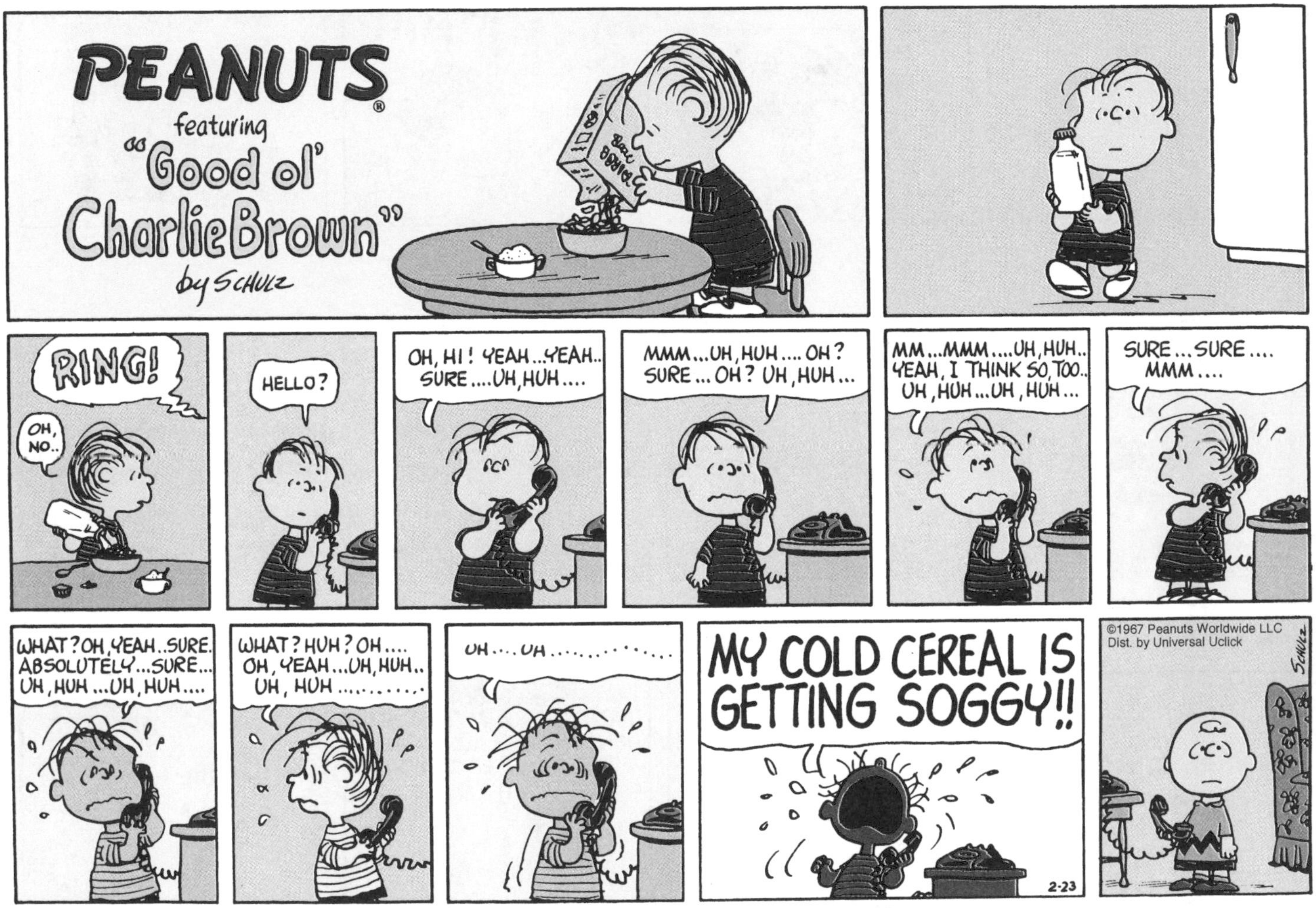
PEANUTS®
featuring
"Good ol' CharlieBrown"
by SCHULZ
RING!
OH, NO..
HELLO?
OH, HI! YEAH...YEAH.. SURE....UH, HUH....
MMM...UH, HUH.... OH? SURE... OH? UH, HUH...
MM...MMM....UH, HUH.. YEAH, I THINK SO, TOO.. UH, HUH...UH, HUH...
SURE... SURE.... MMM....
WHAT? OH, YEAH..SURE. ABSOLUTELY...SURE... UH, HUH...UH, HUH....
WHAT? HUH? OH.... OH, YEAH...UH, HUH.. UH, HUH ....
UH.... UH ....
MY COLD CEREAL IS GETTING SOGGY!!
2-23
©1967 Peanuts Worldwide LLC
Dist. by Universal Uclick
SCHULZ

IN KITE-FLYING, THE RATIO OF WEIGHT TO SAIL-AREA IS VERY IMPORTANT
2-25
THIS RATIO IS KNOWN AS "SAIL LOADING" AND IT IS MEASURED IN OUNCES PER SQUARE FOOT..FOR EXAMPLE, A THREE-FOOT FLAT KITE WITH A SAIL AREA OF FOUR AND ONE-HALF SQUARE FEET SHOULD WEIGH ABOUT TWO OR THREE OUNCES...
© 1987 Peanuts Worldwide LLC, Dist. by Universal Uclick
YOU KNOW A LOT ABOUT KITES, DON'T YOU, CHARLIE BROWN?
YES, I THINK I CAN SAY THAT I DO...
www.snoopy.com
THEN WHY IS YOUR KITE DOWN THE SEWER?
SCHULZ

HOW CAN YOU TELL A "KITE-EATING" TREE FROM AN ORDINARY TREE?
YOU CAN'T UNTIL YOU SEE A KITE CAUGHT BY ONE... AN ORDINARY TREE WILL LET A KITE GO RIGHT AWAY, BUT A KITE-EATING TREE WILL HANG ON TO A KITE FOR WEEKS!
2-26
© 1987 Peanuts Worldwide LLC, Dist. by Universal Uclick
THEY CLUTCH KITES IN THEIR GREEDY BRANCHES, AND SLOWLY DEVOUR THEM! IT'S A SHOCKING SIGHT... THEY EAT THE PAPER LIKE IT WAS FRIED CHICKEN, AND SPIT OUT THE STICKS LIKE BONES!
www.snoopy.com
ANY ONE OF THESE TREES COULD BE A MONSTROUS KITE-EATING TREE... YOU JUST CAN'T TELL..
BRRR!

MY KITE IS UP! IT'S UP! IT'S UP!
NO, IT'S GOING DOWN! STAY UP, YOU FOOL!
DON'T GET NEAR THAT KITE-EATING TREE!
LOOK OUT! LOOK OUT!
OH, NO! OH, GOOD GRIEF! OH, NO! OH, NO!
2-27
© 1987 Peanuts Worldwide LLC, Dist. by Universal Uclick
OH, NO!
AAUGH!
www.snoopy.com
THAT'S THE MOST GRUESOME THING I'VE EVER SEEN.....
SCHULZ

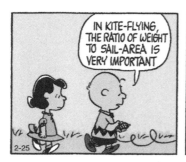

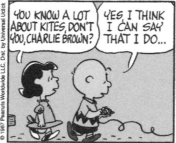

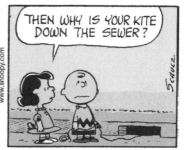

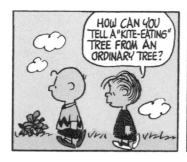

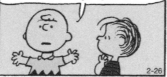

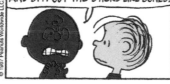

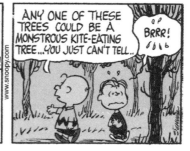

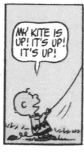

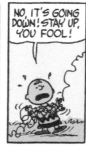

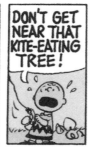

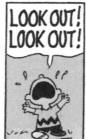

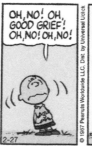

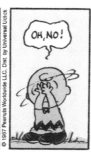

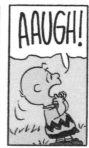

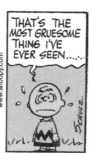

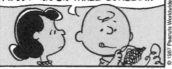

WHAT'S GOING ON HERE?
DON'T LOOK! DON'T LOOK!
THIS IS A "KITE-EATING" TREE! IT HAS ONE OF MY KITES...DON'T LOOK! IT'S A TERRIBLE SIGHT! WHATEVER YOU DO, DON'T LOOK!
2-28
© 1967 Peanuts Worldwide LLC, Dist. by Universal Uclick
AAUGH!
www.snoopy.com
SHE LOOKED!
SCHULZ

"THIS STUPID "KITE-EATING" TREE HAS MY KITE!
3-1
IF YOU DON'T LET GO OF THAT KITE, I'LL KICK YOU RIGHT IN THE STOMACH!!
© 1967 Peanuts Worldwide LLC, Dist. by Universal Uclick
BAM!
www.snoopy.com
THESE KITE-EATING TREES HAVE HARD STOMACHS...
SCHULZ

PERHAPS YOU CAN GIVE ME AN ANSWER, LINUS..
2-24
WHAT WOULD YOU DO IF YOU FELT THAT NO ONE LIKED YOU?
© 1967 Peanuts Worldwide LLC, Dist. by Universal Uclick
I'D TRY TO LOOK AT MYSELF OBJECTIVELY, AND SEE WHAT I COULD DO TO IMPROVE... THAT'S MY ANSWER, CHARLIE BROWN
www.snoopy.com
I HATE THAT ANSWER!
SCHULZ

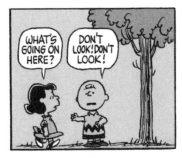

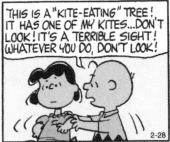

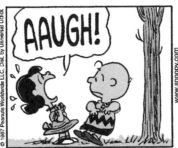

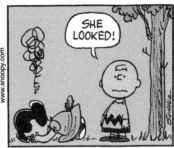

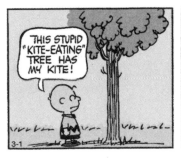

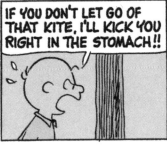

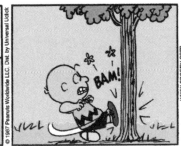

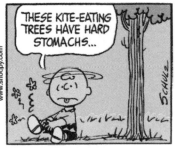

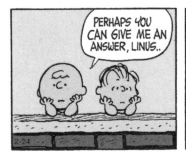

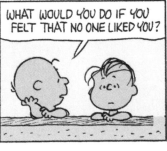

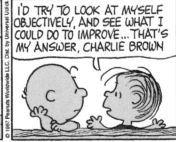

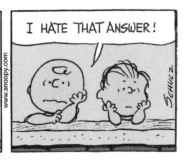

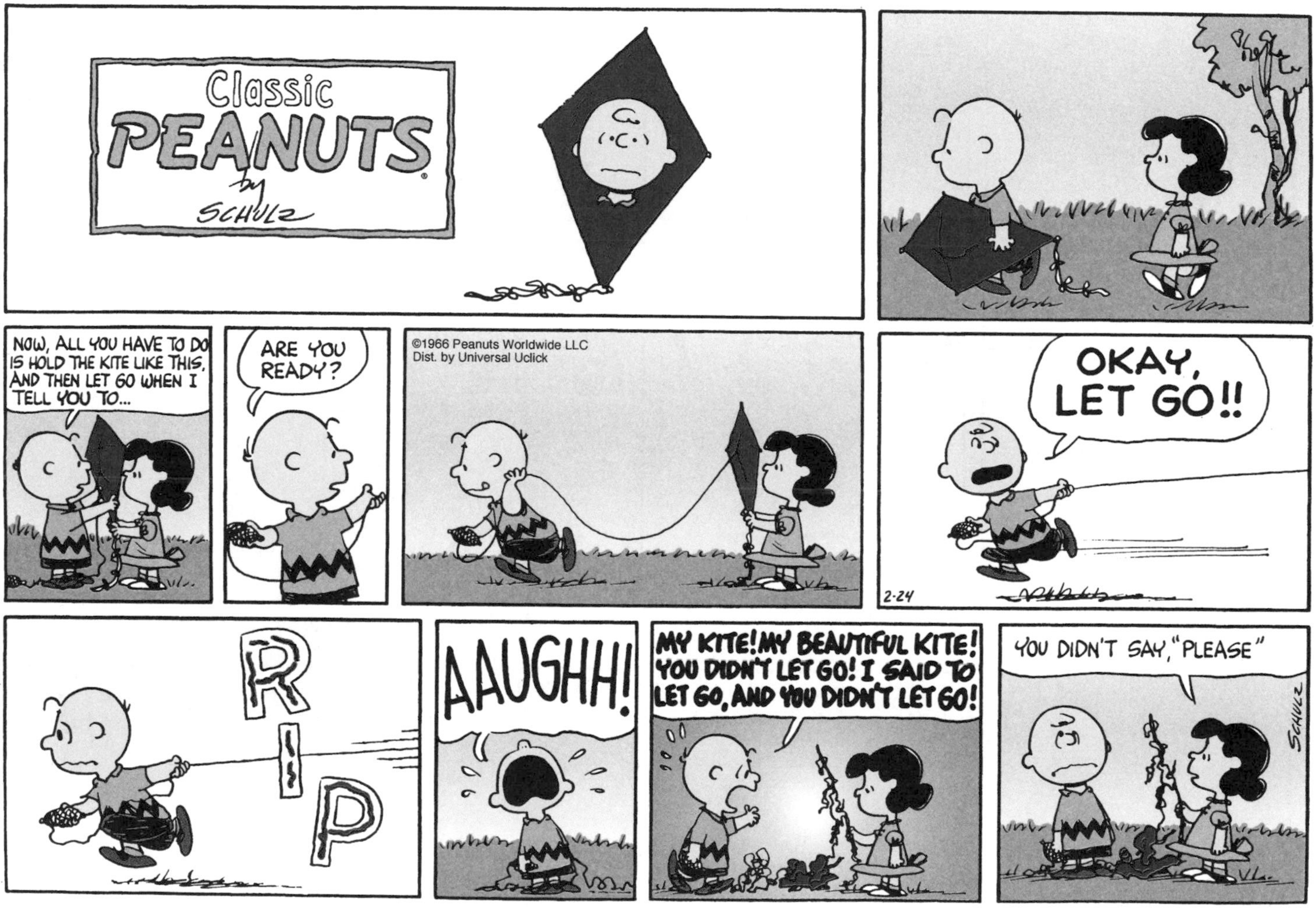
Classic
PEANUTS
by
SCHULZ
NOW, ALL YOU HAVE TO DO IS HOLD THE KITE LIKE THIS, AND THEN LET GO WHEN I TELL YOU TO...
ARE YOU READY?
©1966 Peanuts Worldwide LLC
Dist. by Universal Uclick
OKAY, LET GO!!
2-24
R I P
AAUGHH!
MY KITE! MY BEAUTIFUL KITE! YOU DIDN'T LET GO! I SAID TO LET GO, AND YOU DIDN'T LET GO!
YOU DIDN'T SAY, "PLEASE"
SCHULZ

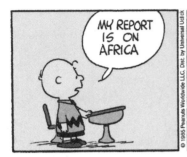

MY REPORT IS ON AFRICA
ACTUALLY, WHAT I MEAN TO SAY IS THAT MY REPORT WOULD HAVE BEEN ON AFRICA IF.... WELL, MY INTENTIONS WERE.....
IT SEEMS THAT I JUST NEVER QUITE GOT AROUND TO...WELL, YOU KNOW HOW IT GOES SOMETIMES, AND I JUST...I JUST NEVER..
I THROW MYSELF UPON THE MERCY OF THE COURT!
© 1965 Peanuts Worldwide LLC, Dist. by Universal Uclick
www.snoopy.com
2-27
SCHULZ

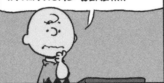

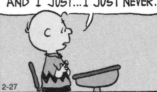

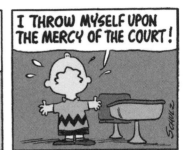

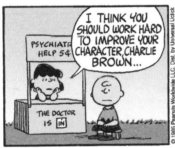

PSYCHIATRIC HELP 5¢
THE DOCTOR IS IN
I THINK YOU SHOULD WORK HARD TO IMPROVE YOUR CHARACTER, CHARLIE BROWN...
ONCE A CHILD GETS TO BE FIVE YEARS OLD, YOU KNOW, HIS CHARACTER IS PRETTY WELL ESTABLISHED
BUT I'M ALREADY FIVE YEARS OLD! I'M **MORE** THAN FIVE!
THAT'S RIGHT, YOU ARE, AREN'T YOU?
TOO BAD...THAT'S THE WAY IT GOES!
THE DOCTOR IS IN
© 1965 Peanuts Worldwide LLC, Dist. by Universal Uclick
www.snoopy.com
2-29
SCHULZ

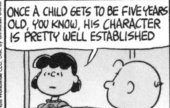

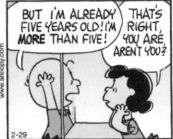

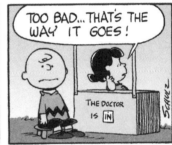

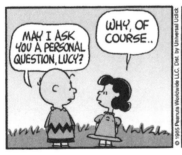

MAY I ASK YOU A PERSONAL QUESTION, LUCY?
WHY, OF COURSE..
I DON'T WANT TO UPSET YOU..
DON'T BE SILLY, CHARLIE BROWN... NOTHING YOU ASK COULD POSSIBLY UPSET ME..
DO YOU PRAY BEFORE YOU GO TO BED, OR AFTER YOU GET UP IN THE MORNING?
AAUGH!
© 1965 Peanuts Worldwide LLC, Dist. by Universal Uclick
www.snoopy.com
3-2
SCHULZ

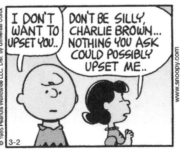

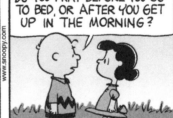

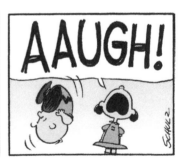

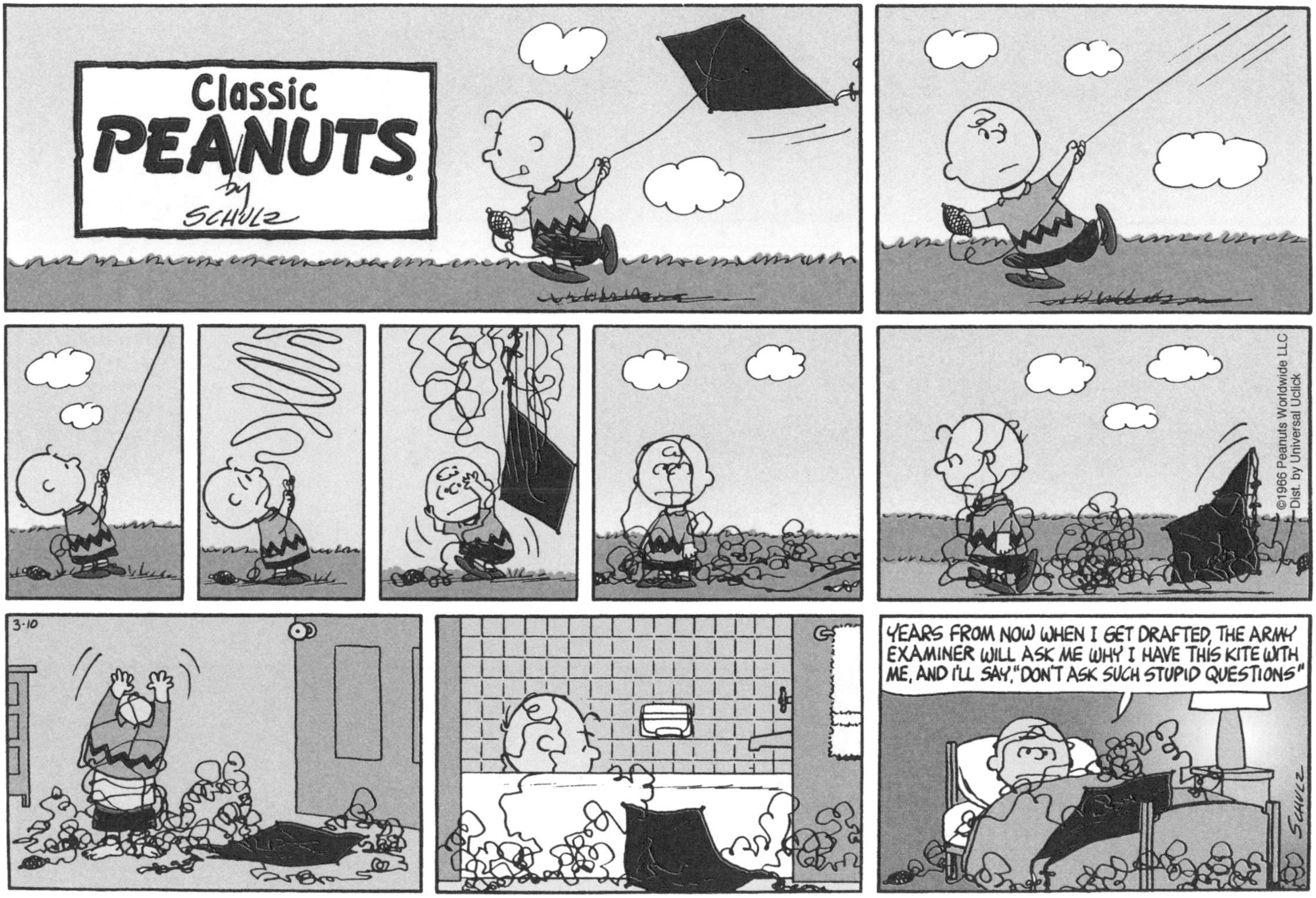
Classic
PEANUTS
by
SCHULZ
©1966 Peanuts Worldwide LLC
Dist. by Universal Uclick
3-10
YEARS FROM NOW WHEN I GET DRAFTED, THE ARMY EXAMINER WILL ASK ME WHY I HAVE THIS KITE WITH ME, AND I'LL SAY, "DON'T ASK SUCH STUPID QUESTIONS"
SCHULZ

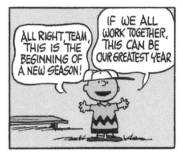

ALL RIGHT, TEAM, THIS IS THE BEGINNING OF A NEW SEASON!
IF WE ALL WORK TOGETHER, THIS CAN BE OUR GREATEST YEAR
NOW, THE FIRST THING WE HAVE TO DO IS START A PROGRAM OF VIGOROUS CALISTHENICS...
3-3
© 1967 Peanuts Worldwide LLC, Dist. by Universal Uclick
www.snoopy.com
HOW ABOUT ONE PUSH-UP ?
SCHULZ

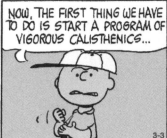

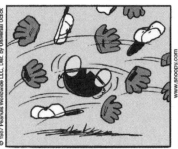

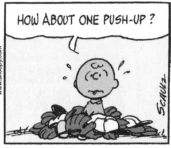

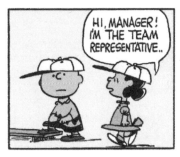

HI, MANAGER! I'M THE TEAM REPRESENTATIVE..
AS SPOKESMAN FOR THE TEAM, MAY I WISH YOU THE VERY BEST OF LUCK DURING THE NEW SEASON
3-4
© 1967 Peanuts Worldwide LLC, Dist. by Universal Uclick
WELL, THANK YOU....
www.snoopy.com
SPEAKING JUST FOR MYSELF, MAY I SAY YOU'RE GOING TO NEED IT!
SCHULZ

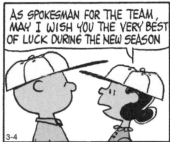

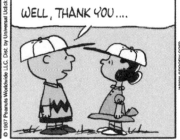

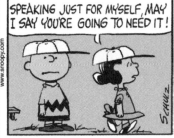

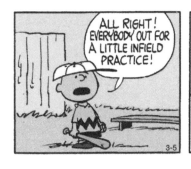

ALL RIGHT! EVERYBODY OUT FOR A LITTLE INFIELD PRACTICE!
3-5
I'LL HIT THE BALL TO THIRD BASE..YOU THROW IT TO FIRST..FIRST THROWS IT HOME, THE CATCHER WHIPS IT BACK TO THIRD AND WE THROW IT AROUND THE HORN! OKAY? LET'S GET IT RIGHT THE FIRST TIME! OKAY, HERE WE GO!!
© 1967 Peanuts Worldwide LLC, Dist. by Universal Uclick
CLIP
www.snoopy.com
SCHULZ

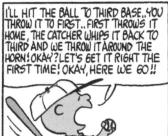

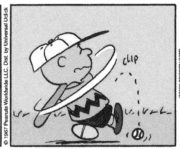

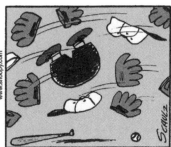

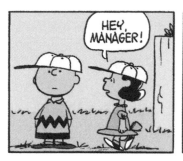

HEY, MANAGER!
AS TEAM SPOKESMAN, I'VE BEEN REQUESTED TO ASK YOU FOR MORE TIME OFF
3-6
© 1967 Peanuts Worldwide LLC, Dist. by Universal Uclick
WHAT SORT OF TIME OFF WOULD YOU LIKE?
www.snoopy.com
WE'D PREFER NOT TO SHOW UP FOR THE GAMES!
SCHULZ

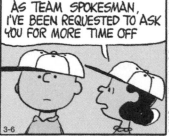

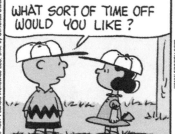

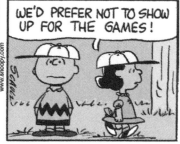

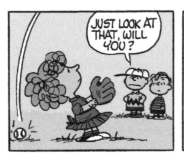

JUST LOOK AT THAT, WILL YOU?
OUR TEAM ISN'T READY TO START A NEW SEASON... WE'RE JUST NOT READY...
3-7
© 1967 Peanuts Worldwide LLC, Dist. by Universal Uclick
WHERE DID THE TIME GO? WHY DOES THE SEASON HAVE TO START SO SOON?
www.snoopy.com
CHARLIE BROWN, OUR TEAM WOULDN'T BE READY IF THE SEASON STARTED IN NOVEMBER!
SCHULZ

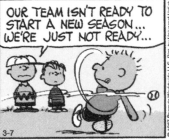

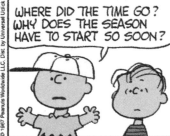

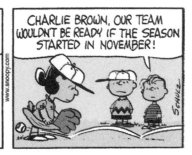

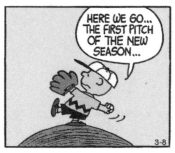

HERE WE GO... THE FIRST PITCH OF THE NEW SEASON...
3-8
© 1967 Peanuts Worldwide LLC, Dist. by Universal Uclick
POW!
www.snoopy.com
SOMETIMES I HAVE DIFFICULTY TELLING ONE SEASON FROM ANOTHER...
SCHULZ

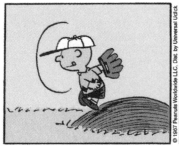

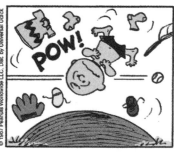

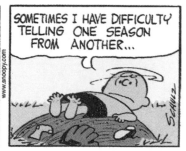

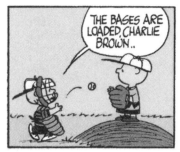

THE BASES ARE LOADED, CHARLIE BROWN..
ALREADY?
3-10
© 1987 Peanuts Worldwide LLC, Dist. by Universal Uclick
WHAT DO YOU MEAN, "ALREADY"?
www.snoopy.com
THE SEASON JUST STARTED!
SCHULZ

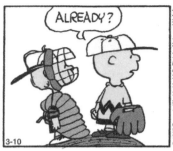

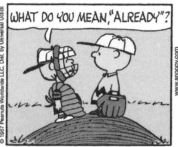

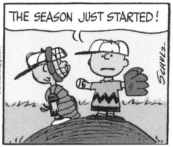

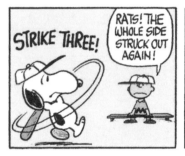

STRIKE THREE!
RATS! THE WHOLE SIDE STRUCK OUT AGAIN!
IN THE BIG LEAGUES WHEN A MANAGER GETS MAD, HE KICKS THE WATER COOLER! WHAT DO I HAVE TO KICK?
© 1987 Peanuts Worldwide LLC, Dist. by Universal Uclick
3-11
A HOSE!
www.snoopy.com
SCHULZ

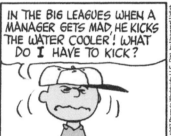

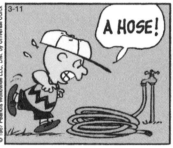

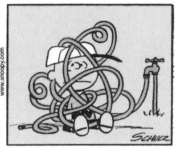

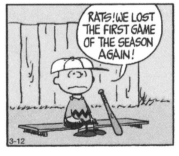

RATS! WE LOST THE FIRST GAME OF THE SEASON AGAIN!
3-12
LOSING A BALL GAME IS LIKE DROPPING AN ICE CREAM CONE ON THE SIDEWALK...
© 1987 Peanuts Worldwide LLC, Dist. by Universal Uclick
IT JUST LAYS THERE, AND YOU KNOW YOU'VE DROPPED IT AND THERE'S NOTHING YOU CAN DO.... IT'S TOO LATE....
www.snoopy.com
RATS!
SCHULZ

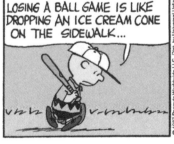

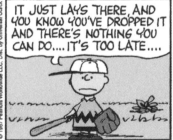

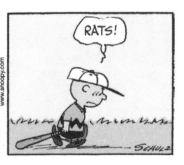

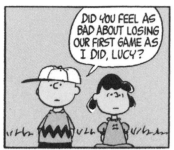

DID YOU FEEL AS BAD ABOUT LOSING OUR FIRST GAME AS I DID, LUCY?
OH, YES, CHARLIE BROWN... I SAT UP ALL NIGHT CRYING MY EYES OUT!
3-13
© 1967 Peanuts Worldwide LLC, Dist. by Universal Uclick
HAHAHAHAHA
www.snoopy.com
NO JURY WOULD EVER CONVICT ME!
SCHULZ

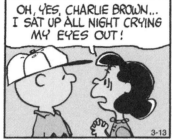

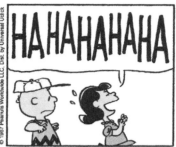

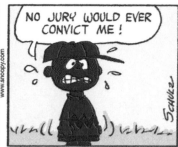

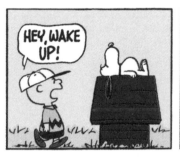

HEY, WAKE UP!
HOW CAN YOU LIE THERE SLEEPING SO PEACEFULLY WHEN WE LOST OUR FIRST GAME OF THE SEASON? DON'T YOU HAVE ANY FEELINGS ?!
© 1967 Peanuts Worldwide LLC, Dist. by Universal Uclick
DON'T THESE THINGS BOTHER YOU? DON'T THEY NAG AT YOU AND TEAR AT YOU AND..
3-14
www.snoopy.com
SIGH..
Z
SCHULZ

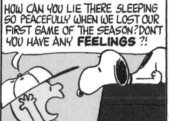

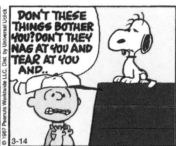

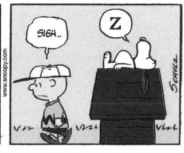

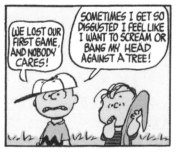

WE LOST OUR FIRST GAME, AND NOBODY CARES!
SOMETIMES I GET SO DISGUSTED I FEEL LIKE I WANT TO SCREAM OR BANG MY HEAD AGAINST A TREE!
3-15
© 1967 Peanuts Worldwide LLC, Dist. by Universal Uclick
www.snoopy.com
THANKS...I NEEDED THAT!
SCHULZ

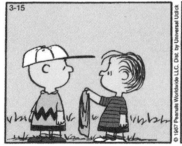

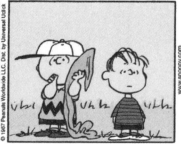

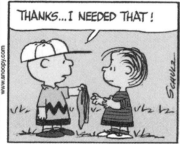

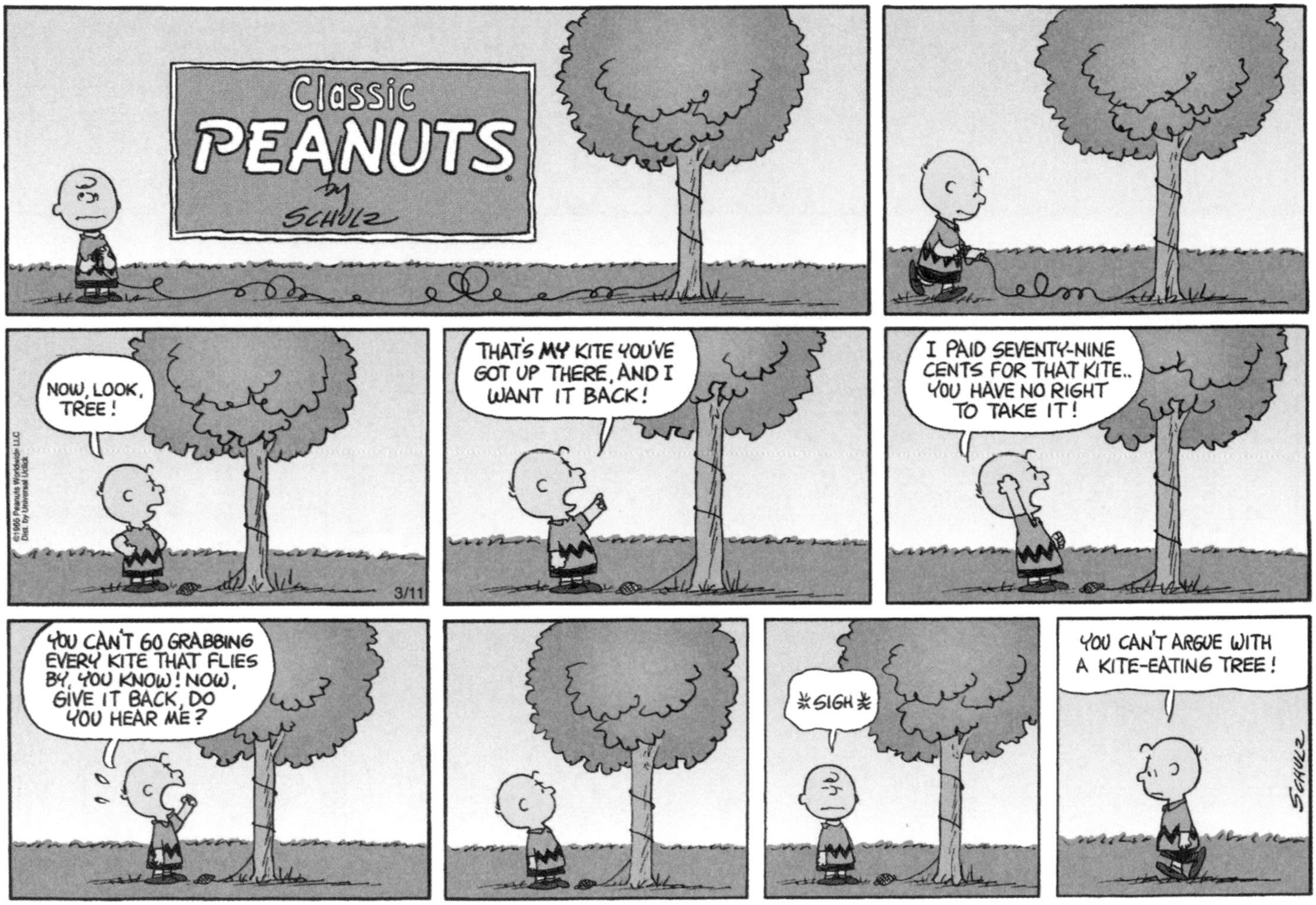
Classic
PEANUTS
by
SCHULZ
NOW, LOOK, TREE!
©1966 Peanuts Worldwide LLC
Dist. by Universal Uclick
3/11
THAT'S MY KITE YOU'VE GOT UP THERE, AND I WANT IT BACK!
I PAID SEVENTY-NINE CENTS FOR THAT KITE.. YOU HAVE NO RIGHT TO TAKE IT!
YOU CAN'T GO GRABBING EVERY KITE THAT FLIES BY, YOU KNOW! NOW, GIVE IT BACK, DO YOU HEAR ME?
SIGH
YOU CAN'T ARGUE WITH A KITE-EATING TREE!
SCHULZ

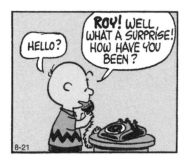

HELLO?
ROY! WELL, WHAT A SURPRISE! HOW HAVE YOU BEEN?
8-21
CHARLIE BROWN, I HAVE A FRIEND HERE WHO WANTS TO MEET YOU... SHE LOVES BASEBALL, AND WANTS TO PLAY ON YOUR TEAM... HER NAME IS "PEPPERMINT" PATTY...
© 1956 Peanuts Worldwide LLC, Dist. by Universal Uclick
HI, CHUCK!
www.snoopy.com
"CHUCK"!?!
SCHULZ

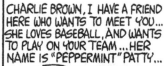

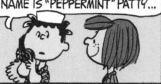

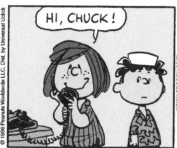

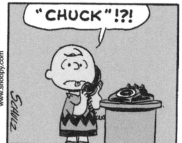

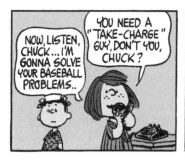

NOW, LISTEN, CHUCK... I'M GONNA SOLVE YOUR BASEBALL PROBLEMS..
YOU NEED A "TAKE-CHARGE" GUY, DON'T YOU, CHUCK?
" CHUCK " ?
© 1956 Peanuts Worldwide LLC, Dist. by Universal Uclick
I'M HEADIN' ACROSS TOWN RIGHT NOW, SO YOU GET YOUR TEAM TOGETHER... TELL 'EM "PEPPERMINT" PATTY IS ON HER WAY! SO LONG, CHUCK!
8-22
www.snoopy.com
" CHUCK " ?!?
SCHULZ

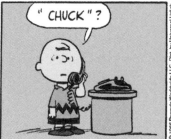

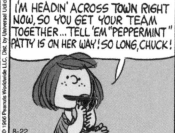

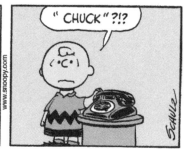

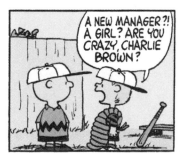

A NEW MANAGER?! A GIRL? ARE YOU CRAZY, CHARLIE BROWN?
ALL I KNOW IS THIS GIRL SAID SHE COULD HELP OUR TEAM..
BUT THE SEASON'S ALMOST OVER!
8-23
© 1956 Peanuts Worldwide LLC, Dist. by Universal Uclick
WE COULD STILL COME IN FOURTH PLACE, AND WIN A SPOT IN THE PLAYOFF! I THINK IT'S WORTH A CHANCE... I THINK WE COULD..
www.snoopy.com
HEY, MAC, I'M LOOKING FOR A KID NAMED CHUCK BROWN!
"CHUCK BROWN"?!
SCHULZ

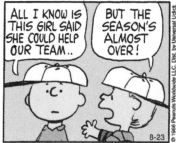

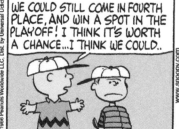

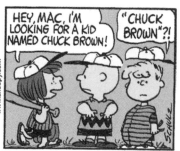

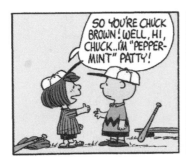

SO YOU'RE CHUCK BROWN! WELL, HI, CHUCK..I'M "PEPPERMINT" PATTY!
AREN'T YOU GONNA INTRODUCE ME TO YOUR TEAM? ROY TOLD ME ALL ABOUT YOUR TEAM..
8-24
© 1966 Peanuts Worldwide LLC. Dist. by Universal Uclick
THE GUY I REALLY WANNA MEET IS LINUS
www.snoopy.com
THIS IS LINUS...
SCHULZ

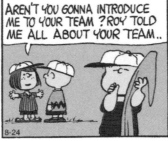

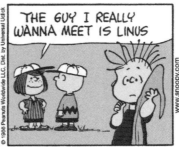

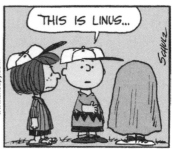

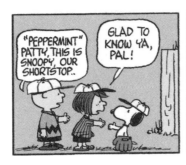

"PEPPERMINT" PATTY, THIS IS SNOOPY, OUR SHORTSTOP..
GLAD TO KNOW YA, PAL!
NOW, IF YOU'LL COME OVER HERE, I'LL INTRODUCE YOU TO LUCY AND SOME OF THE OTHER GIRLS...
© 1966 Peanuts Worldwide LLC. Dist. by Universal Uclick
8-26
Y'KNOW WHAT?
www.snoopy.com
THAT SHORTSTOP IS THE FUNNIEST LOOKIN' KID I'VE EVER SEEN!
SCHULZ

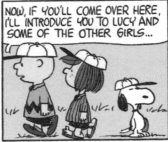

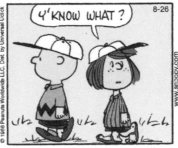

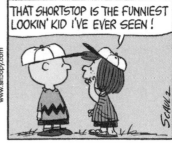

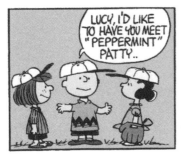

LUCY, I'D LIKE TO HAVE YOU MEET "PEPPERMINT" PATTY..
SHE'S COME CLEAR ACROSS TOWN TO HELP US WIN A FEW BALL GAMES
GLAD TO KNOW YA, LUCILLE, OL' GIRL!
8-27
© 1966 Peanuts Worldwide LLC. Dist. by Universal Uclick
WE'LL SHOW CHUCK HERE HOW THIS GAME IS REALLY PLAYED, WON'T WE?
www.snoopy.com
"LUCILLE"?! "CHUCK"?!?
SCHULZ

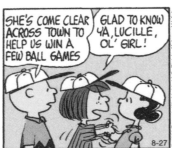

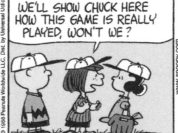

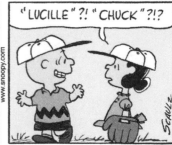

I'LL TAKE OVER THE MOUND CHORES, CHUCK..YOU PLAY LEFT-FIELD...
PSST! HEY, CHUCK! BEFORE THE GAME STARTS, HOW ABOUT A LITTLE KISS ON THE NOSE FOR GOOD LUCK?
8-28
© 1966 Peanuts Worldwide LLC, Dist. by Universal Uclick
THANKS, CHUCK!
SMAK
www.snoopy.com
I'M SURPRISED AT MYSELF...I NEVER REALIZED HOW FAR I'D GO TO WIN A BALL GAME....
SCHULZ

HI! I HEAR YOU'RE MY CATCHER..
WELL, WE WON'T NEED ANY SIGNALS...I'LL JUST FOG IT BY 'EM, AND YOU CATCH 'EM, OKAY? BY THE WAY, WHAT WAS THAT YOU WERE WHISTLING?
8-29
© 1966 Peanuts Worldwide LLC, Dist. by Universal Uclick
JUST A LITTLE SOMETHING BY BEETHOVEN
OH...
www.snoopy.com
I COME CLEAR ACROSS TOWN TO PLAY BALL, AND WHO DO I GET FOR A CATCHER? A MINIATURE LEONARD BERNSTEIN!
SCHULZ

OKAY, TEAM, LET'S GET THIS NEXT GUY!
WE CAN DO IT! WE CAN GET HIM EASY! HE'S NO HITTER! HE'S NO HITTER AT ALL!
© 1966 Peanuts Worldwide LLC, Dist. by Universal Uclick
C'MON, TEAM, LET'S BEAR DOWN OUT THERE! LET'S REALLY GET THIS GUY!
www.snoopy.com
THAT'S THE ONLY PITCHER I'VE EVER KNOWN WHO SUPPLIED HER OWN INFIELD CHATTER!
8-31
SCHULZ

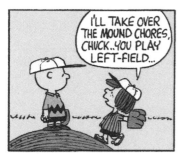

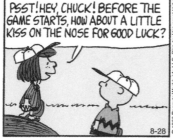

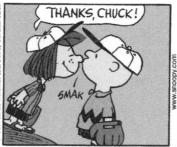

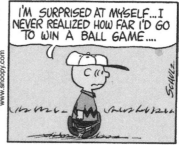

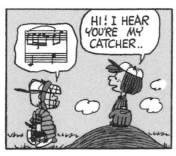

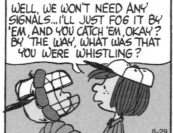

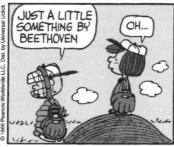

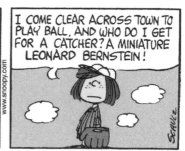

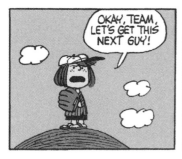

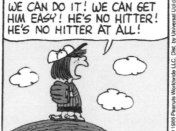

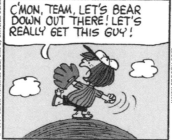

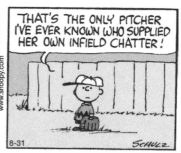

THIS IS RIDICULOUS!
I'VE HIT FIVE HOME RUNS AND PITCHED A NO-HIT GAME, AND WE'RE BEHIND THIRTY-SEVEN TO FIVE! WHOEVER HEARD OF THIRTY-SEVEN UNEARNED RUNS? THIS IS RIDICULOUS!
9-2
© 1966 Peanuts Worldwide LLC, Dist. by Universal Uclick
I THOUGHT I COULD HELP YOUR TEAM, CHUCK, BUT IT'S HOPELESS! I'M GOING BACK WHERE I CAME FROM!
www.snoopy.com
THAT MUST BE A NICE THING TO BE ABLE TO DO...
SCHULZ

DEAR PEPPERMINT PATTY, I HOPE YOU HAD A NICE WALK HOME.
I JUST WANTED YOU TO KNOW THAT I APPRECIATED YOUR COMING CLEAR ACROSS TOWN TO HELP OUR TEAM.
SINCERELY,
© 1966 Peanuts Worldwide LLC, Dist. by Universal Uclick
www.snoopy.com
" CHUCK"
9-4
SCHULZ

HELP!
© 1965 Peanuts Worldwide LLC, Dist. by Universal Uclick
IT'S AFTER ME! IT'S AFTER ME!
?
www.snoopy.com
SAVE ME, CHARLIE BROWN! SAVE ME! I'M BEING CHASED BY A BLANKET!
3-20
I NEVER DREAMED THAT SHE'D BE THE FIRST IN OUR LITTLE GROUP TO CRACK UP!
SCHULZ

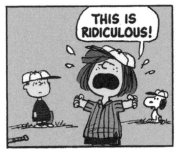

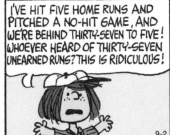

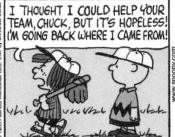

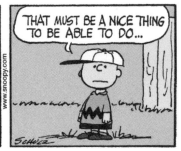

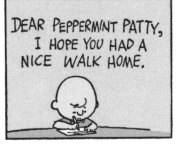

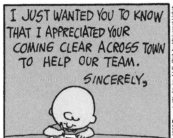

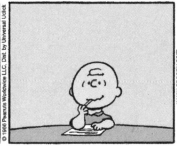

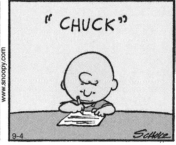

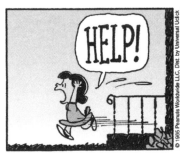

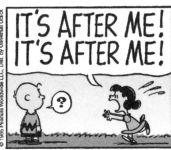

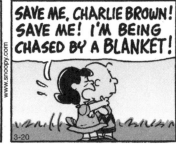

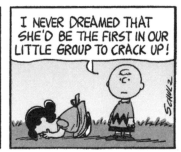

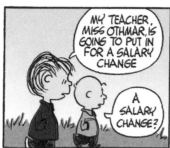

MY TEACHER, MISS OTHMAR, IS GOING TO PUT IN FOR A SALARY CHANGE
A SALARY CHANGE?
© 1965 Peanuts Worldwide LLC. Dist. by Universal Uclick
3-5
YES, SHE SAYS SHE TAKES CHILDREN TO THE MOVIE ROOM FOR MOVIES, TO THE ART ROOM FOR ART, BACK TO THE MOVIE ROOM FOR FILM STRIPS...
www.snoopy.com
TO THE LIBRARY FOR BOOKS, TO THE CAFETERIA FOR LUNCH, TO THE GYM FOR PHYSICAL EDUCATION AND AROUND AND AROUND THE SCHOOL BUILDING FOR YARD DUTIES...
SHE'S DECIDED SHE WANTS TO BE PAID BY THE MILE!
SCHULZ

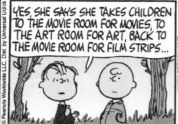

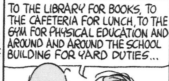

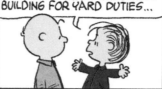

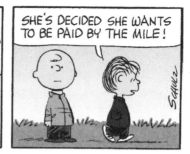

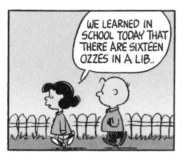

WE LEARNED IN SCHOOL TODAY THAT THERE ARE SIXTEEN OZZES IN A LIB..
WE'VE BEEN STUDYING PINTS AND QUARTS, AND FEET AND INCHES AND OZZES AND LIBS...
3-7
© 1966 Peanuts Worldwide LLC. Dist. by Universal Uclick
I GET KIND OF CONFUSED ON QUARTS AND FEET, BUT I'M GOOD ON OZZES AND LIBS..
www.snoopy.com
DID YOU KNOW THERE ARE SIXTEEN OZZES IN A LIB?
I NEVER KNOW HOW TO ANSWER A QUESTION LIKE THAT..
SCHULZ

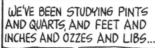

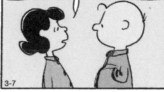

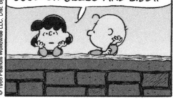

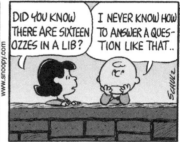

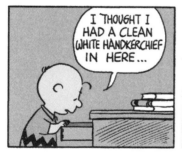

I THOUGHT I HAD A CLEAN WHITE HANDKERCHIEF IN HERE...
THERE'S A BLUE ONE... A GREEN ONE..ANOTHER BLUE ONE...
3-18
© 1966 Peanuts Worldwide LLC. Dist. by Universal Uclick
WHAT IN THE WORLD HAPPENED TO MY WHITE HANDKERCHIEF?
www.snoopy.com
THERE IT IS, MEN... FORT ZINDERNEUF!!
SCHULZ

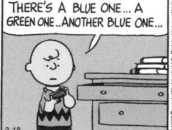

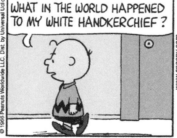

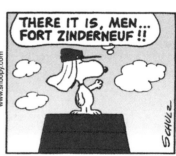

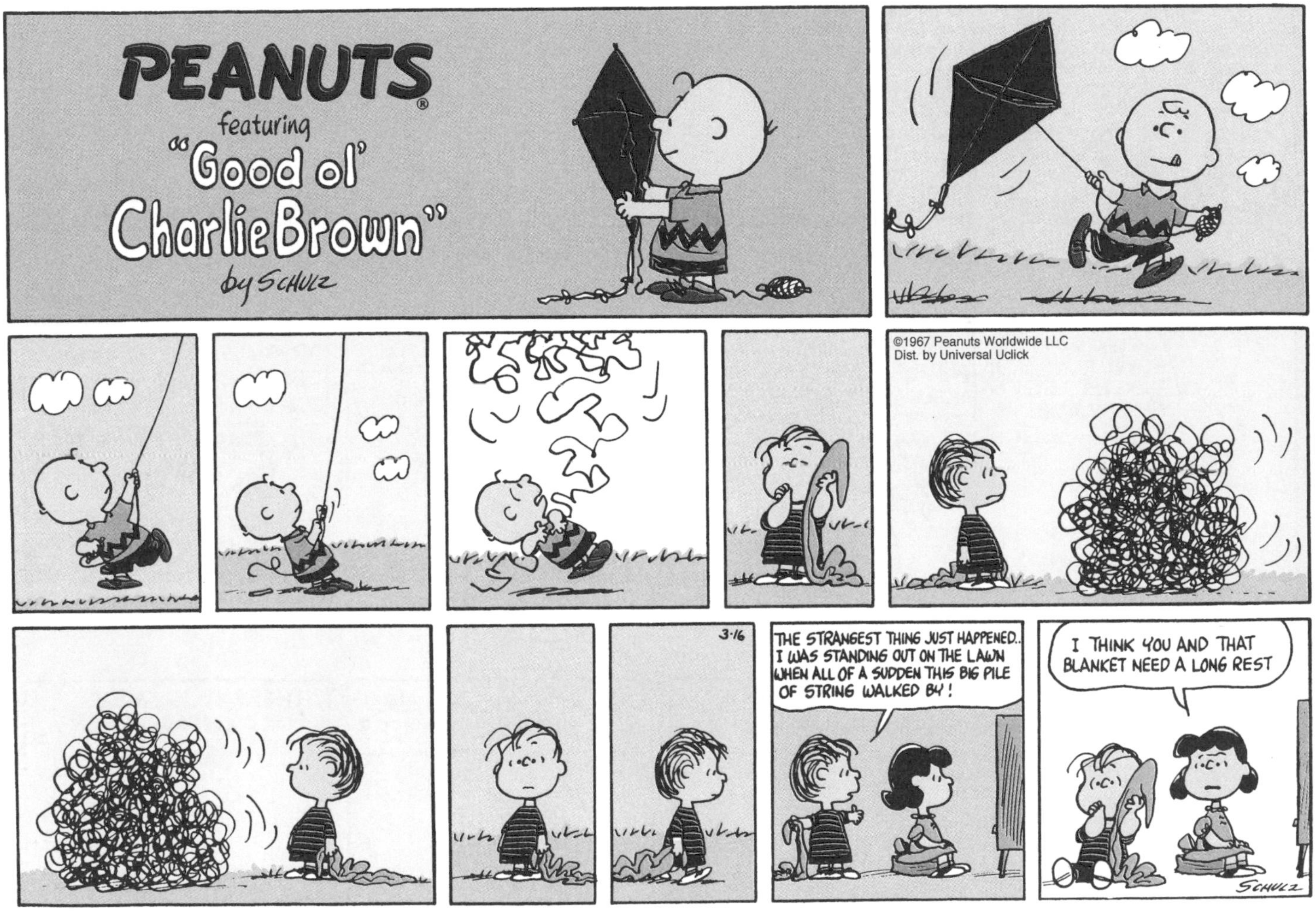
PEANUTS®
featuring
"Good ol' CharlieBrown"
by SCHULZ
©1967 Peanuts Worldwide LLC
Dist. by Universal Uclick
3-16
THE STRANGEST THING JUST HAPPENED.. I WAS STANDING OUT ON THE LAWN WHEN ALL OF A SUDDEN THIS BIG PILE OF STRING WALKED BY!
I THINK YOU AND THAT BLANKET NEED A LONG REST
SCHULZ

HELLO?
HELLO, CHUCK? THIS IS OL' PEPPERMINT PATTY! HAVE I GOT A SURPRISE FOR YOU! I'VE FOUND YOU A NEW BALL PLAYER....
3-17
© 1967 Peanuts Worldwide LLC. Dist. by Universal Uclick
THIS GUY IS TERRIFIC! HE'S NOT VERY BIG, BUT HE CAN REALLY PLAY! HIS NAME?
www.snoopy.com
JOSÉ PETERSON!
SCHULZ

CHUCK, I'D LIKE TO HAVE YOU MEET JOSÉ PETERSON..
NOW, THE WAY I SEE IT, CHUCK, YOU CAN PLAY JOSÉ PETERSON HERE AT SECOND WHERE HE CAN WORK WITH THAT FUNNY-LOOKING KID YOU'VE GOT PLAYING SHORTSTOP...
© 1967 Peanuts Worldwide LLC. Dist. by Universal Uclick
WHAT ABOUT LINUS? HE'S ALWAYS PLAYED A PRETTY GOOD SECOND BASE...
DON'T WORRY ABOUT LINUS... I'LL EXPLAIN THE WHOLE THING TO HIM..
3-18
www.snoopy.com
HI, SWEETIE!
SCHULZ

.640
THAT'S THE WAY JOSÉ PETERSON HIT THE YEAR HIS FAMILY LIVED IN NEW MEXICO...
3-19
© 1967 Peanuts Worldwide LLC. Dist. by Universal Uclick
.850
www.snoopy.com
THAT'S THE WAY JOSÉ PETERSON HIT THE YEAR HIS FAMILY LIVED IN NORTH DAKOTA...
SCHULZ

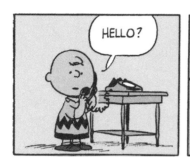

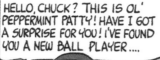

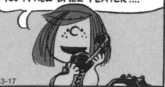

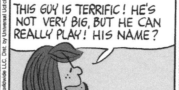

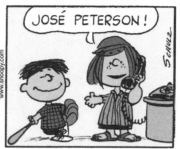

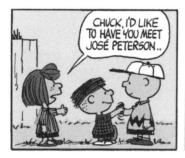

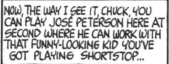

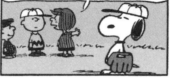

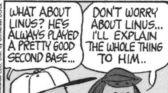

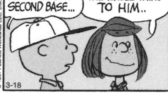

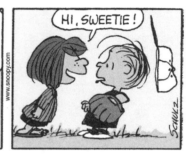

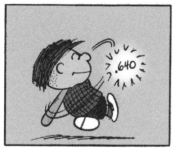

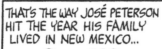

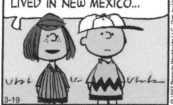

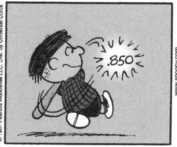

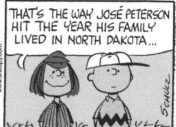

NOW, LOOK, CHUCK... HERE'S THE WAY YOUR NEW LINEUP CAN GO...

WITH JOSÉ PETERSON AT SECOND AND ME TAKING OVER THE MOUND CHORES, YOU'RE GOING TO HAVE A GREAT TEAM, YES, SIR!

3-20

NOBODY WILL BE ABLE TO BEAT US! WHY, YOU'LL PROBABLY BE SELECTED "MANAGER OF THE YEAR"!

© 1967 Peanuts Worldwide LLC, Dist. by Universal Uclick

FOR WHAT?

www.snoopy.com

HOW DO YOU LIKE PLAYING IN THE OUTFIELD, CHARLIE BROWN?

TERRIBLE! I'D RATHER BE UP THERE ON THE MOUND..

WE HAVE A BETTER TEAM NOW, BUT IT ISN'T **MY** TEAM..I THINK I'LL JUST HAVE TO TELL PEPPERMINT PATTY THAT I PREFER TO RUN THIS TEAM MYSELF

3-21

✻ AHEM ✻ EXCUSE ME...YOU...UH... YOU'RE...UH... YOU'RE PITCHING A GREAT GAME...

THANKS, "CHUCK," OL' PAL...

© 1967 Peanuts Worldwide LLC, Dist. by Universal Uclick

WHAT HAPPENED?

I WAS SUDDENLY OVERCOME BY A BURST OF WISHY-WASHINESS!

www.snoopy.com

I'VE GOT BAD NEWS, "CHUCK"...JOSÉ PETERSON AND I HAVE DECIDED TO FORM A TEAM IN OUR OWN NEIGHBORHOOD...

FRANKLY, I DON'T THINK YOUR TEAM IS EVER GOING TO AMOUNT TO MUCH, "CHUCK"...YOU JUST DON'T HAVE IT... MAYBE YOU COULD TRY SHUFFLEBOARD OR SOMETHING LIKE THAT...

3-24

WELL, WE'VE GOT A LONG WAY TO GO SO WE'D BETTER SAY GOOD-BY... JOSÉ PETERSON'S MOM IS HAVING ME OVER TONIGHT FOR TORTILLAS AND SWEDISH MEAT-BALLS!

© 1967 Peanuts Worldwide LLC, Dist. by Universal Uclick

www.snoopy.com

"SHUFFLEBOARD"?!

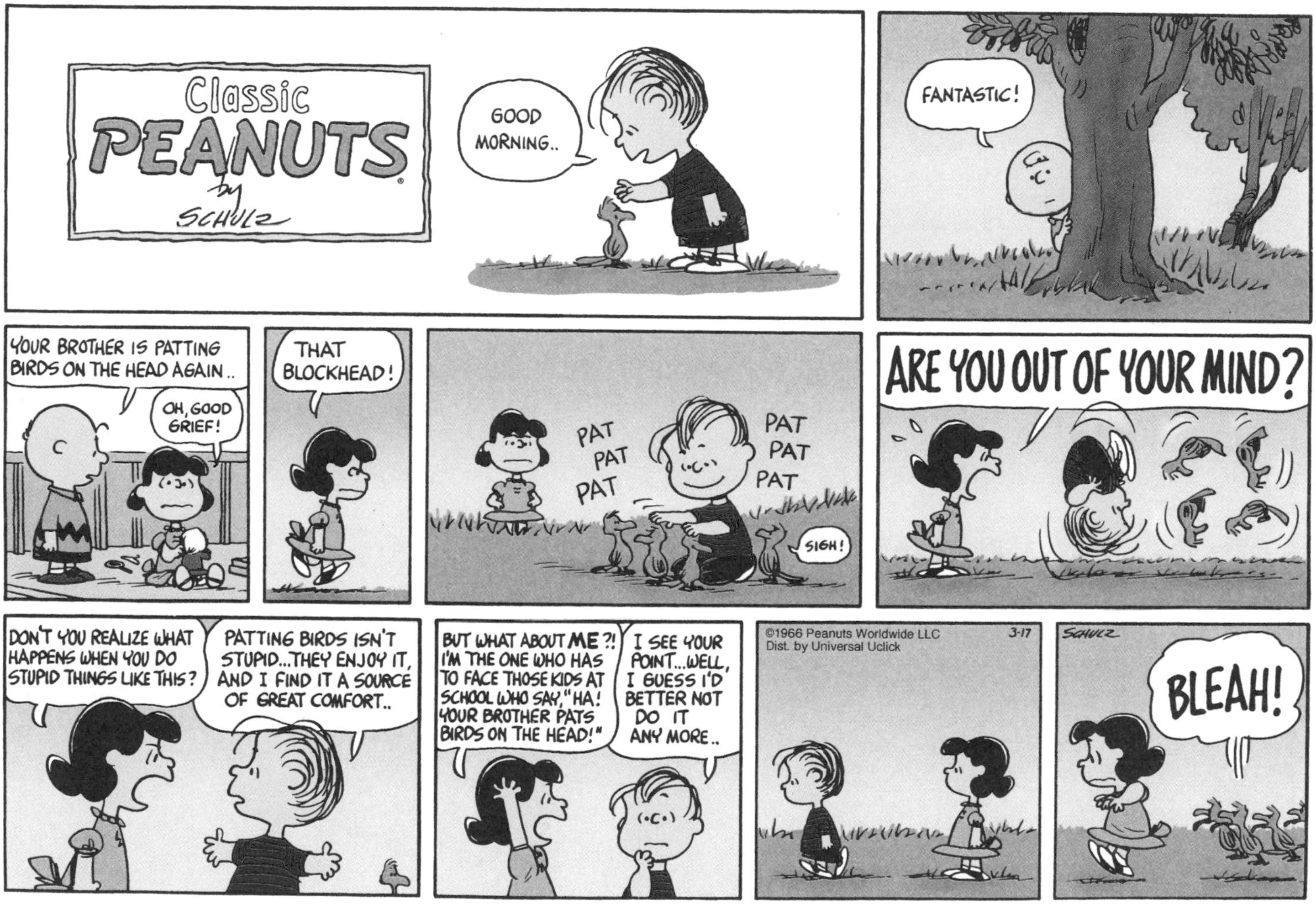
Classic PEANUTS by SCHULZ
GOOD MORNING..
FANTASTIC!
YOUR BROTHER IS PATTING BIRDS ON THE HEAD AGAIN..
OH, GOOD GRIEF!
THAT BLOCKHEAD!
PAT PAT PAT
PAT PAT PAT
SIGH!
ARE YOU OUT OF YOUR MIND?
DON'T YOU REALIZE WHAT HAPPENS WHEN YOU DO STUPID THINGS LIKE THIS?
PATTING BIRDS ISN'T STUPID...THEY ENJOY IT, AND I FIND IT A SOURCE OF GREAT COMFORT..
BUT WHAT ABOUT ME?! I'M THE ONE WHO HAS TO FACE THOSE KIDS AT SCHOOL WHO SAY, "HA! YOUR BROTHER PATS BIRDS ON THE HEAD!"
I SEE YOUR POINT...WELL, I GUESS I'D BETTER NOT DO IT ANY MORE..
©1966 Peanuts Worldwide LLC
Dist. by Universal Uclick
3-17
SCHULZ
BLEAH!

YOU KNOW WHAT?
WHAT?
A PEANUT BUTTER SANDWICH IS JUST THE SANDWICH TO BE EATING WHEN YOU'RE LOOKING ACROSS THE PLAYGROUND AT A LITTLE RED-HAIRED GIRL YOU ADMIRE, BUT KNOW YOU HAVEN'T A CHANCE OF EVER MEETING
3-19
© 1966 Peanuts Worldwide LLC, Dist. by Universal Uclick
WHY IS THAT?
www.snoopy.com
IF YOU HAVE TO ASK, YOU'LL NEVER UNDERSTAND!
SCHULZ

IT'S STUPID TO JUST SIT HERE AND ADMIRE THAT LITTLE RED-HAIRED GIRL FROM A DISTANCE
3-20
IT'S STUPID NOT TO GET UP AND GO OVER AND TALK TO HER..IT'S REALLY STUPID...IT'S JUST PLAIN STUPID...
© 1966 Peanuts Worldwide LLC, Dist. by Universal Uclick
SO WHY DON'T I GO OVER AND TALK TO HER?
www.snoopy.com
BECAUSE I'M STUPID!
SCHULZ

I'D GIVE ANYTHING TO BE ABLE TO TALK WITH THAT LITTLE RED-HAIRED GIRL..
3-21
THE AMAZING THING IS THAT I KNOW I'M THE SORT OF PERSON SHE'D LIKE! I MEAN I'M NOT ROUGH OR CRUDE OR ANYTHING
© 1966 Peanuts Worldwide LLC, Dist. by Universal Uclick
I'M NOT THE GREATEST PERSON WHO EVER LIVED, OF COURSE, BUT AFTER ALL, WHO IS? I'M JUST A NICE SORT OF GUY WHO....
www.snoopy.com
..WHO NEVER GETS TO MEET LITTLE RED-HAIRED GIRLS!
SCHULZ

WHAT'S THIS? THAT LITTLE RED-HAIRED GIRL DROPPED HER PENCIL...
GEE... IT'S GOT TEETH MARKS ALL OVER IT...
© 1966 Peanuts Worldwide LLC, Dist. by Universal Uclick
SHE NIBBLES ON HER PENCIL...
www.snoopy.com
SHE'S HUMAN!
SCHULZ
3-22

WHAT'S THAT YOU'RE HOLDING?
3-23
IT'S A PENCIL... IT BELONGS TO THAT LITTLE RED-HAIRED GIRL... I'M GOING TO STAND HERE UNTIL SHE WALKS BY, AND THEN I'M GOING TO TELL HER HOW I FOUND IT...
© 1966 Peanuts Worldwide LLC, Dist. by Universal Uclick
I HATE TO SEE YOU GO TO ALL THAT TROUBLE, CHARLIE BROWN... WHY DON'T I JUST GIVE IT TO HER?
www.snoopy.com
HEY! HERE'S YOUR STUPID PENCIL!!
SCHULZ

I ALMOST GOT AN "A" ON MY SPELLING TEST
3/28
THE ONLY WORD I MISSED WAS "CUCUMBER"
© 1967 Peanuts Worldwide LLC, Dist. by Universal Uclick
DON'T WORRY ABOUT IT..
www.snoopy.com
THE WAY I SEE IT, A WORD LIKE "CUCUMBER" DESERVES TO BE MISSPELLED!
SCHULZ

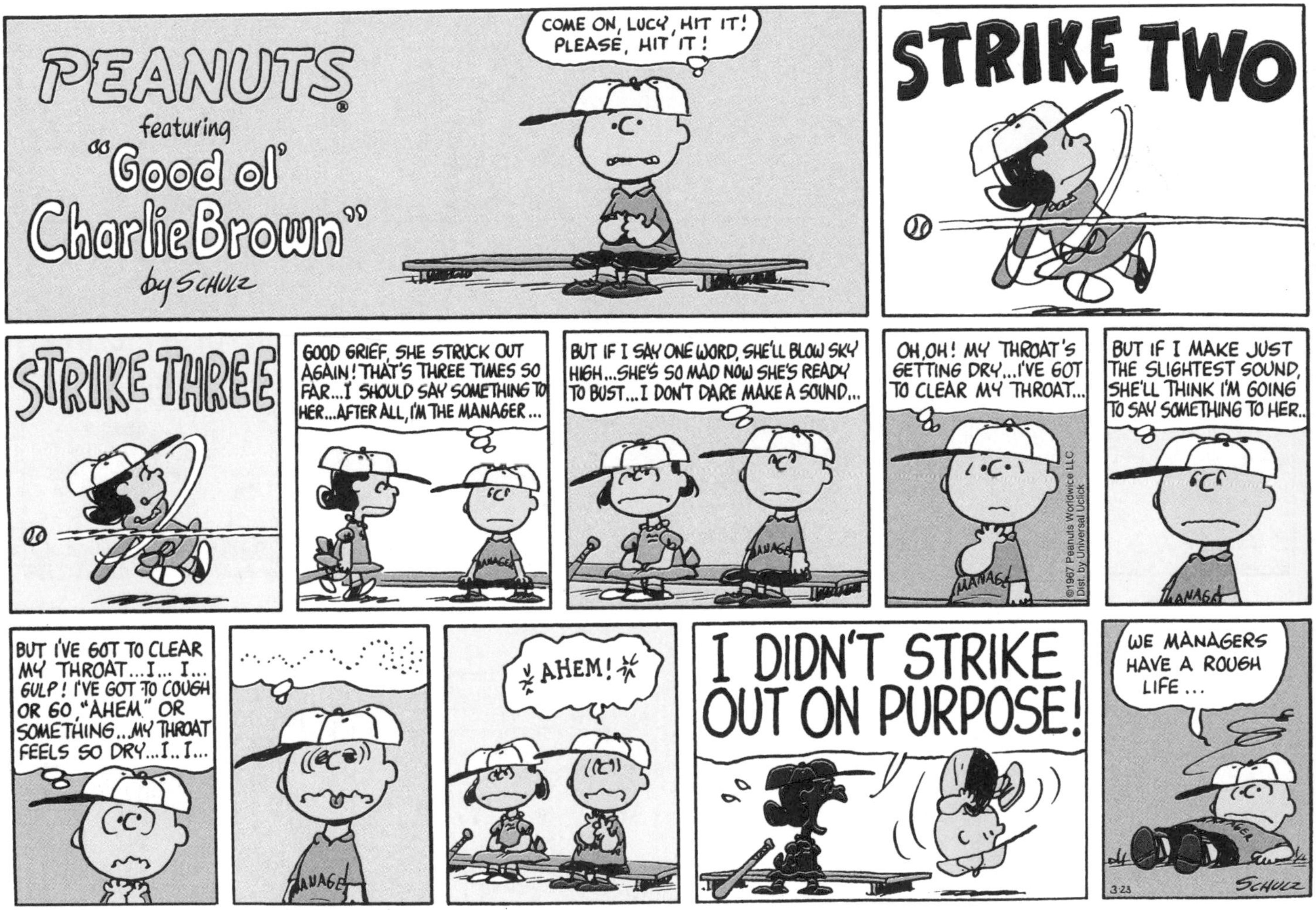
PEANUTS
featuring
"Good ol' CharlieBrown"
by SCHULZ
COME ON, LUCY, HIT IT! PLEASE, HIT IT!
STRIKE TWO
STRIKE THREE
GOOD GRIEF, SHE STRUCK OUT AGAIN! THAT'S THREE TIMES SO FAR...I SHOULD SAY SOMETHING TO HER...AFTER ALL, I'M THE MANAGER...
BUT IF I SAY ONE WORD, SHE'LL BLOW SKY HIGH...SHE'S SO MAD NOW SHE'S READY TO BUST...I DON'T DARE MAKE A SOUND...
OH, OH! MY THROAT'S GETTING DRY...I'VE GOT TO CLEAR MY THROAT...
©1967 Peanuts Worldwide LLC
Dist. by Universal Uclick
BUT IF I MAKE JUST THE SLIGHTEST SOUND, SHE'LL THINK I'M GOING TO SAY SOMETHING TO HER..
BUT I'VE GOT TO CLEAR MY THROAT...I... I... GULP! I'VE GOT TO COUGH OR GO, "AHEM" OR SOMETHING...MY THROAT FEELS SO DRY...I..I...
AHEM!
I DIDN'T STRIKE OUT ON PURPOSE!
WE MANAGERS HAVE A ROUGH LIFE...
3-23
SCHULZ

I HAVE GREAT NEWS FOR YOU, MANAGER!
THIS YEAR I'M GOING TO CONCENTRATE ON MY HITTING...
3-26
© 1966 Peanuts Worldwide LLC, Dist. by Universal Uclick
I HAVE IT ALL FIGURED OUT...
www.snoopy.com
ALL I NEED IS ONE HIT, AND I CAN RAISE MY LIFETIME BATTING AVERAGE TO .001 !
SCHULZ

HEY, SNOOPY! WAKE UP! THE BASEBALL SEASON HAS BEGUN!
I SAID, WAKE UP! IT'S TIME TO PLAY BALL!
3-25
© 1966 Peanuts Worldwide LLC, Dist. by Universal Uclick
BLEAH!
www.snoopy.com
MY FIRST HOLDOUT!
SCHULZ

WHAP
3-27
CLOMP
© 1966 Peanuts Worldwide LLC, Dist. by Universal Uclick
GOOD CATCH, SNOOPY..
PTUI!
THANK YOU..
www.snoopy.com
BLEAH! HORSEHIDE TASTES TERRIBLE IN THE MORNING!
SCHULZ

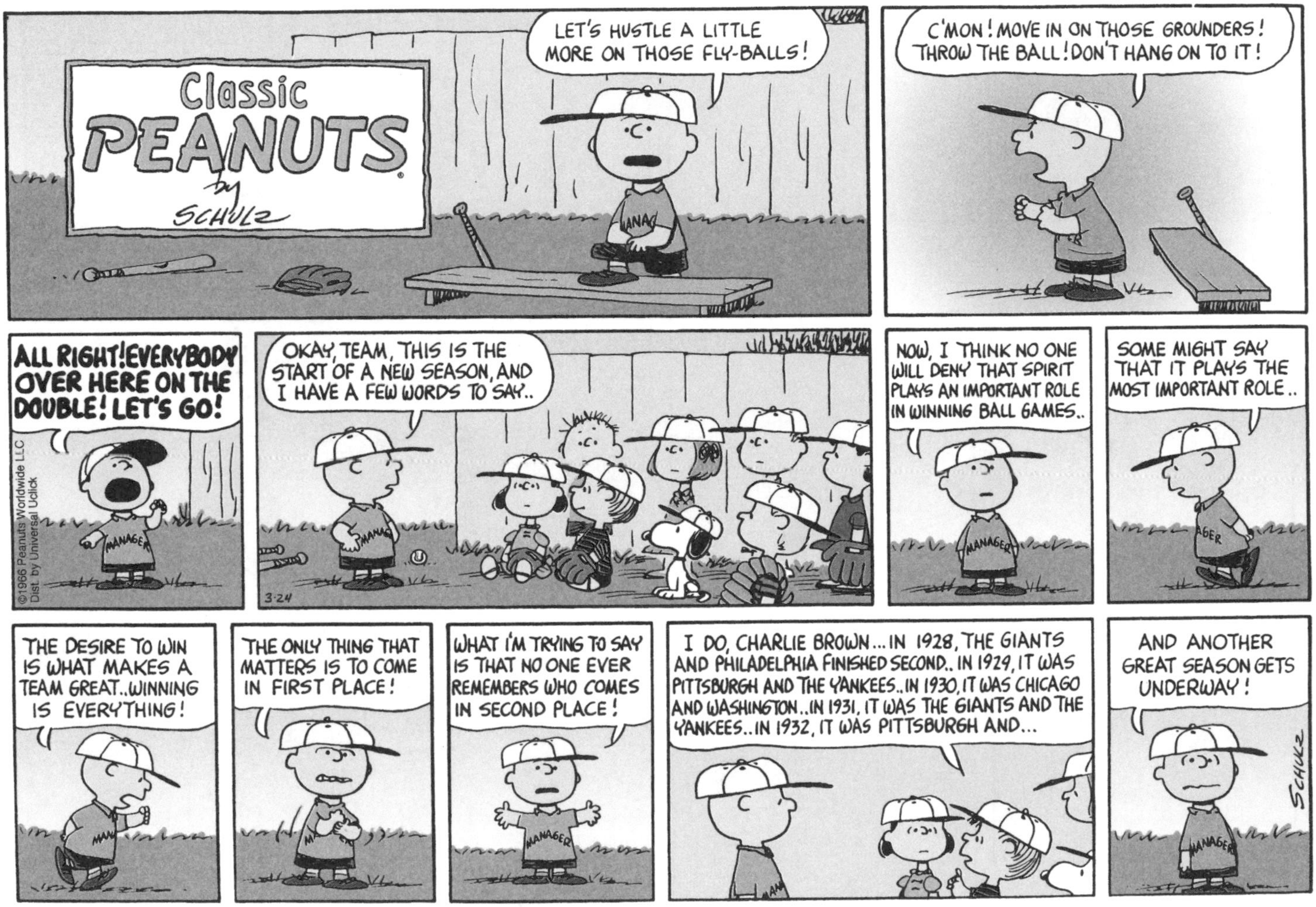
Classic PEANUTS by SCHULZ
LET'S HUSTLE A LITTLE MORE ON THOSE FLY-BALLS!
C'MON! MOVE IN ON THOSE GROUNDERS! THROW THE BALL! DON'T HANG ON TO IT!
ALL RIGHT! EVERYBODY OVER HERE ON THE DOUBLE! LET'S GO!
©1966 Peanuts Worldwide LLC
Dist. by Universal Uclick
OKAY, TEAM, THIS IS THE START OF A NEW SEASON, AND I HAVE A FEW WORDS TO SAY..
3-24
NOW, I THINK NO ONE WILL DENY THAT SPIRIT PLAYS AN IMPORTANT ROLE IN WINNING BALL GAMES..
SOME MIGHT SAY THAT IT PLAYS THE MOST IMPORTANT ROLE..
THE DESIRE TO WIN IS WHAT MAKES A TEAM GREAT..WINNING IS EVERYTHING!
THE ONLY THING THAT MATTERS IS TO COME IN FIRST PLACE!
WHAT I'M TRYING TO SAY IS THAT NO ONE EVER REMEMBERS WHO COMES IN SECOND PLACE!
I DO, CHARLIE BROWN... IN 1928, THE GIANTS AND PHILADELPHIA FINISHED SECOND.. IN 1929, IT WAS PITTSBURGH AND THE YANKEES.. IN 1930, IT WAS CHICAGO AND WASHINGTON.. IN 1931, IT WAS THE GIANTS AND THE YANKEES.. IN 1932, IT WAS PITTSBURGH AND...
AND ANOTHER GREAT SEASON GETS UNDERWAY!
SCHULZ

3-26
© 1965 Peanuts Worldwide LLC, Dist. by Universal Uclick
www.snoopy.com
SURF'S UP!
SCHULZ

DON'T TELL ME THAT'S YOUR LUNCH ?!
© 1965 Peanuts Worldwide LLC, Dist. by Universal Uclick
SOME OF IT...
3-27
www.snoopy.com
WHAT ELSE DO YOU HAVE IN THERE?
MY SKATE BOARD!
SCHULZ

3-28
© 1965 Peanuts Worldwide LLC, Dist. by Universal Uclick
AAUGH!
www.snoopy.com
THAT'S WHAT I CALL A REAL "WIPE-OUT"!
SCHULZ

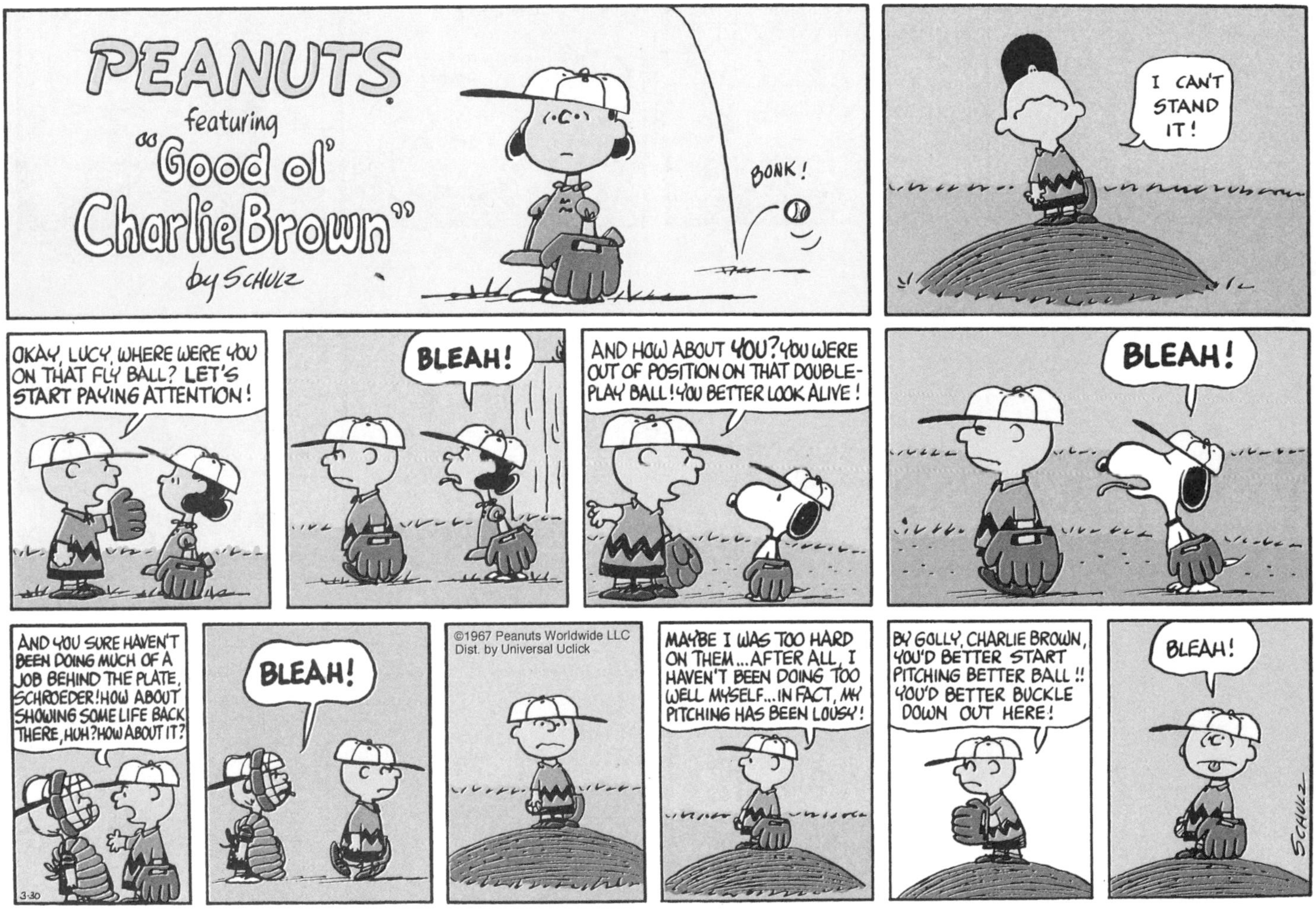

PEANUTS
featuring "Good ol' CharlieBrown"
by SCHULZ
BONK!
I CAN'T STAND IT!
OKAY, LUCY, WHERE WERE YOU ON THAT FLY BALL? LET'S START PAYING ATTENTION!
BLEAH!
AND HOW ABOUT YOU? YOU WERE OUT OF POSITION ON THAT DOUBLE-PLAY BALL! YOU BETTER LOOK ALIVE!
BLEAH!
AND YOU SURE HAVEN'T BEEN DOING MUCH OF A JOB BEHIND THE PLATE, SCHROEDER! HOW ABOUT SHOWING SOME LIFE BACK THERE, HUH? HOW ABOUT IT?
3-30
BLEAH!
©1967 Peanuts Worldwide LLC
Dist. by Universal Uclick
MAYBE I WAS TOO HARD ON THEM...AFTER ALL, I HAVEN'T BEEN DOING TOO WELL MYSELF...IN FACT, MY PITCHING HAS BEEN LOUSY!
BY GOLLY, CHARLIE BROWN, YOU'D BETTER START PITCHING BETTER BALL!! YOU'D BETTER BUCKLE DOWN OUT HERE!
BLEAH!
SCHULZ

MY HEART IS FULL ON THE DAY I FIRST GO OUT TO THE OL' BALL FIELD...
© 1965 Peanuts Worldwide LLC, Dist. by Universal Uclick
I LOVE THE SMELL OF THE HORSEHIDE, THE GRASSY OUTFIELD AND THE DUSTY INFIELD...I LOVE THE MEMORIES..THE HOPES...AND THE DREAMS FOR THE NEW SEASON..
3-29
www.snoopy.com
AH! THERE IT IS! MY PITCHER'S MOUND...COVERED WITH TRADITION..
AND DANDELIONS!
SCHULZ

THIS PITCHER'S MOUND IS COVERED WITH DANDELIONS
DON'T TOUCH THEM, CHARLIE BROWN!
© 1965 Peanuts Worldwide LLC, Dist. by Universal Uclick
DON'T YOU DARE HURT ALL THOSE INNOCENT DANDELIONS! THEY'RE BEAUTIFUL! DON'T YOU DARE CUT THEM DOWN!
3-30
www.snoopy.com
BESIDES, YOU MAY NOT KNOW IT, BUT YOU LOOK KIND OF CUTE STANDING THERE SURROUNDED BY DANDELIONS..
I DON'T WANT TO LOOK CUTE!!
SCHULZ

HERE WE GO... THE FIRST PITCH OF THE SEASON..
© 1965 Peanuts Worldwide LLC, Dist. by Universal Uclick
www.snoopy.com
POW!
IT'S KIND OF PEACEFUL LYING HERE AMONG THE DANDELIONS..
SCHULZ
3-31

WHAT IN THE WORLD ARE ALL THESE DANDELIONS DOING ON THE PITCHER'S MOUND?
THEY GREW THERE! AND MY STUPID GIRL-OUTFIELDERS WON'T LET ME CUT THEM DOWN! THEY SAY THEY'RE PRETTY, AND I LOOK CUTE STANDING HERE AMONG THEM!
4-2
© 1965 Peanuts Worldwide LLC, Dist. by Universal Uclick
THEY'RE RIGHT...YOU DO LOOK KIND OF CUTE STANDING THERE..
www.snoopy.com
SCHULZ

HOLD YOUR CHIN UP, CHARLIE BROWN..
4-3
I'M GOING TO TICKLE YOU WITH THIS DANDELION..IF YOUR CHIN TURNS YELLOW, IT MEANS YOU LIKE BUTTER..
?
© 1965 Peanuts Worldwide LLC, Dist. by Universal Uclick
HEY, LOOK! CHARLIE BROWN LIKES BUTTER!
www.snoopy.com
I WONDER IF MY FONDNESS FOR DAIRY PRODUCTS WILL HELP US WIN BALL GAMES
SCHULZ

WHY, CHARLIE BROWN! YOU CUT DOWN ALL THE DANDELIONS!
YES, I CUT DOWN ALL THE DANDELIONS! THIS IS A PITCHER'S MOUND, NOT A FLOWER GARDEN!
4-4
© 1965 Peanuts Worldwide LLC, Dist. by Universal Uclick
SPEAKING OF FLOWER GARDENS, I'LL BET A CIRCLE OF DAFFODILS WOULD LOOK NICE AROUND THIS MOUND, DON'T YOU THINK SO?
www.snoopy.com
OH, YES, VERY NICE...OR EVEN SOME MARIGOLDS..
I CAN'T STAND IT!
SCHULZ

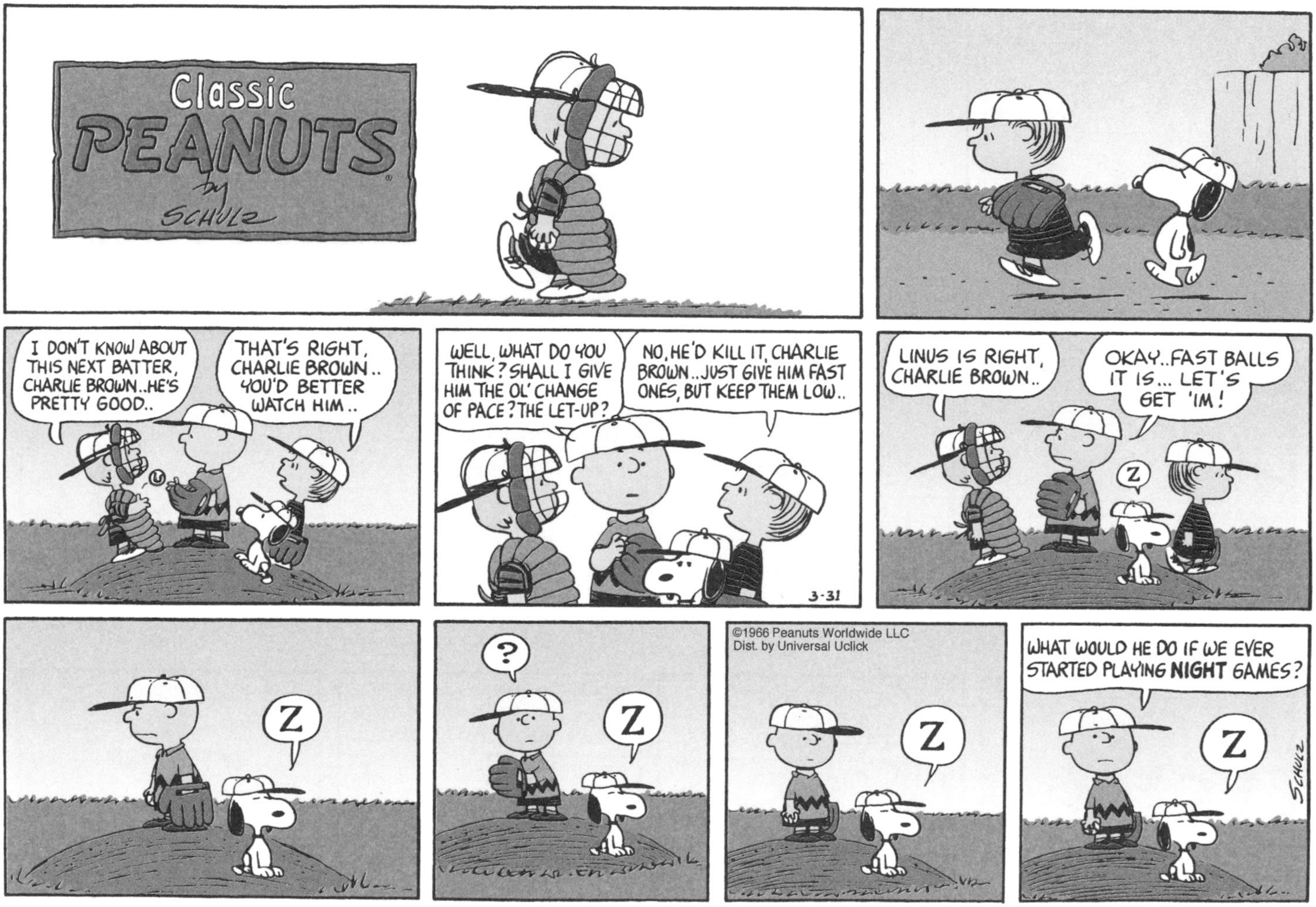
Classic
PEANUTS
by
SCHULZ
I DON'T KNOW ABOUT THIS NEXT BATTER, CHARLIE BROWN..HE'S PRETTY GOOD..
THAT'S RIGHT, CHARLIE BROWN.. YOU'D BETTER WATCH HIM..
WELL, WHAT DO YOU THINK? SHALL I GIVE HIM THE OL' CHANGE OF PACE? THE LET-UP?
NO, HE'D KILL IT, CHARLIE BROWN...JUST GIVE HIM FAST ONES, BUT KEEP THEM LOW..
3-31
LINUS IS RIGHT, CHARLIE BROWN..
OKAY..FAST BALLS IT IS... LET'S GET 'IM!
Z
Z
?
Z
©1966 Peanuts Worldwide LLC
Dist. by Universal Uclick
Z
WHAT WOULD HE DO IF WE EVER STARTED PLAYING NIGHT GAMES?
Z
SCHULZ

THIS IS THE ONE MOMENT OF THE YEAR I CHERISH..
THIS IS THE FIRST TIME I CLIMB UP ON THAT OL' PITCHER'S MOUND..
THIS IS THE MOMENT OF MOMENTS.. THE BEGINNING OF A NEW SEASON... THIS IS A MOMENT TO SAVOR THOUGHTFULLY..A MOMENT TO...
© 1966 Peanuts Worldwide LLC, Dist. by Universal Uclick
GET UP THERE AND PITCH, YOU BLOCKHEAD!
www.snoopy.com
3-28
IT'S OVER!
SCHULZ

YOU KNOW, A THOUGHT JUST OCCURRED TO ME..
I PUT UP WITH AN AWFUL LOT BEING YOUR CATCHER, AND SOMETHING JUST OCCURRED TO ME..
© 1966 Peanuts Worldwide LLC, Dist. by Universal Uclick
THE THOUGHT OCCURRED TO ME THAT BEETHOVEN NEVER WOULD HAVE PUT UP WITH WHAT I PUT UP WITH... AT LEAST I DON'T THINK HE WOULD HAVE...
3-29
www.snoopy.com
ANYWAY, THAT'S THE THOUGHT THAT JUST OCCURRED TO ME..
THANKS, FRIEND!
SCHULZ

3-30
AH! HE HIT IT RIGHT TO MY SHORTSTOP! THIS'LL BE AN EASY OUT...
© 1966 Peanuts Worldwide LLC, Dist. by Universal Uclick
HERE'S THE WORLD WAR I FLYING ACE ZOOMING THROUGH THE AIR IN HIS SOPWITH CAMEL..
www.snoopy.com
* SIGH *
SCHULZ

ONE HUNDRED AND TWENTY-THREE TO NOTHING!
NO ONE SHOULD EVER HAVE TO LOSE THE FIRST GAME OF THE SEASON BY A SCORE OF 123 TO 0!
© 1986 Peanuts Worldwide LLC, Dist. by Universal Uclick
IT'S JUST NOT RIGHT..
4-1
www.snoopy.com
BESIDES, HOW COULD WE POSSIBLY LOSE A GAME 123 TO 0?
WE NEVER GOT ANY BREAKS!
SCHULZ

WELL, WE LOST THE FIRST GAME OF THE SEASON AGAIN!
4-5
I SHOULDN'T LET IT BOTHER ME, BUT IT DOES...
© 1985 Peanuts Worldwide LLC, Dist. by Universal Uclick
WE ALWAYS SEEM TO LOSE THE FIRST GAME OF THE SEASON AND THE LAST GAME OF THE SEASON..
www.snoopy.com
AND ALL THE STUPID GAMES IN-BETWEEN!
SCHULZ

HERE, TAKE THIS BAT, AND HIT ME A FEW FLIES...
4-7
© 1987 Peanuts Worldwide LLC, Dist. by Universal Uclick
www.snoopy.com
I MEANT ONE AT A TIME!
SCHULZ

Classic PEANUTS by SCHULZ
IT'S STARTING TO RAIN, CHARLIE BROWN... AREN'T WE GOING TO CALL THE GAME?
NO, WE'RE NOT GOING TO CALL THE GAME, SO YOU MIGHT AS WELL GET BACK OUT THERE IN CENTER FIELD WHERE YOU BELONG!
AND TRY TO PAY ATTENTION TO WHAT YOU'RE DOING!
POW!
BONK
©1965 Peanuts Worldwide LLC
Dist. by Universal Uclick
THIS IS GOING TO BE ANOTHER GREAT SEASON!
SCHULZ

I'LL BE GLAD WHEN I GROW UP, AND CAN MOVE OUT OF THIS NEIGHBORHOOD!
I NEED TO SEE NEW PLACES, AND MEET NEW PEOPLE
EVERYONE AROUND HERE BORES ME!
"EVERYONE"?
ESPECIALLY "EVERYONE"!!!
4-12
© 1968 Peanuts Worldwide LLC. Dist. by Universal Uclick
www.snoopy.com
SCHULZ

IF YOU HAVE SOME PROBLEM IN YOUR LIFE, DO YOU BELIEVE YOU SHOULD TRY TO SOLVE IT RIGHT AWAY OR THINK ABOUT IT FOR AWHILE?
OH, THINK ABOUT IT...BY ALL MEANS...I BELIEVE YOU SHOULD THINK ABOUT IT FOR AWHILE...
TO GIVE YOURSELF TIME TO DO THE RIGHT THING ABOUT THE PROBLEM?
NO, TO GIVE IT TIME TO GO AWAY!
4-12
© 1967 Peanuts Worldwide LLC. Dist. by Universal Uclick
www.snoopy.com
SCHULZ

AND ALSO WHEN I TALK TO PEOPLE, I FIND THAT THEY DON'T REALLY LISTEN TO ME..
I FIND THAT I CAN'T SEEM TO HOLD A PERSON'S ATTENTION...WHEN I TALK TO PEOPLE, THEIR MINDS SORT OF WANDER OFF, AND THEY STARE INTO SPACE, AND...
...AND...AND....
SIGH
HELP 5¢
THE DOCTOR IS IN
4-12
© 1965 Peanuts Worldwide LLC. Dist. by Universal Uclick
www.snoopy.com
SCHULZ

Classic PEANUTS by SCHULZ
BEEN WAITING LONG?
YOU STUPID TREE!
4-8
YOU THINK YOU'RE GOING TO GET THIS KITE, DON'T YOU? WELL, YOU'RE NOT!
I'M GOING TO START THIS KITE FROM HERE, AND I'M GOING TO FLY IT WHERE YOU CAN'T GET IT...
THIS IS ONE KITE THAT ISN'T GOING TO GET TANGLED IN A TREE!
ALL YOU TREES ARE ALIKE...YOU THINK YOU CAN JUST..
WUMP!
©1965 Peanuts Worldwide LLC
Dist. by Universal Uclick
SIGH!
SCHULZ

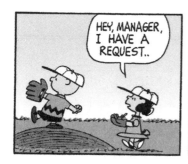

HEY, MANAGER, I HAVE A REQUEST..
TRY TO PITCH SO THAT NO ONE HITS ME A FLY BALL THIS INNING...I DON'T HAVE ANY ROOM IN MY GLOVE FOR A FLY BALL...
4-10
© 1966 Peanuts Worldwide LLC. Dist. by Universal Uclick
WHAT'S THAT YOU HAVE IN IT?
www.snoopy.com
TAPIOCA PUDDING!
SCHULZ

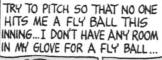

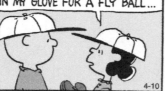

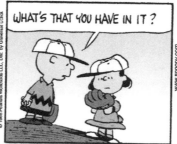

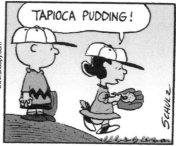

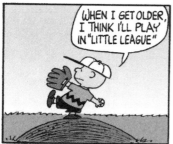

WHEN I GET OLDER, I THINK I'LL PLAY IN "LITTLE LEAGUE"
LATER ON I'LL PLAY FOR MY SCHOOL TEAM, THEN A LITTLE COLLEGE BALL AND THEN THE MAJOR LEAGUES!
© 1966 Peanuts Worldwide LLC. Dist. by Universal Uclick
POW!
www.snoopy.com
IN THE MEANTIME, I HAVE MY PROBLEMS!
SCHULZ
4-19

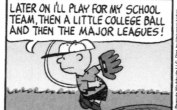

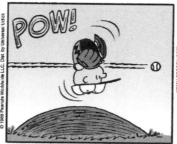

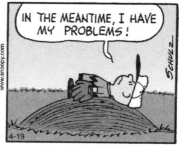

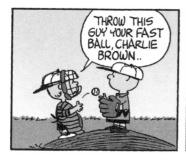

THROW THIS GUY YOUR FAST BALL, CHARLIE BROWN..
I THINK YOU'D BETTER KEEP THE BALL LOW TO THIS GUY, CHARLIE BROWN...GIVE HIM A LOW CURVE..
4-19
© 1965 Peanuts Worldwide LLC. Dist. by Universal Uclick
THROW THIS GUY ALL KNUCKLE BALLS, CHARLIE BROWN...YOU'LL FOOL HIM WITH KNUCKLE BALLS...
www.snoopy.com
THIS IS THE LATEST THING... PITCHING BY COMMITTEE!
SCHULZ

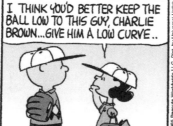

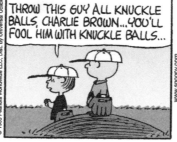

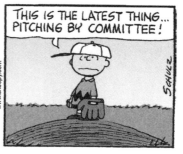

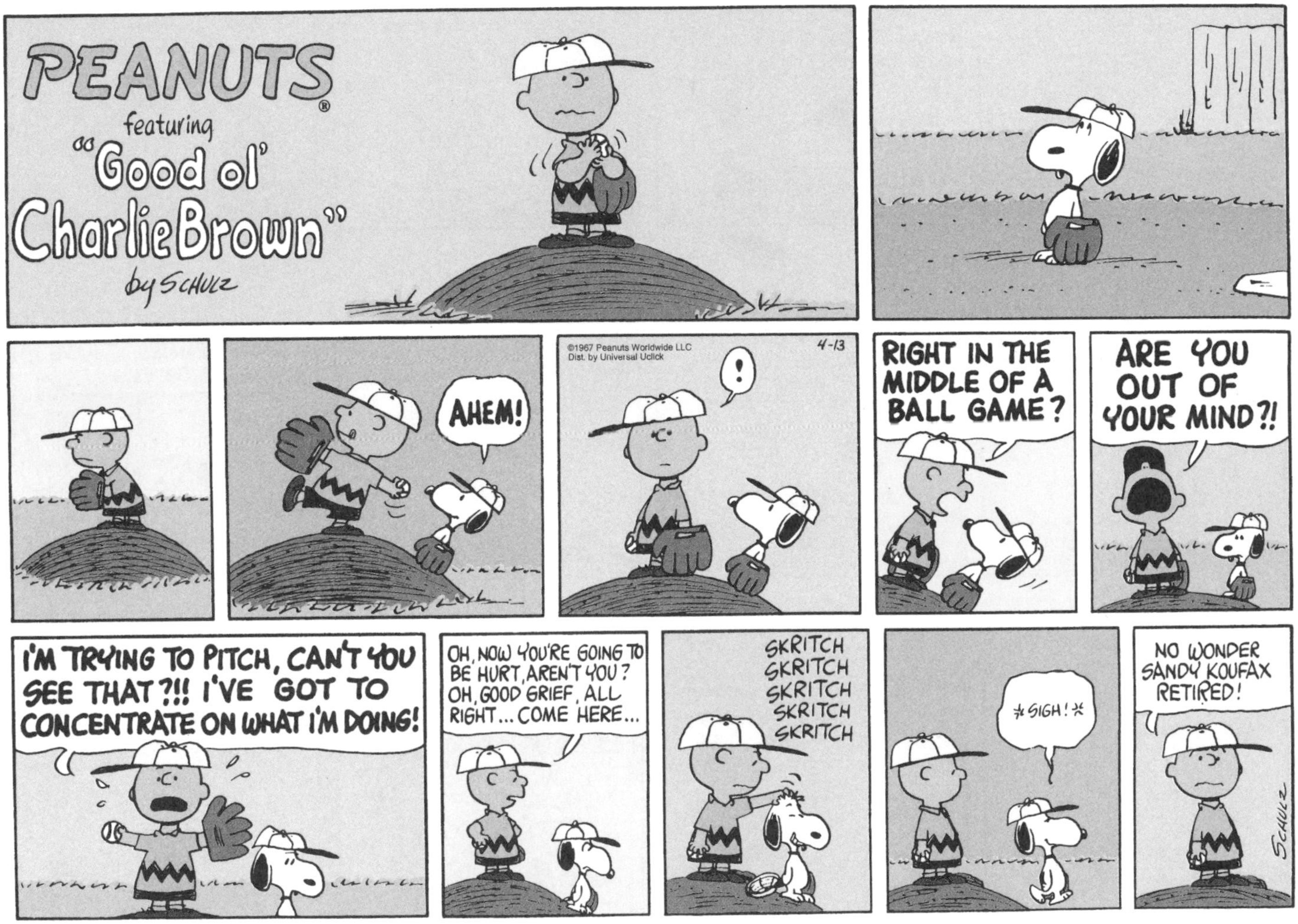
PEANUTS®
featuring
"Good ol' Charlie Brown"
by SCHULZ
©1967 Peanuts Worldwide LLC
Dist. by Universal Uclick
4-13
AHEM!
!
RIGHT IN THE MIDDLE OF A BALL GAME?
ARE YOU OUT OF YOUR MIND?!
I'M TRYING TO PITCH, CAN'T YOU SEE THAT?!! I'VE GOT TO CONCENTRATE ON WHAT I'M DOING!
OH, NOW YOU'RE GOING TO BE HURT, AREN'T YOU? OH, GOOD GRIEF, ALL RIGHT... COME HERE...
SKRITCH SKRITCH SKRITCH SKRITCH SKRITCH
SIGH!
NO WONDER SANDY KOUFAX RETIRED!
SCHULZ

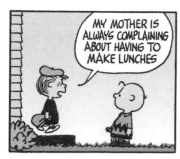

MY MOTHER IS ALWAYS COMPLAINING ABOUT HAVING TO MAKE LUNCHES
WHAT'S SO HARD ABOUT IT? THIS MORNING I TOLD HER I'D MAKE MY OWN LUNCH
© 1966 Peanuts Worldwide LLC. Dist. by Universal Uclick
AND I DID, TOO! SEE? I MADE MY OWN LUNCH..
4-22
www.snoopy.com
EIGHT CANDY BARS!
SCHULZ

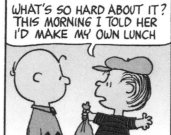

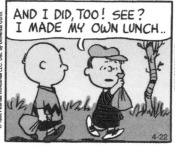

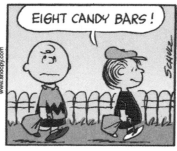

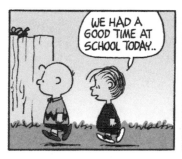

WE HAD A GOOD TIME AT SCHOOL TODAY..
OUR TEACHER TOOK US ON A FIELD TRIP...WE WENT OUT, AND WE SAW THIS GREAT BIG FIELD
4-25
© 1966 Peanuts Worldwide LLC. Dist. by Universal Uclick
IT WAS A REAL FIELD, AND WE SAW IT! WE STOOD RIGHT THERE, AND WE SAW THAT FIELD!
www.snoopy.com
DO YOU THINK YOU'LL BE GOING ON ANY MORE FIELD TRIPS?
I DOUBT IT..WHEN YOU'VE SEEN ONE FIELD, YOU'VE SEEN THEM ALL
SCHULZ

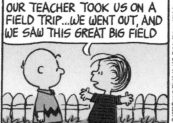

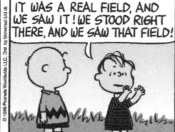

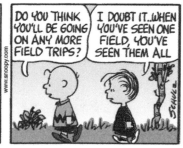

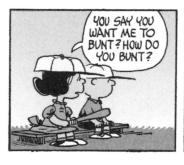

YOU SAY YOU WANT ME TO BUNT? HOW DO YOU BUNT?
JUST HOLD THE BAT OUT IN FRONT OF YOU, AND TRY TO TAP THE BALL LIGHTLY...
© 1965 Peanuts Worldwide LLC. Dist. by Universal Uclick
www.snoopy.com
I'M A GOOD MANAGER...IT'S ONLY THE MIDDLE OF MAY, AND ALREADY MY STOMACH HURTS!
SCHULZ
5-17

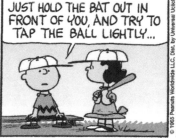

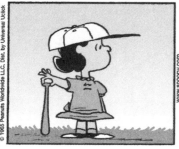

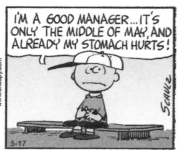

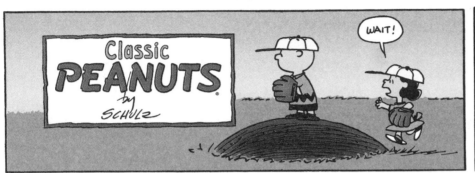

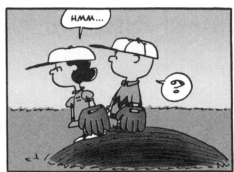

Classic
PEANUTS
by SCHULZ
WAIT!
HMM...
?
BRUSH THIS GUY BACK, CHARLIE BROWN! GIVE 'IM THE OL' BEAN-BALL!
NO, I CAN'T DO THAT... IT WOULDN'T BE RIGHT...
IT WOULDN'T BE RIGHT ?!
LISTEN TO WHO'S GONE MORAL ON US ALL OF A SUDDEN! OL' WISHY-WASHY HERE IS TOO MORAL TO THROW A BEAN-BALL!
?
WHAT ABOUT THE WAY THE EARLY SETTLERS TREATED THE INDIANS? WAS THAT MORAL? HOW ABOUT THE CHILDREN'S CRUSADE? WAS THAT MORAL?
YEAH, AND HOW ABOUT THOSE AWFUL MOVIE ADS YOU SEE NOWADAYS?
DO YOU CALL THOSE MORAL, CHARLIE BROWN?
4-15
DO YOU THINK THAT INCIDENT AT HARPER'S FERRY WAS CONSISTENT WITH MORALITY?
DEFINE MORALITY!
OUR WHOLE SYSTEM OF FREEWAYS IS A PERFECT EXAMPLE OF WHAT I'M TRYING TO SAY!
HAVE YOU LISTENED TO RADIO LATELY?
HOW ABOUT THIS WHOLE CONSERVATION SITUATION?
©1965 Peanuts Worldwide LLC
Dist. by Universal Uclick
SCHULZ
WE NEVER WIN ANY BALL GAMES, BUT WE HAVE SOME INTERESTING DISCUSSIONS!

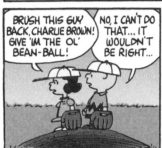

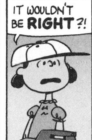

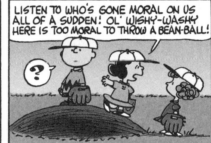

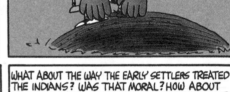

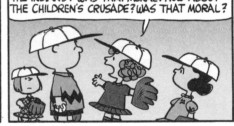

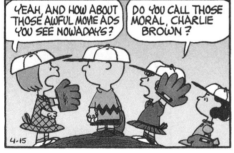

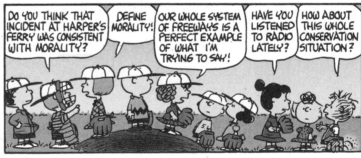

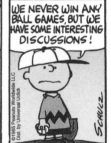

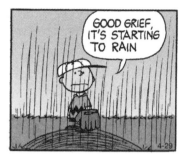

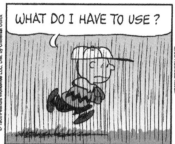

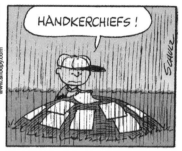

GOOD GRIEF, IT'S STARTING TO RAIN
4-29
IN THE BIG LEAGUES WHEN IT STARTS TO RAIN, THE GROUNDSKEEPER COVERS THE PITCHER'S MOUND WITH A TARP
© 1966 Peanuts Worldwide LLC. Dist. by Universal Uclick
WHAT DO I HAVE TO USE ?
www.snoopy.com
HANDKERCHIEFS !
SCHULZ

THE RAIN WASHED AWAY MY PITCHER'S MOUND !
WHY DON'T YOU WRITE TO COMMISSIONER ECKERT, AND ASK HIM TO SEND YOU A NEW ONE ?
4-30
© 1966 Peanuts Worldwide LLC. Dist. by Universal Uclick
www.snoopy.com
YOU'RE NOT MUCH FOR TAKING SUGGESTIONS, ARE YOU ?
SCHULZ

THE RAIN WASHED AWAY MY PITCHER'S MOUND...
I'M A PITCHER WITHOUT A MOUND...I'M A LOST SOUL... I'M LIKE A POLITICIAN OUT OF OFFICE
5-1
© 1966 Peanuts Worldwide LLC. Dist. by Universal Uclick
OR A SAILOR WITHOUT AN OCEAN...
www.snoopy.com
OR A BOY WITHOUT A GIRL.......
SCHULZ

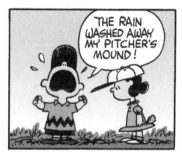

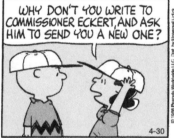

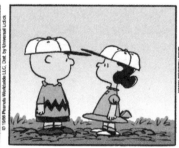

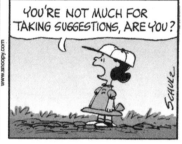

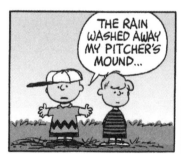

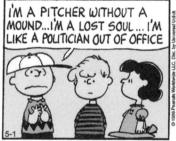

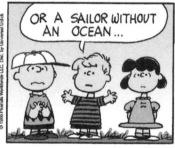

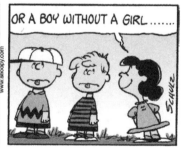

GUESS WHAT... I MADE YOU A NEW PITCHER'S MOUND...
YOU'RE KIDDING!
NO, I'M NOT.. COME, AND SEE...
5-2
© 1986 Peanuts Worldwide LLC. Dist. by Universal Uclick
www.snoopy.com
DID I GET IT A LITTLE TOO HIGH?
SCHULZ

HEY, CHARLIE BROWN! I'VE GOT YOUR MOUND ALL FIXED UP!
WELL, WHAT DO YOU THINK?
IT LOOKS GREAT...
© 1986 Peanuts Worldwide LLC. Dist. by Universal Uclick
GO AHEAD...TRY IT..
www.snoopy.com
OF COURSE, IT NEEDS A LITTLE PATTING DOWN..
SCHULZ
5-3

WELL, THE RAIN MAY HAVE WASHED AWAY MY PITCHER'S MOUND, BUT NOW IT'S BACK IN SHAPE!
I'M UP HERE LIKE I USED TO BE! UP HERE ON THE OL' MOUND THROWING MY OL' FAST BALL, AND..
© 1986 Peanuts Worldwide LLC. Dist. by Universal Uclick
POW!
www.snoopy.com
WHAT WE NEED AROUND HERE IS A LITTLE MORE RAIN...
5-4
SCHULZ

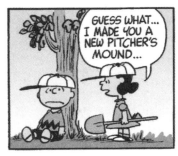

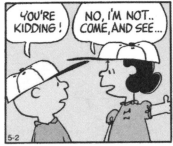

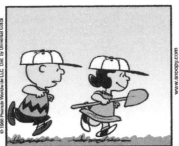

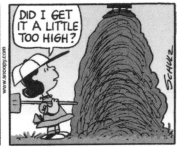

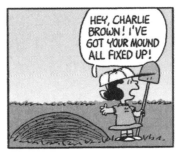

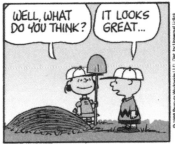

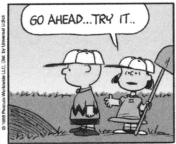

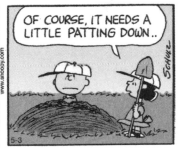

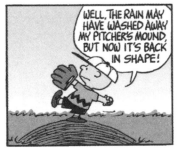

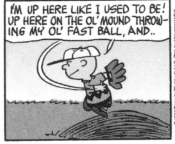

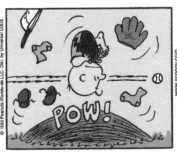

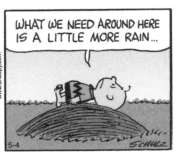

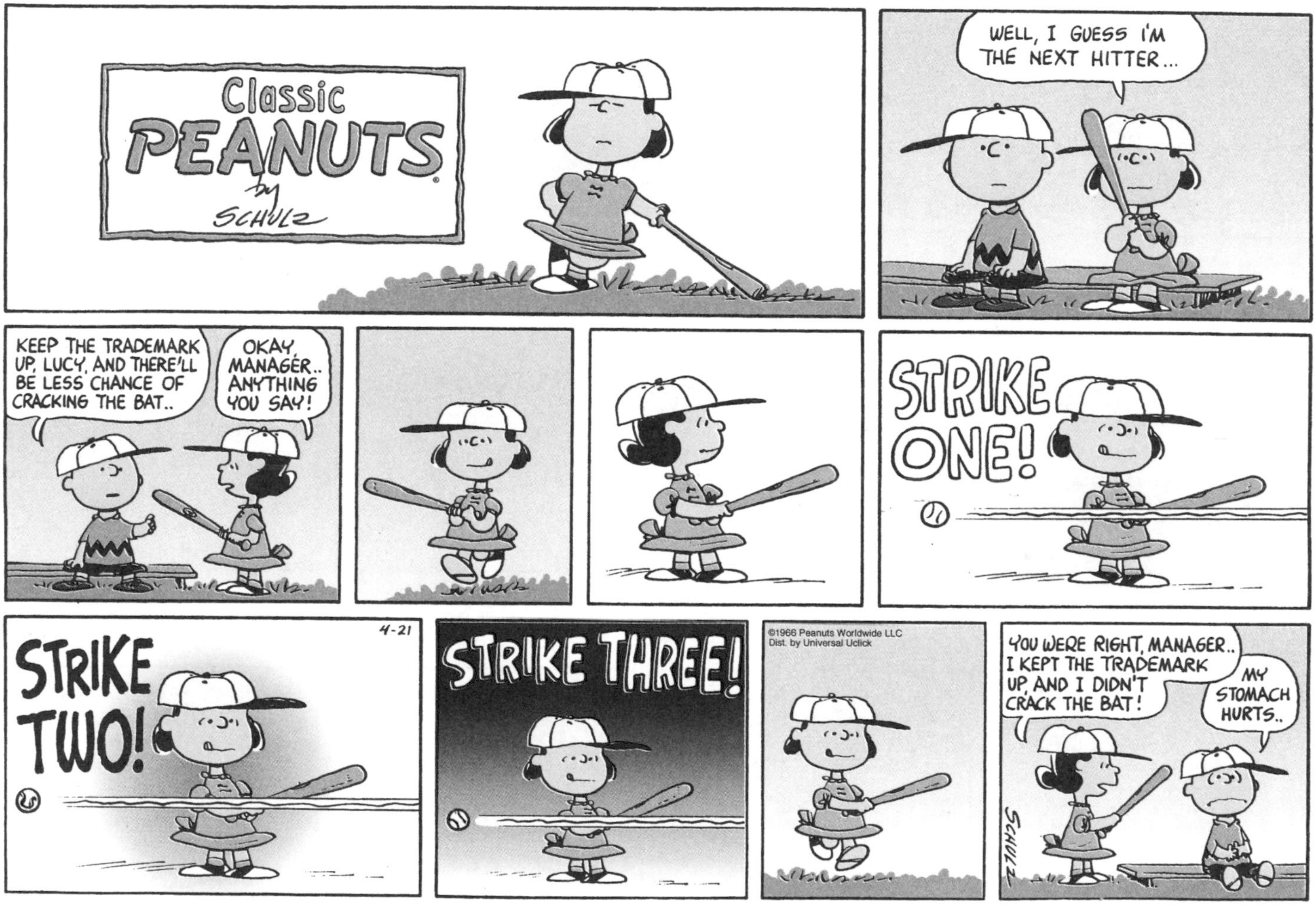
Classic PEANUTS by SCHULZ
WELL, I GUESS I'M THE NEXT HITTER...
KEEP THE TRADEMARK UP, LUCY, AND THERE'LL BE LESS CHANCE OF CRACKING THE BAT..
OKAY, MANAGER.. ANYTHING YOU SAY!
STRIKE ONE!
4-21
STRIKE TWO!
STRIKE THREE!
©1966 Peanuts Worldwide LLC Dist. by Universal Uclick
YOU WERE RIGHT, MANAGER.. I KEPT THE TRADEMARK UP, AND I DIDN'T CRACK THE BAT!
MY STOMACH HURTS..
SCHULZ

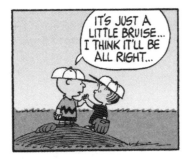

IT'S JUST A LITTLE BRUISE... I THINK IT'LL BE ALL RIGHT...
DO I THINK IT'S GOING TO RAIN? NO, I DOUBT IT...THOSE DON'T LOOK LIKE RAIN CLOUDS TO ME..
4-25
© 1965 Peanuts Worldwide LLC, Dist. by Universal Uclick
SUPPERTIME? OH, YES...I THINK WE'LL BE FINISHED WELL BEFORE SUPPERTIME..
www.snoopy.com
SOMETIMES I GET TO PITCH IN-BETWEEN QUESTIONS!
SCHULZ

4-28
PTUI!
© 1965 Peanuts Worldwide LLC, Dist. by Universal Uclick
www.snoopy.com
I MUST ADMIT I HAVE THE MOST UNIQUE DOUBLE-PLAY COMBINATION IN BASEBALL!
SCHULZ

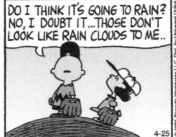

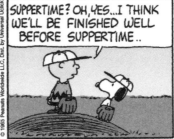

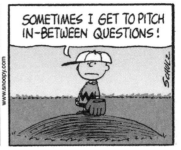

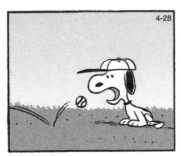

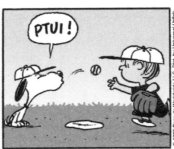

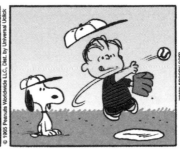

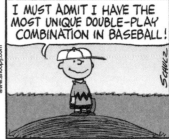

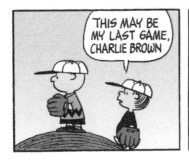

THIS MAY BE MY LAST GAME, CHARLIE BROWN
MY DAD'S BEEN TRANSFERRED... WE'RE MOVING TO A NEW CITY... I'LL PROBABLY NEVER SEE YOU AGAIN...
5-7
UNLESS, OF COURSE, WE HAPPEN TO GO TO THE SAME COLLEGE.. WHAT COLLEGE DO YOU THINK YOU'LL BE GOING TO?
www.snoopy.com
IT'S KIND OF HARD TO DECIDE IN THE LAST HALF OF THE NINTH INNING
SCHULZ

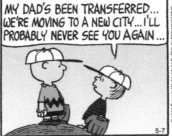

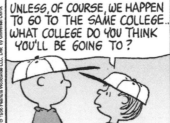

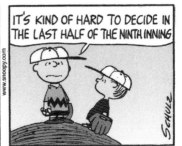

GOOD-BYE, CHARLIE BROWN.. IT'S BEEN NICE KNOWING YOU..
THIS IS REALLY HAPPENING! I CAN'T BELIEVE IT!
SO LONG, YOU OL' BLOCKHEAD...IT'S BEEN NICE KNOWING YOU..
I DON'T KNOW WHAT TO SAY.. I CAN'T BELIEVE IT...I....I.....
5-10
HERE, CHARLIE BROWN...I WANT YOU TO HAVE THIS...
YOUR BLANKET!
© 1968 Peanuts Worldwide LLC. Dist. by Universal Uclick
www.snoopy.com
SCHULZ

WHAT DO YOU MEAN, LINUS IS GONE?
HE'S GONE! HE AND LUCY HAVE MOVED AWAY...THEIR WHOLE FAMILY JUST PLAIN MOVED AWAY....
THAT'S RIDICULOUS! HE CAN'T MOVE AWAY! I LIKED HIM! I REALLY LIKED HIM!
5-11
THINGS LIKE THIS JUST DON'T HAPPEN!
HOW CAN I LOSE LINUS AND HAVE AMBLYOPIA BOTH IN ONE YEAR?!
© 1968 Peanuts Worldwide LLC. Dist. by Universal Uclick
www.snoopy.com
SCHULZ

WHERE WAS THAT BIG TRUCK GOING?
THAT'S A MOVING VAN...LINUS AND LUCY HAVE MOVED AWAY..
BUT I THOUGHT SHE WAS JUST KIDDING! I DIDN'T THINK THEY'D REALLY GO!
WELL, WHAT DO YOU CARE? YOU NEVER LIKED LUCY ANYWAY! YOU WERE ALWAYS INSULTING HER!
BUT I DIDN'T UNDERSTAND... I MEAN, I...
OH, STOP MAKING EXCUSES! GO ON HOME, AND PLAY YOUR OL' BEETHOVEN!
SCHROEDER, WHAT IF YOU AND I GOT MARRIED SOMEDAY, AND
I NEVER EVEN SAID GOOD-BYE..
5-13
© 1968 Peanuts Worldwide LLC. Dist. by Universal Uclick
www.snoopy.com
SCHULZ

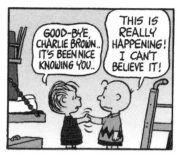

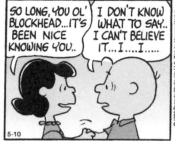

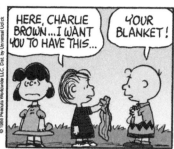

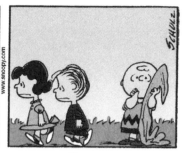

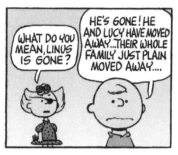

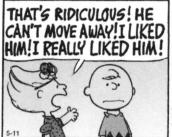

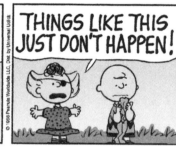

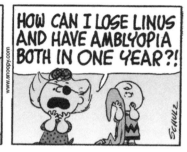

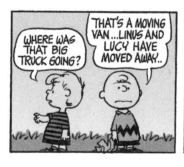

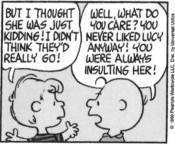

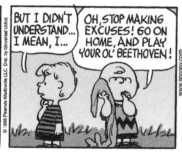

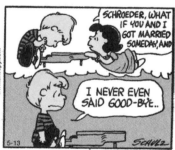

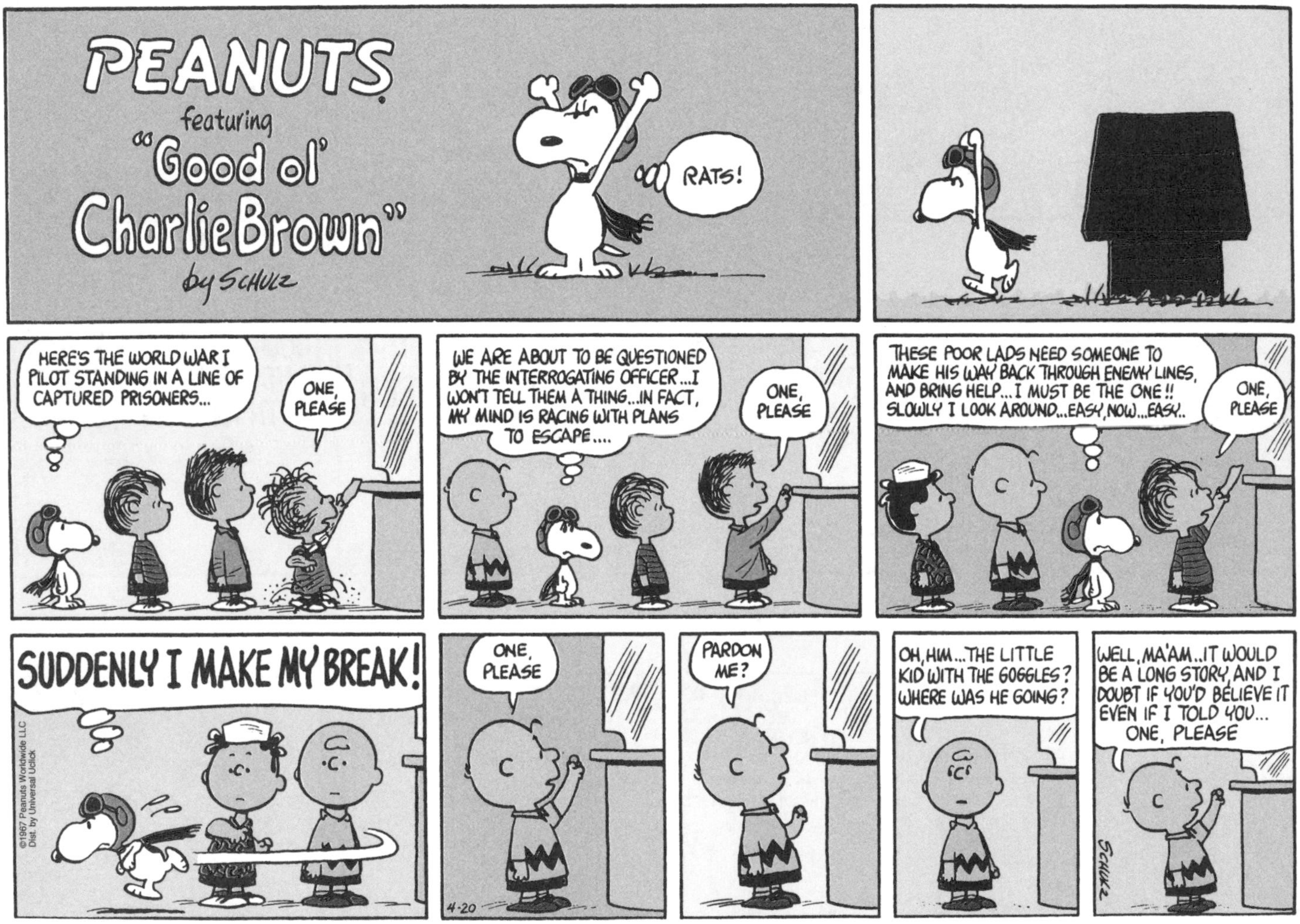
PEANUTS
featuring "Good ol' CharlieBrown"
by SCHULZ
RATS!
HERE'S THE WORLD WAR I PILOT STANDING IN A LINE OF CAPTURED PRISONERS...
ONE, PLEASE
WE ARE ABOUT TO BE QUESTIONED BY THE INTERROGATING OFFICER...I WON'T TELL THEM A THING...IN FACT, MY MIND IS RACING WITH PLANS TO ESCAPE....
ONE, PLEASE
THESE POOR LADS NEED SOMEONE TO MAKE HIS WAY BACK THROUGH ENEMY LINES, AND BRING HELP...I MUST BE THE ONE!! SLOWLY I LOOK AROUND...EASY, NOW...EASY..
ONE, PLEASE
SUDDENLY I MAKE MY BREAK!
©1967 Peanuts Worldwide LLC Dist. by Universal Uclick
ONE, PLEASE
4-20
PARDON ME?
OH, HIM...THE LITTLE KID WITH THE GOGGLES? WHERE WAS HE GOING?
WELL, MA'AM...IT WOULD BE A LONG STORY, AND I DOUBT IF YOU'D BELIEVE IT EVEN IF I TOLD YOU... ONE, PLEASE
SCHULZ

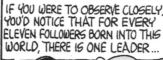

THERE ARE LEADERS IN THIS WORLD, CHARLIE BROWN, AND THERE ARE FOLLOWERS...

YOU ARE DOOMED ALWAYS TO BE A FOLLOWER! YOU WERE DOOMED FROM BIRTH...NOW, I HAVE A NEW THEORY....

5-19

IF YOU WERE TO OBSERVE CLOSELY, YOU'D NOTICE THAT FOR EVERY ELEVEN FOLLOWERS BORN INTO THIS WORLD, THERE IS ONE LEADER...

THAT'S MY NEW THEORY... BABIES ARE BORN IN SQUADS!

www.snoopy.com

© 1965 Peanuts Worldwide LLC, Dist. by Universal Uclick

NOW, IN CASE OF A FOUL BALL, RIP OFF YOUR MASK AND CATCH IT...

RIGHT

5-20

POW!

www.snoopy.com

IN ALL THE TIME WE'VE BEEN PLAYING, I'VE NEVER SEEN A FOUL BALL...

© 1965 Peanuts Worldwide LLC, Dist. by Universal Uclick

GOOD GRIEF, MY CENTER-FIELDER IS FACING THE WRONG WAY!

HEY, THE BALL GAME IS **THIS** WAY!

I CAN'T FACE THAT WAY.. THE SUN SHINES IN MY EYES..I HAVE VERY SENSITIVE AND BEAUTIFUL EYES...

MAYBE YOU'D LIKE TO HAVE US MOVE THE WHOLE BALL FIELD AROUND IN FRONT OF YOU?

THAT'S A GOOD IDEA, CHARLIE BROWN...YOU DO THAT...I'LL STAY RIGHT HERE

I CAN'T STAND IT...I JUST CAN'T STAND IT!

© 1965 Peanuts Worldwide LLC, Dist. by Universal Uclick

www.snoopy.com

5-21

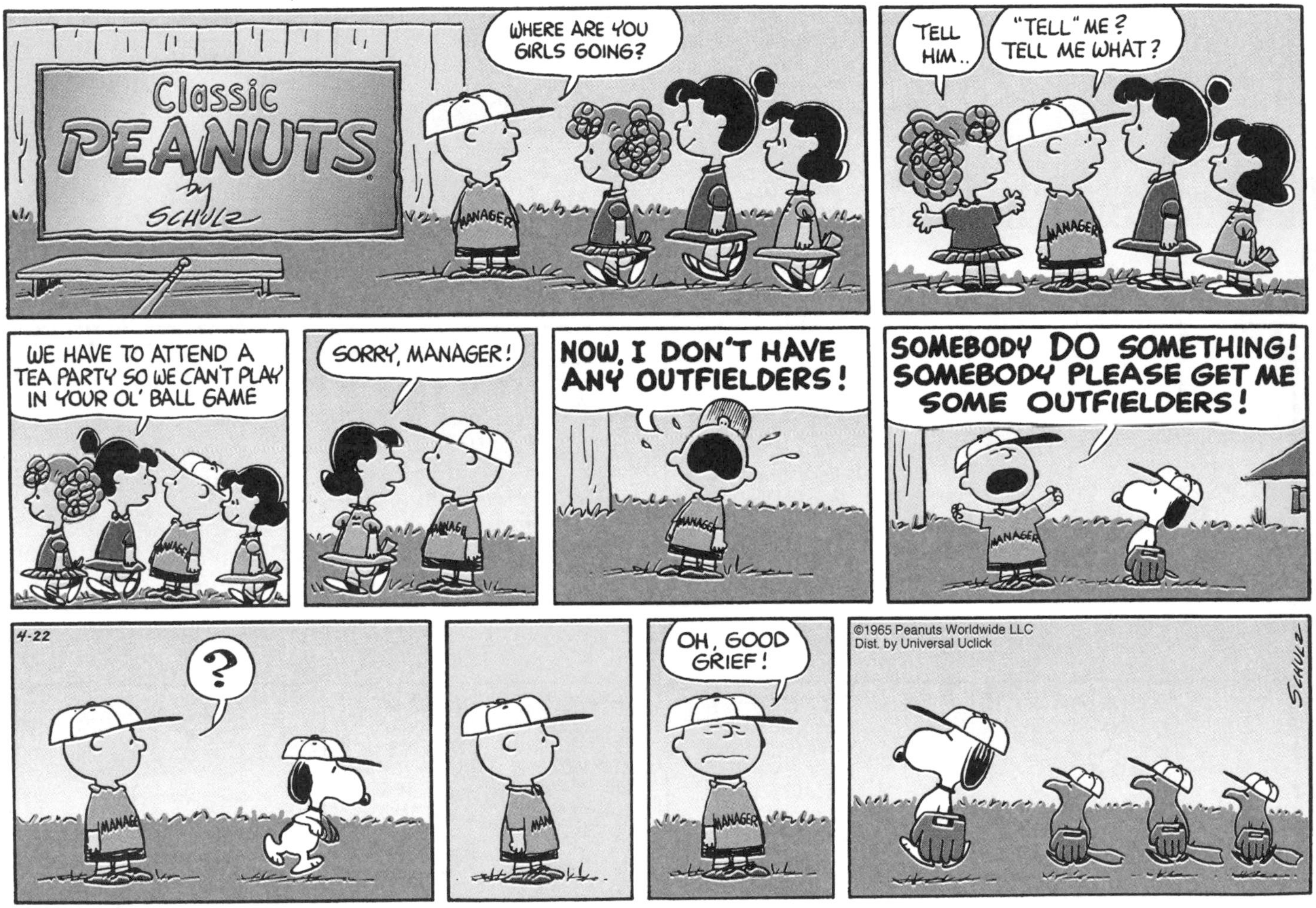
Classic PEANUTS by SCHULZ
WHERE ARE YOU GIRLS GOING?
TELL HIM..
"TELL" ME? TELL ME WHAT?
WE HAVE TO ATTEND A TEA PARTY SO WE CAN'T PLAY IN YOUR OL' BALL GAME
SORRY, MANAGER!
NOW, I DON'T HAVE ANY OUTFIELDERS!
SOMEBODY DO SOMETHING! SOMEBODY PLEASE GET ME SOME OUTFIELDERS!
4-22
?
OH, GOOD GRIEF!
©1965 Peanuts Worldwide LLC
Dist. by Universal Uclick
SCHULZ

YOU'RE NOT A GOOD MANAGER.. YOU KNOW WHY?
YOU SHOULD BE OUT THERE ARGUING WITH THE UMPIRE, AND KICKING DIRT ON HIS SHOES
© 1966 Peanuts Worldwide LLC. Dist. by Universal Uclick
I'VE NEVER SEEN YOU KICK DIRT ON THE UMPIRE'S SHOES... YOU'RE JUST NOT A GOOD MANAGER, CHARLIE BROWN...
www.snoopy.com
I **MUST** BE A GOOD MANAGER..MY STOMACH HURTS!
SCHULZ
5-22

WHAT'S GOING ON?
CHARLIE BROWN DOESN'T FEEL WELL.. HIS STOMACH HURTS...
IT'S NERVES, CHARLIE BROWN... YOU TAKE THIS GAME TOO SERIOUSLY.. BE LIKE FRIEDA AND ME...WE DON'T CARE IF WE WIN OR LOSE! **LA DE DA!** WHO CARES?
5-23
© 1966 Peanuts Worldwide LLC. Dist. by Universal Uclick
LA DE DA! WIN OR LOSE! WHO CARES? LA DE DA! WE DON'T CARE! WE DON'T CARE!
www.snoopy.com
FOR SOME REASON, THE PAIN HAS SUDDENLY INCREASED...
SCHULZ

I'M GOING TO SEE MY OPHTHALMOLOGIST.. I THINK HE'S GOING TO TAKE OFF THIS EYE-PATCH TODAY....
ASK HIM WHY MY STOMACH HURTS ALL THE TIME
I CAN'T ASK AN EYE DOCTOR ABOUT YOUR STUPID OL' STOMACH!
5-24
© 1966 Peanuts Worldwide LLC. Dist. by Universal Uclick
NO, I SUPPOSE YOU CAN'T...
www.snoopy.com
WELL, ANYWAY, GOOD LUCK WITH YOUR EYE-PATCH
THANK YOU... GOOD LUCK WITH YOUR STOMACH..
SCHULZ

PSYCHIATRIC HELP 5¢

THE DOCTOR IS IN

I THINK I KNOW WHAT'S WRONG WITH YOU...

5-25

WALK UP ONTO THAT PITCHER'S MOUND... DOES YOUR STOMACH HURT NOW?

YES!! OW! OOO!! YES!

ALL RIGHT, NOW COME DOWN OFF THE MOUND... THERE...HAS IT STOPPED HURTING?

YES...YES, I THINK IT HAS!

THERE'S YOUR TROUBLE... FIVE CENTS, PLEASE!

LINUS, I'M GOING TO LET YOU PITCH.. THE TENSION UP HERE ON THE MOUND IS TOO HARD ON MY STOMACH...

I'M GOING OUT HERE, AND PLAY LEFT-FIELD... I THINK IT WILL HELP ME TO RELAX...

WHAT ABOUT MY STOMACH?

I THINK I DID THE RIGHT THING WHEN I GAVE UP PITCHING..

IT'S MUCH MORE RELAXING OUT HERE IN LEFT-FIELD... IT WAS GETTING SO MY STOMACH WOULD START TO HURT AS SOON AS I'D WALK UP ONTO THE PITCHER'S MOUND

6-1

OUT HERE I DON'T HAVE ALL THAT TENSION...I CAN JUST SORT OF..

ALL RIGHT, YOU BLOCKHEAD, KEEP YOUR EYES OPEN!!

70

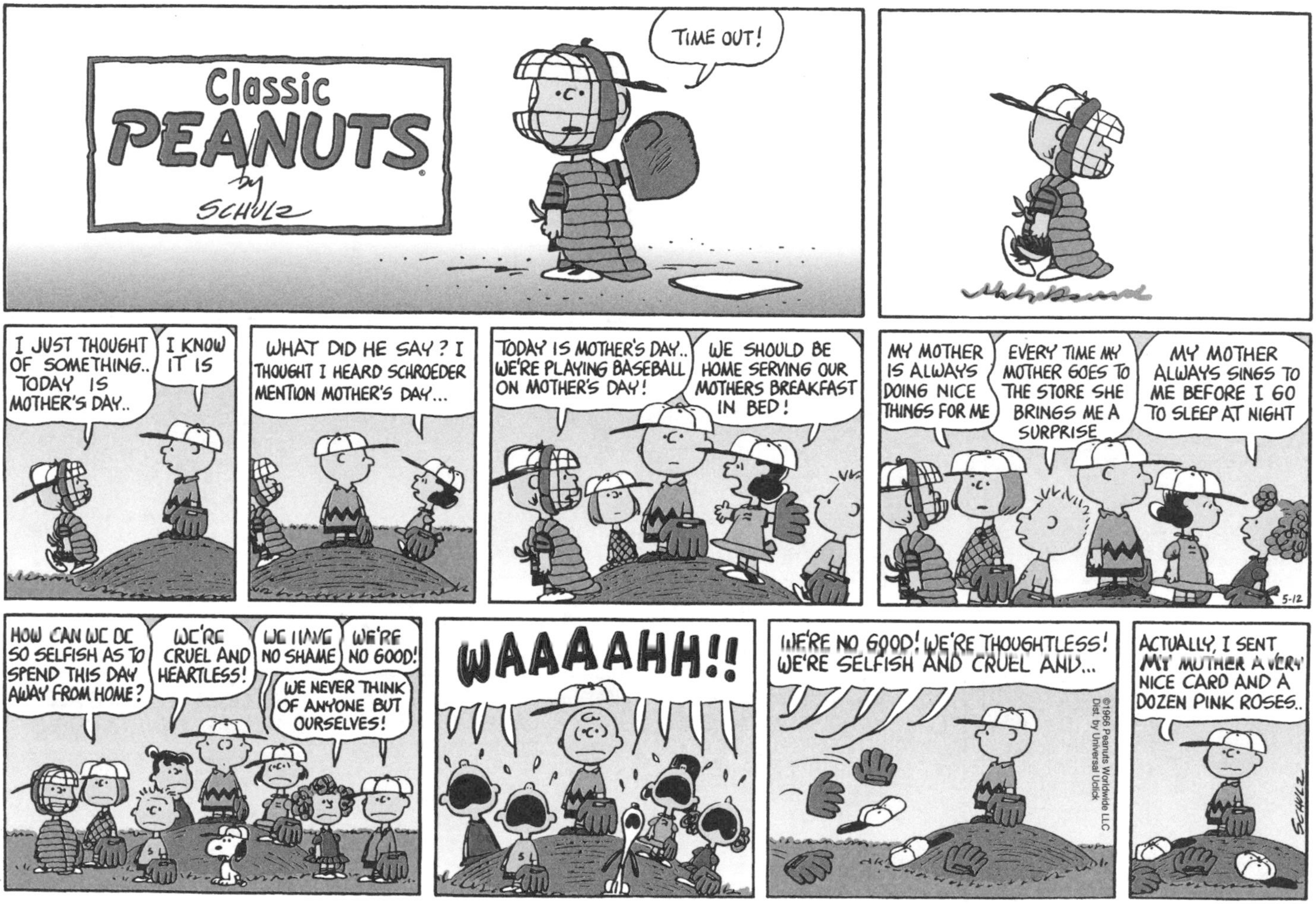
Classic PEANUTS by SCHULZ
TIME OUT!
I JUST THOUGHT OF SOMETHING.. TODAY IS MOTHER'S DAY..
I KNOW IT IS
WHAT DID HE SAY? I THOUGHT I HEARD SCHROEDER MENTION MOTHER'S DAY...
TODAY IS MOTHER'S DAY.. WE'RE PLAYING BASEBALL ON MOTHER'S DAY!
WE SHOULD BE HOME SERVING OUR MOTHERS BREAKFAST IN BED!
MY MOTHER IS ALWAYS DOING NICE THINGS FOR ME
EVERY TIME MY MOTHER GOES TO THE STORE SHE BRINGS ME A SURPRISE
MY MOTHER ALWAYS SINGS TO ME BEFORE I GO TO SLEEP AT NIGHT
5-12
HOW CAN WE BE SO SELFISH AS TO SPEND THIS DAY AWAY FROM HOME?
WE'RE CRUEL AND HEARTLESS!
WE HAVE NO SHAME
WE'RE NO GOOD!
WE NEVER THINK OF ANYONE BUT OURSELVES!
WAAAAAHH!!
WE'RE NO GOOD! WE'RE THOUGHTLESS! WE'RE SELFISH AND CRUEL AND...
©1966 Peanuts Worldwide LLC Dist. by Universal Uclick
ACTUALLY, I SENT MY MOTHER A VERY NICE CARD AND A DOZEN PINK ROSES..
SCHULZ

AS SOON AS SCHOOL IS OVER, I HAVE TO GO TO CAMP FOR TWO WEEKS..
5-29
I DON'T REALLY CARE MUCH ABOUT GOING TO CAMP...I'M AFRAID I'LL GET LONESOME
© 1965 Peanuts Worldwide LLC, Dist. by Universal Uclick
I'M AFRAID THAT WHEN I'M MILES AWAY FROM HOME, I'LL START TO MISS MY FRIENDS
www.snoopy.com
WHAT FRIENDS?
SCHULZ

IF YOU DON'T WANT TO GO TO CAMP, CHARLIE BROWN, WHY GO?
I FEEL OBLIGATED
5-30
MY MOM AND DAD THINK THEY'RE DOING ME A FAVOR...THEY'RE HAPPY BECAUSE THEY THINK THIS WILL BE A GOOD EXPERIENCE FOR ME
© 1965 Peanuts Worldwide LLC, Dist. by Universal Uclick
RATS!
www.snoopy.com
POOR GOOD OL' CHARLIE BROWN...
SCHULZ

PSYCHIATRIC HELP 5¢
THIS FEAR OF GOING TO CAMP IS SOMETHING YOU'VE GOT TO OVERCOME!
THE DOCTOR IS IN
5-31
IT'LL BE GOOD FOR YOU! IT'LL TEACH YOU TO STAND ON YOUR OWN TWO FEET! THIS IS JUST THE SORT OF EXPERIENCE YOU NEED!
THE DOCTOR
© 1965 Peanuts Worldwide LLC, Dist. by Universal Uclick
HOW ABOUT YOU? ARE YOU GOING TO CAMP THIS SUMMER?
PSYCHIATRIC HELP 5¢
THE DOCTOR IS IN
www.snoopy.com
AND LEAVE MY GOOD HOME? DON'T BE RIDICULOUS!!!
THE DOCTOR IS IN
SCHULZ

WELL, OLD FRIEND, I'M OFF TO CAMP FOR TWO WEEKS..
I JUST WANTED TO SAY, "GOOD-BY" BEFORE I LEFT... I KNOW I'M GOING TO MISS YOU..
6-1
© 1965 Peanuts Worldwide LLC, Dist. by Universal Uclick
I SUPPOSE YOU'LL MISS ME, TOO, BUT I GUESS WE...
www.snoopy.com
Z
SIGH
SCHULZ

WELL, HERE I AM ON A BUS GOING TO CAMP
6-2
THESE CAMP BUSES ARE PRETTY NICE, I GUESS...
© 1965 Peanuts Worldwide LLC, Dist. by Universal Uclick
SIGH WE'VE ONLY BEEN ON THIS BUS FOR TEN MINUTES, AND ALREADY I'M LONESOME..
www.snoopy.com
I FEEL LIKE I'M BEING DRAFTED!
SCHULZ

WELL, HERE I AM AT CAMP STANDING IN MY FIRST CHOW LINE...LUNCH IS GONNA TASTE GOOD
WHAT'S YOUR NAME, KID?
CHARLIE BROWN
© 1965 Peanuts Worldwide LLC, Dist. by Universal Uclick
HEY, GET A LOAD OF THE KID WITH THE FUNNY NAME!
www.snoopy.com
LUNCH IS GONNA TASTE AWFUL!
SCHULZ
6-4

DEAR MOM AND DAD, HOW ARE YOU?
I AM FINE.
MY FIRST DAY OF CAMP IS OVER.
I LIVED THROUGH IT.
© 1965 Peanuts Worldwide LLC, Dist. by Universal Uclick
www.snoopy.com
6-5
SCHULZ

A LETTER FROM LINUS! WELL, I'LL BE!
DEAR CHARLIE BROWN...HOW ARE YOU ENJOYING CAMP? I SUPPOSE YOU ARE WORRIED ABOUT YOUR BASEBALL TEAM..
WELL, DON'T WORRY...WE'RE DOING FINE...IN FACT, YESTERDAY WE WON THE FIRST GAME WE'VE WON ALL SEASON!
SIGH
© 1965 Peanuts Worldwide LLC, Dist. by Universal Uclick
www.snoopy.com
6-7
SCHULZ

SNIF!
?
EXCUSE ME, BUT I COULDN'T HELP OVERHEARING YOU CRYING.. WHAT'S THE MATTER?
I DON'T KNOW...I GUESS I'M JUST LONESOME..
FRIEND!!
© 1965 Peanuts Worldwide LLC, Dist. by Universal Uclick
www.snoopy.com
6-8
SCHULZ

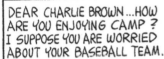

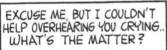

ROY, YOU'VE GOT TO SNAP OUT OF IT!

A CAMP LIKE THIS IS THE BEST PLACE FOR SOMEONE LIKE YOU...IT HELPS YOU TO BREAK THOSE OLD APRON STRINGS!

LIFE IS FULL OF EXPERIENCES THAT HAVE TO BE FACED ALONE!

BUT YOU SAID YOU WERE LONESOME, TOO...

I TALK A GOOD CAMP...

DEAR MOM AND DAD, THINGS ARE GOING BETTER HERE AT CAMP.

Yesterday I met this kid named Charlie Brown.

HE WAS VERY LONESOME, BUT I THINK I HAVE HELPED HIM.

He's the kind who makes a good temporary friend.

C'MON, ROY, WE'LL BE LATE FOR THE "SING OUT"

WE'RE ALL GOING TO SIT AROUND THE CAMPFIRE, AND SING SONGS...

MAYBE I SHOULDN'T GO...

THOSE WORLD WAR I SONGS ALWAYS GET ME RIGHT HERE

75

STRIKE THREE!
WHAT'S THE MATTER, KID? AIN'TCHA NEVER PLAYED BASEBALL BEFORE?!!
6-13
© 1965 Peanuts Worldwide LLC, Dist. by Universal Uclick
WHY DIDN'T YOU TELL HIM, CHARLIE BROWN? WHY DIDN'T YOU TELL HIM ABOUT HOW YOU'RE THE MANAGER OF A TEAM AT HOME?
www.snoopy.com
SOMEHOW, MENTIONING A TEAM THAT HAS THREE GIRL-OUTFIELDERS AND A DOG-SHORTSTOP DIDN'T SEEM QUITE APPROPRIATE!
SCHULZ

WELL, SO LONG, CHARLIE BROWN... IT'S BEEN NICE KNOWING YOU..
IT'S BEEN NICE KNOWING YOU, TOO, ROY....HAVE A GOOD TRIP HOME..
6-14
© 1965 Peanuts Worldwide LLC, Dist. by Universal Uclick
FOR THE FIRST TIME IN MY LIFE I FEEL I REALLY HELPED SOMEONE...HE WAS LONESOME, AND I BECAME HIS FRIEND...
www.snoopy.com
WHAT AN ACCOMPLISHMENT!
SCHULZ

WELL, HERE I AM ON THE BUS RETURNING HOME FROM CAMP
6-15
HERE'S THE STATION..I'M ALMOST HOME...I CAN'T BELIEVE IT...
© 1965 Peanuts Worldwide LLC, Dist. by Universal Uclick
LOOK! THERE'S SOME KIDS ALL LINED UP JUST GETTING READY TO LEAVE FOR CAMP...
www.snoopy.com
LET 'EM GO! I'VE DONE MY HITCH!!
SCHULZ

Classic PEANUTS by SCHULZ
GOOD GRIEF! ANOTHER HOME RUN!
BOY, I MUST BE STUPID TO STAND OUT HERE, AND TAKE A BEATING LIKE THIS!
MY TEAM HATES ME, I'M A LOUSY PITCHER, MY STOMACH HURTS..... I DON'T KNOW WHY I PLAY THIS GAME..I MUST REALLY BE STUPID!
CHARLIE BROWN, YOU CAN'T GO ON LIKE THIS..YOU'VE GOT TO CHANGE YOUR ATTITUDE! THE YEARS ARE GOING BY, AND YOU'RE NOT ENJOYING LIFE AT ALL!
5-5
JUST REMEMBER, CHARLIE BROWN... THE MOMENTS YOU SPEND OUT HERE ON THIS PITCHER'S MOUND ARE MOMENTS TO BE TREASURED!
WE'RE NOT GOING TO BE KIDS FOREVER, CHARLIE BROWN, SO TREASURE THESE MOMENTS...
©1966 Peanuts Worldwide LLC
Dist. by Universal Uclick
POW!
THIS IS A DIFFICULT MOMENT TO TREASURE!
SCHULZ

OH, BOY! IS IT EVER GOOD TO BE BACK HOME!
6-16
HI, LUCY! I'M BACK!
YOU'RE WHAT?
© 1965 Peanuts Worldwide LLC, Dist. by Universal Uclick
I SAID, I'M BACK!
www.snoopy.com
HAVE YOU BEEN AWAY?
SCHULZ

THAT STUPID TREE HAS MY KITE!
IT'S A KITE-EATING TREE, THAT'S WHAT IT IS! IT GRABS KITES, AND CHEWS THEM UP!
5-28
© 1965 Peanuts Worldwide LLC, Dist. by Universal Uclick
WHAT'S IT DOING NOW?
www.snoopy.com
IT'S SPITTING OUT THE BONES!

WHAT IN THE WORLD DO YOU CALL THIS?
I CAN'T PITCH WITHOUT MY BLANKET, CHARLIE BROWN..YOU KNOW THAT!
GET OUTA HERE! I'LL DO THE PITCHING MYSELF EVEN IF IT KILLS MY STOMACH!
© 1966 Peanuts Worldwide LLC, Dist. by Universal Uclick
BY GOLLY, IF YOU'RE EVER GOING TO GET ANYTHING DONE, YOU JUST HAVE TO DO IT YOURSELF...
www.snoopy.com
POW!
UNFORTUNATELY!
6-3
SCHULZ

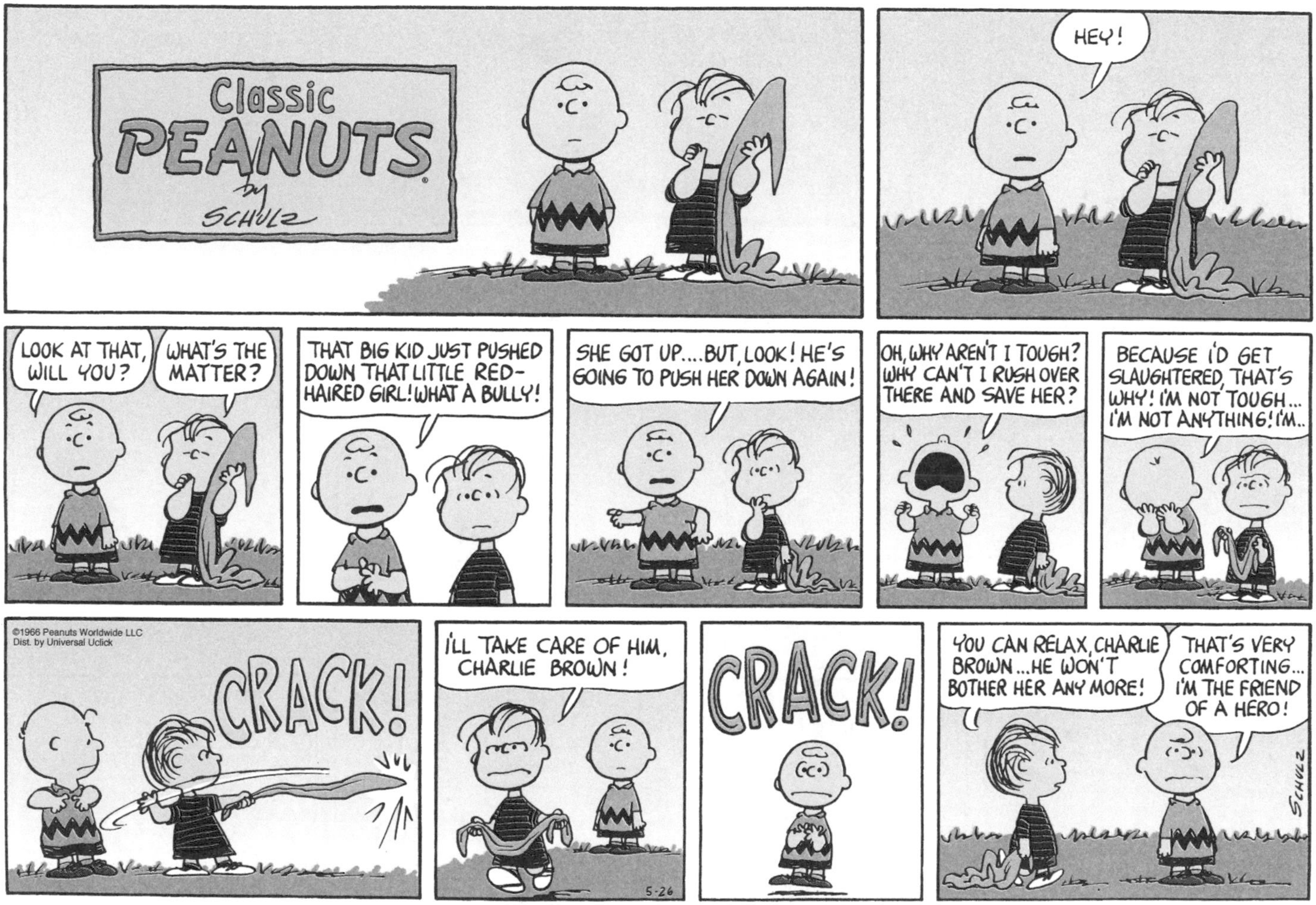
Classic
PEANUTS
by
SCHULZ
HEY!
LOOK AT THAT, WILL YOU?
WHAT'S THE MATTER?
THAT BIG KID JUST PUSHED DOWN THAT LITTLE RED-HAIRED GIRL! WHAT A BULLY!
SHE GOT UP....BUT, LOOK! HE'S GOING TO PUSH HER DOWN AGAIN!
OH, WHY AREN'T I TOUGH? WHY CAN'T I RUSH OVER THERE AND SAVE HER?
BECAUSE I'D GET SLAUGHTERED, THAT'S WHY! I'M NOT TOUGH... I'M NOT ANYTHING! I'M..
©1966 Peanuts Worldwide LLC
Dist. by Universal Uclick
CRACK!
I'LL TAKE CARE OF HIM, CHARLIE BROWN!
5-26
CRACK!
YOU CAN RELAX, CHARLIE BROWN... HE WON'T BOTHER HER ANY MORE!
THAT'S VERY COMFORTING... I'M THE FRIEND OF A HERO!
SCHULZ

WHY ARE YOU STANDING HERE, CHARLIE BROWN?
I'M WAITING FOR THAT LITTLE RED-HAIRED GIRL TO WALK BY..
I'M GOING TO SAY HELLO TO HER AND ASK HER HOW SHE'S ENJOYING HER SUMMER VACATION, AND JUST SORT OF TALK TO HER..YOU KNOW...
6-7
YOU'LL NEVER DO IT, CHARLIE BROWN...YOU'LL PANIC..
© 1986 Peanuts Worldwide LLC. Dist. by Universal Uclick
BESIDES THAT, SHE'S ALREADY WALKED BY!
www.snoopy.com
SCHULZ

WELL, SO LONG, LINUS...HAVE A GOOD TIME AT CAMP...
THANK YOU, CHARLIE BROWN... I MAY HAVE A GOOD TIME IF THE QUEEN SNAKES DON'T GET ME...
6-12
HOW ABOUT YOUR BLANKET? ARE YOU GOING TO TAKE YOUR BLANKET?
BUS LEAVE 3:15
© 1986 Peanuts Worldwide LLC. Dist. by Universal Uclick
WHAT DO YOU THINK **THIS** IS, **MOSQUITO NETTING**?!
www.snoopy.com
SCHULZ

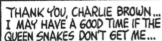

LOOK, LUCY, I GOT A LETTER FROM LINUS!
THAT BLOCKHEAD! HE NEVER WROTE TO **ME**!
HE SAID HE'S MET ROY, THAT SAME KID I MET LAST YEAR... AND HE SAID HE GAVE A LITTLE TALK AROUND THE CAMPFIRE LAST NIGHT
THAT STUPID BLOCKHEAD
6-21
HE SAID HE TOLD ALL THE KIDS ABOUT "THE GREAT PUMPKIN," AND AFTERWARDS THEY ELECTED HIM CAMP PRESIDENT!
© 1986 Peanuts Worldwide LLC. Dist. by Universal Uclick
HE SAID HE'S GOING TO STAY FOR AN EXTRA WEEK, AND TO GREET EVERYONE BACK HERE...
HE WROTE TO YOU, BUT HE DIDN'T WRITE TO ME! THAT BLOCKHEAD!
www.snoopy.com
SCHULZ

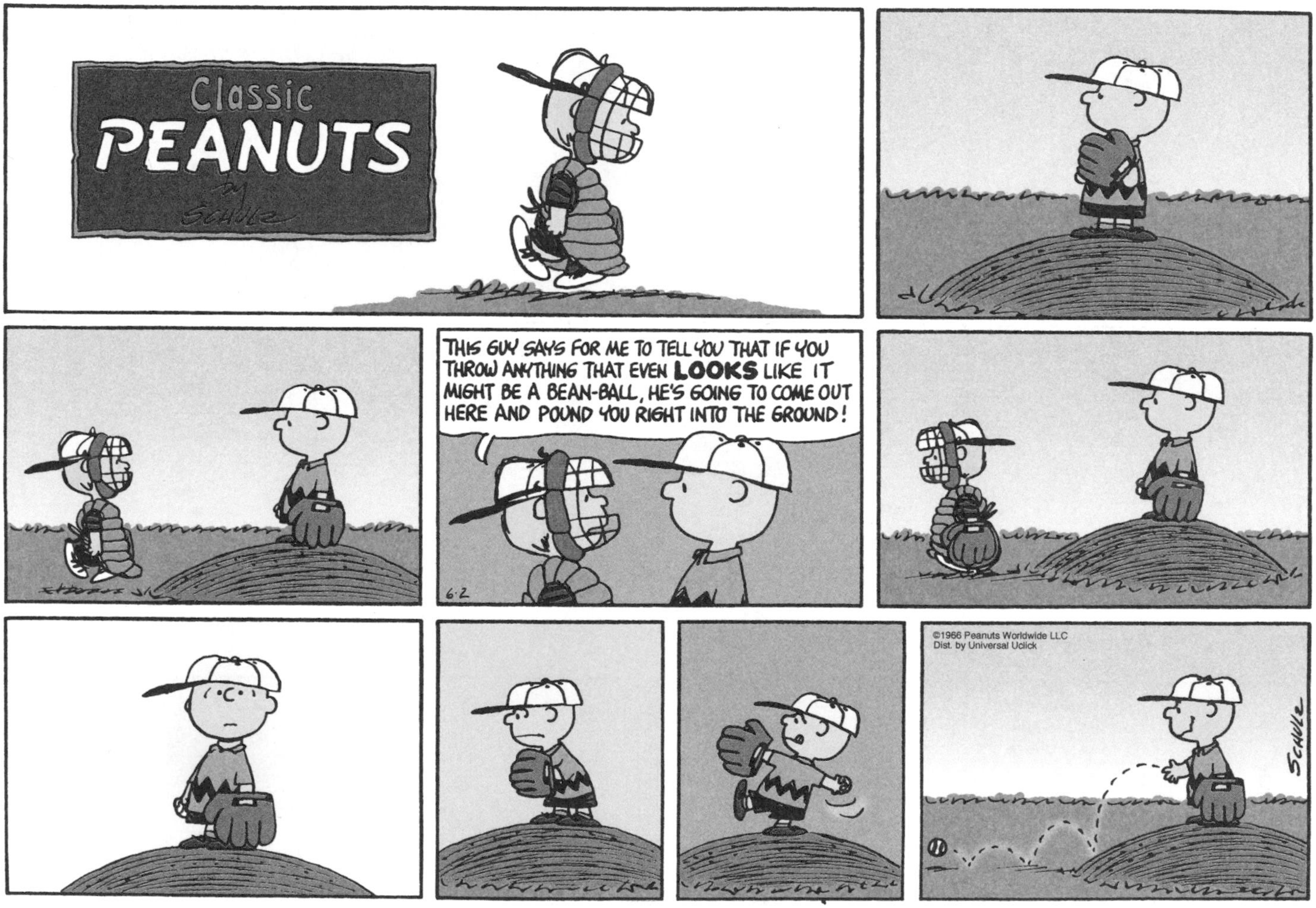
Classic
PEANUTS
by SCHULZ
THIS GUY SAYS FOR ME TO TELL YOU THAT IF YOU THROW ANYTHING THAT EVEN **LOOKS** LIKE IT MIGHT BE A BEAN-BALL, HE'S GOING TO COME OUT HERE AND POUND YOU RIGHT INTO THE GROUND!
6·2
©1966 Peanuts Worldwide LLC
Dist. by Universal Uclick
SCHULZ

WHAT'S THAT?
IT LOOKS LIKE SOMETHING FROM LINUS...
IT IS! HE SENT ME A LITTLE BIRCH-BARK CANOE FROM CAMP! HE SAID HE MADE IT HIMSELF...
6-26
© 1966 Peanuts Worldwide LLC, Dist. by Universal Uclick
SOMETIMES I THINK I DON'T DESERVE A NICE BROTHER LIKE LINUS...
I HAVE OFTEN THOUGHT THE SAME THING
www.snoopy.com
Dear Linus,
Please send me another canoe. The first one broke when I threw it at Charlie Brown!
SCHULZ

YOU KNOW, I FEEL BETTER ALREADY!
THE DOCTOR IS IN
YOU MUST USE VERY MODERN METHODS...
© 1965 Peanuts Worldwide LLC, Dist. by Universal Uclick
OH, YES....ABSOLUTELY THE LATEST TECHNIQUES...
THE DOCTOR IS
6-20
www.snoopy.com
PSYCHIATRY à GO-GO!
THE DOCTOR IS IN
SCHULZ

AREN'T YOU GOING TO BE IN YOUR PSYCHIATRIC BOOTH TODAY?
NOPE! THIS IS MY DAY OFF... IF YOU HAVE A PROBLEM, GO SEE MY ASSISTANT...
© 1965 Peanuts Worldwide LLC, Dist. by Universal Uclick
6-22
www.snoopy.com
HELP 5¢
I THINK I'D FEEL A LITTLE LESS RIDICULOUS IF HE WEREN'T MY OWN DOG...
THE DOCTOR IS IN
SCHULZ

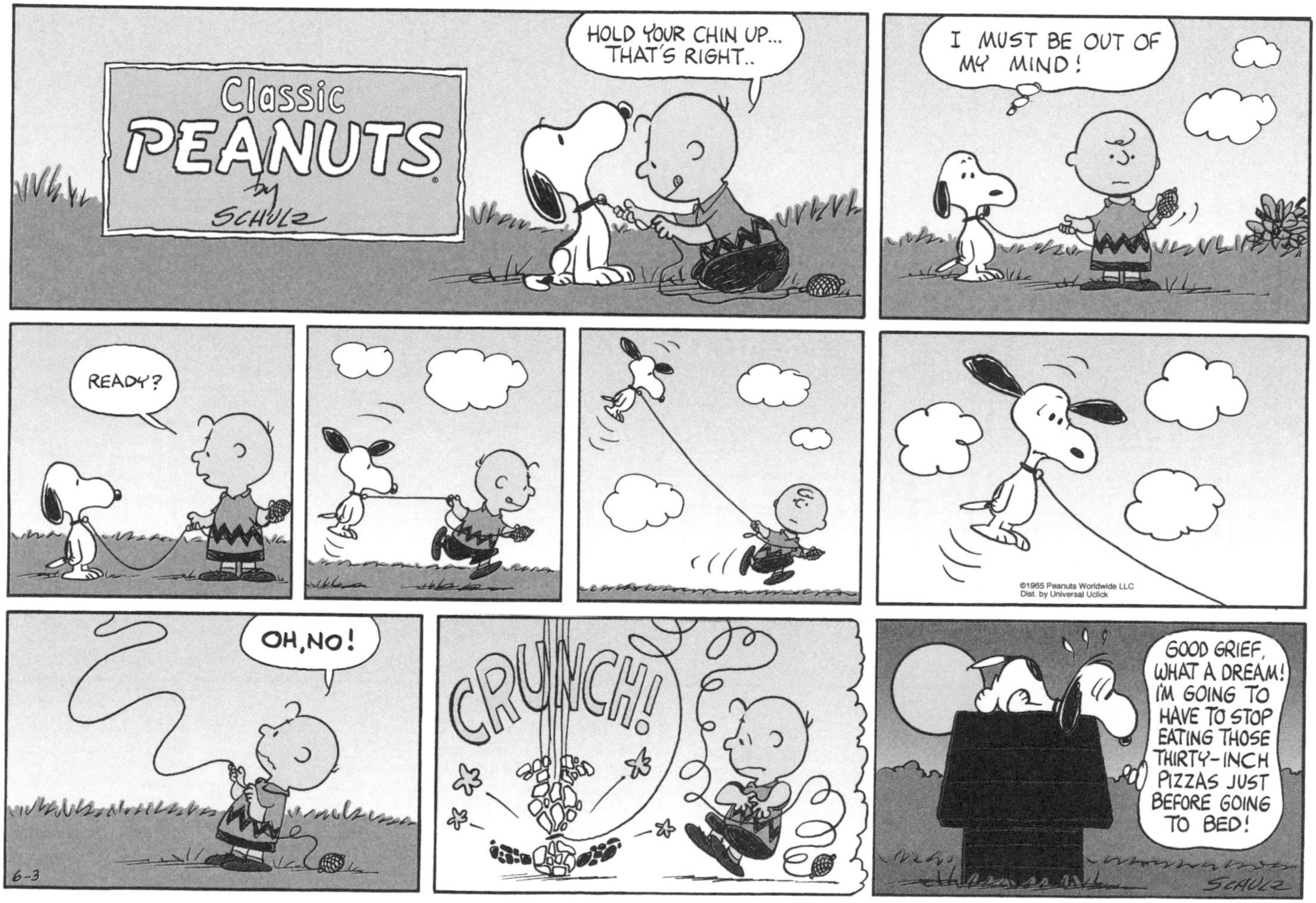
Classic PEANUTS by SCHULZ
HOLD YOUR CHIN UP... THAT'S RIGHT..
I MUST BE OUT OF MY MIND!
READY?
©1965 Peanuts Worldwide LLC
Dist. by Universal Uclick
OH, NO!
6-3
CRUNCH!
GOOD GRIEF, WHAT A DREAM! I'M GOING TO HAVE TO STOP EATING THOSE THIRTY-INCH PIZZAS JUST BEFORE GOING TO BED!
SCHULZ

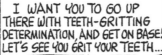
ALL RIGHT, SNOOPY, THIS IS THE LAST OF THE NINTH...WE NEED ONE RUN TO TIE UP THE GAME..

6-25

I WANT YOU TO GO UP THERE WITH TEETH-GRITTING DETERMINATION, AND GET ON BASE! LET'S SEE YOU GRIT YOUR TEETH...

THAT'S FINE...KEEP GRITTING YOUR TEETH, AND YOU'LL GET A HIT!

I FEEL LIKE A FOOL...

© 1965 Peanuts Worldwide LLC, Dist. by Universal Uclick

www.snoopy.com

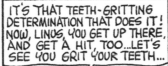
LOOK AT THAT! SNOOPY GOT A HIT! WE'RE STILL IN THE GAME!

IT'S THAT TEETH-GRITTING DETERMINATION THAT DOES IT! NOW, LINUS, YOU GET UP THERE, AND GET A HIT, TOO...LET'S SEE YOU GRIT YOUR TEETH...

6-26

GREAT! IF YOU GRIT YOUR TEETH, YOU CAN'T FAIL!

IF I GET HIT IN THE MOUTH, I CAN SURE FAIL!

© 1965 Peanuts Worldwide LLC, Dist. by Universal Uclick

www.snoopy.com

LOOK AT THAT! LINUS GOT A HIT, TOO! I KNEW WE STILL HAD A CHANCE!

IF YOU GRIT YOUR TEETH, AND SHOW REAL DETERMINATION, YOU ALWAYS HAVE A CHANCE! YOU'RE UP NEXT, LUCY...LET'S SEE YOU GRIT YOUR TEETH...

6-27

FANTASTIC! YOU'LL SCARE THEIR PITCHER TO DEATH! KEEP GRITTING YOUR TEETH, AND GO GET A HIT!

GET A HIT?! I CAN'T EVEN SEE WHERE I'M GOING..

© 1965 Peanuts Worldwide LLC, Dist. by Universal Uclick

www.snoopy.com

LUCY GRITTED HER TEETH, AND GOT AN INFIELD SINGLE! THE BASES ARE LOADED!

IT JUST SHOWS WHAT TEETH-GRITTING DETERMINATION CAN DO! WHO'S OUR NEXT TEETH-GRITTING HERO?

6-28

WHO'S UP NEXT? WHO'S UP NEXT?

YOU ARE!

GRIT YOUR TEETH, CHARLIE BROWN...

© 1965 Peanuts Worldwide LLC, Dist. by Universal Uclick

www.snoopy.com

WHY DO I ALWAYS HAVE TO BE UP WHEN THE BASES ARE LOADED?

JUST DO WHAT YOU TOLD ALL THE OTHERS.... GRIT YOUR TEETH, AND GET A HIT!

COME ON, CHARLIE BROWN... LET'S SEE YOU GRIT YOUR TEETH...THAT'S THE WAY..

6-29

GOOD GRIEF!

CLICKETY CLICK CLICK CHATTER CHATTER

CLICKETY CLICK CLICK CLICK CHATTER

© 1965 Peanuts Worldwide LLC, Dist. by Universal Uclick

www.snoopy.com

STRIKE ONE!

6-30

OOOOOO! C'MON, CHARLIE BROWN, **HIT IT**! FOR ONCE IN YOUR LIFE, **HIT IT**!!

WOULDN'T YOU LIKE JUST FOR ONCE TO SEE CHARLIE BROWN HIT THAT BALL?

NO..

I'M NOT PREPARED TO HAVE THE WORLD COME TO AN END!

© 1965 Peanuts Worldwide LLC, Dist. by Universal Uclick

www.snoopy.com

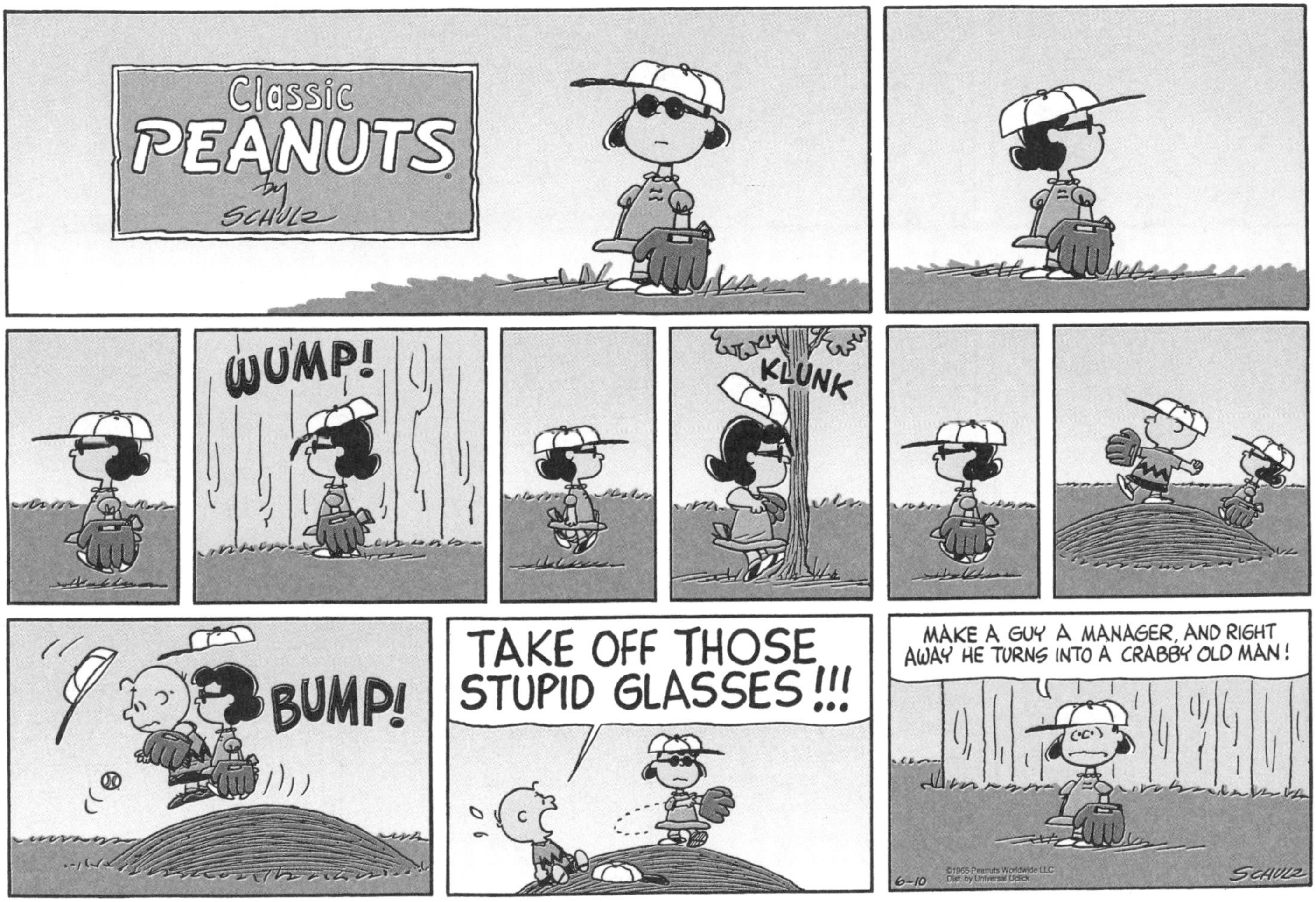
Classic
PEANUTS
by SCHULZ
WUMP!
KLUNK
BUMP!
TAKE OFF THOSE STUPID GLASSES!!!
MAKE A GUY A MANAGER, AND RIGHT AWAY HE TURNS INTO A CRABBY OLD MAN!
6-10
©1965 Peanuts Worldwide LLC
Dist. by Universal Uclick
SCHULZ

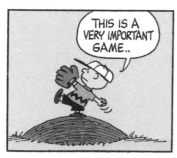

THIS IS A VERY IMPORTANT GAME..
IT'S TRADITIONAL THAT WHOEVER IS IN FIRST PLACE ON THE FOURTH OF JULY GOES ON TO WIN THE PENNANT
7-4
© 1986 Peanuts Worldwide LLC, Dist. by Universal Uclick
POW!
www.snoopy.com
AND WHOEVER IS IN LAST PLACE USUALLY STAYS THERE!
SCHULZ

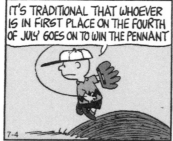

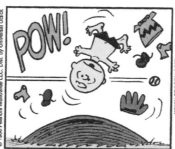

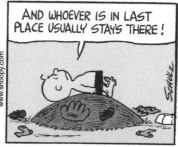

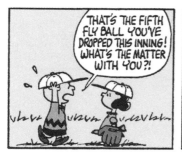

THAT'S THE FIFTH FLY BALL YOU'VE DROPPED THIS INNING! WHAT'S THE MATTER WITH YOU?!
I'M SORRY, CHARLIE BROWN..I'M NOT MYSELF THESE DAYS...MY MOTHER TOOK AWAY OUR TV SET AT HOME, AND I'VE BEEN KIND OF UPSET...
7-11
© 1986 Peanuts Worldwide LLC, Dist. by Universal Uclick
MY HANDS SHAKE ALL THE TIME, AND MY THROAT HURTS...
www.snoopy.com
I THINK I'M GOING THROUGH WITHDRAWAL!
SCHULZ

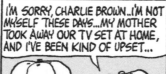

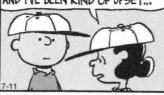

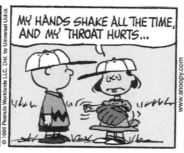

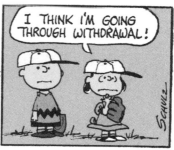

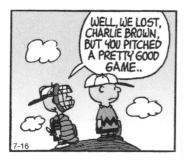

WELL, WE LOST, CHARLIE BROWN, BUT YOU PITCHED A PRETTY GOOD GAME..
7-16
THANK YOU
© 1986 Peanuts Worldwide LLC, Dist. by Universal Uclick
IN THE BIG LEAGUES WHEN A PITCHER FINISHES A GAME, THEY PACK HIS ARM IN ICE...
www.snoopy.com
SCHULZ
I HAVE TO SIT WITH MY ARM IN THE ICE-CUBE TRAY!

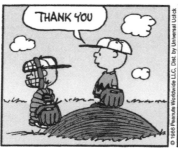

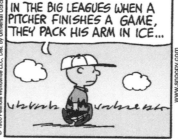

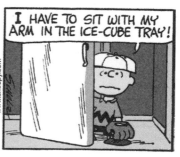

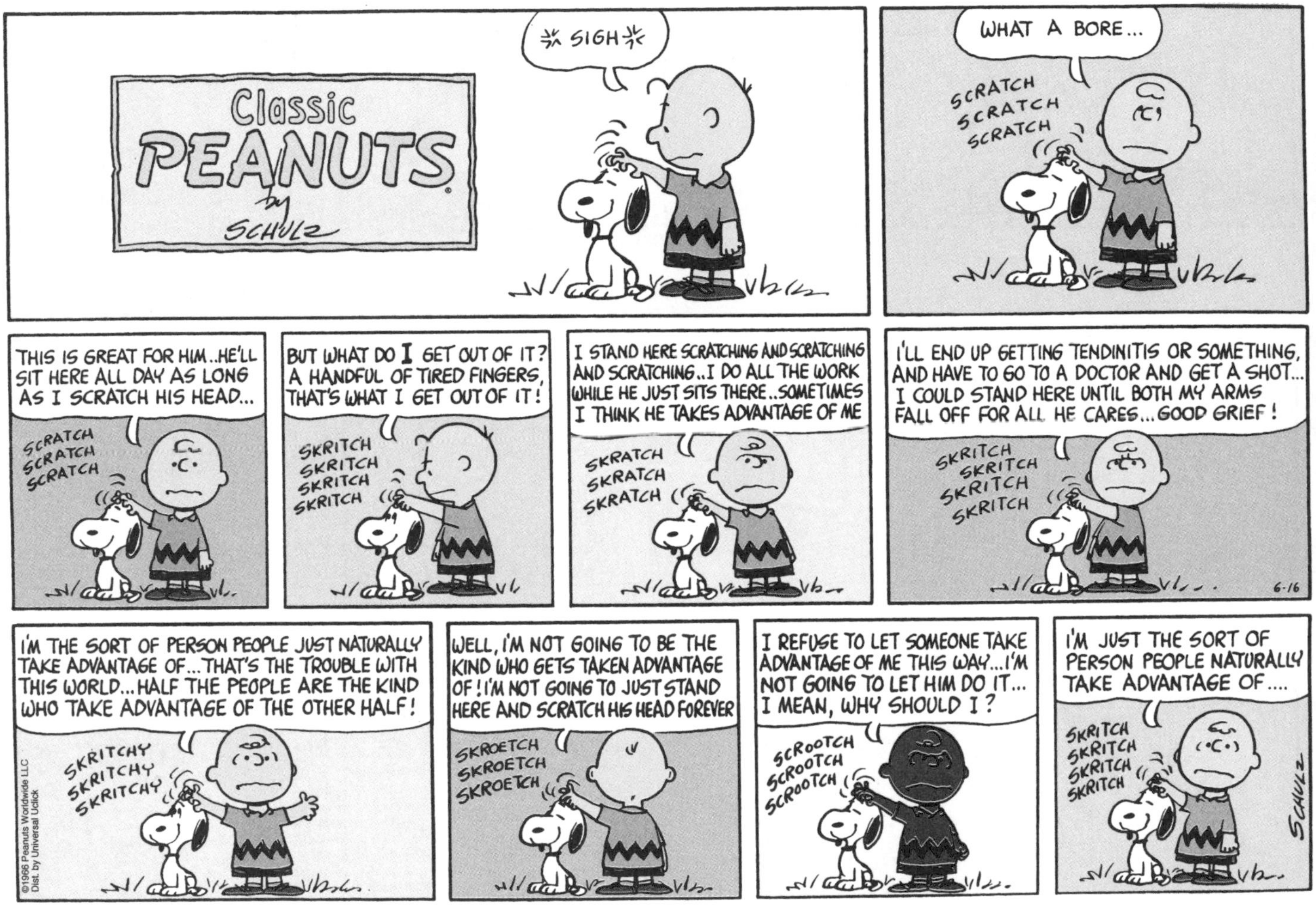
Classic PEANUTS by SCHULZ
SIGH
WHAT A BORE...
SCRATCH SCRATCH SCRATCH
THIS IS GREAT FOR HIM..HE'LL SIT HERE ALL DAY AS LONG AS I SCRATCH HIS HEAD...
SCRATCH SCRATCH SCRATCH
BUT WHAT DO I GET OUT OF IT? A HANDFUL OF TIRED FINGERS, THAT'S WHAT I GET OUT OF IT!
SKRITCH SKRITCH SKRITCH SKRITCH
I STAND HERE SCRATCHING AND SCRATCHING AND SCRATCHING..I DO ALL THE WORK WHILE HE JUST SITS THERE..SOMETIMES I THINK HE TAKES ADVANTAGE OF ME
SKRATCH SKRATCH SKRATCH
I'LL END UP GETTING TENDINITIS OR SOMETHING, AND HAVE TO GO TO A DOCTOR AND GET A SHOT... I COULD STAND HERE UNTIL BOTH MY ARMS FALL OFF FOR ALL HE CARES... GOOD GRIEF!
SKRITCH SKRITCH SKRITCH SKRITCH
6-16
I'M THE SORT OF PERSON PEOPLE JUST NATURALLY TAKE ADVANTAGE OF... THAT'S THE TROUBLE WITH THIS WORLD... HALF THE PEOPLE ARE THE KIND WHO TAKE ADVANTAGE OF THE OTHER HALF!
SKRITCHY SKRITCHY SKRITCHY
©1966 Peanuts Worldwide LLC
Dist. by Universal Uclick
WELL, I'M NOT GOING TO BE THE KIND WHO GETS TAKEN ADVANTAGE OF! I'M NOT GOING TO JUST STAND HERE AND SCRATCH HIS HEAD FOREVER
SKROETCH SKROETCH SKROETCH
I REFUSE TO LET SOMEONE TAKE ADVANTAGE OF ME THIS WAY...I'M NOT GOING TO LET HIM DO IT... I MEAN, WHY SHOULD I?
SCROOTCH SCROOTCH SCROOTCH
I'M JUST THE SORT OF PERSON PEOPLE NATURALLY TAKE ADVANTAGE OF....
SKRITCH SKRITCH SKRITCH SKRITCH
SCHULZ

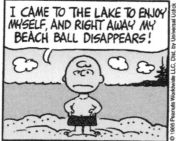

WHERE'S MY BEACH BALL?
I CAME TO THE LAKE TO ENJOY MYSELF, AND RIGHT AWAY MY BEACH BALL DISAPPEARS!
© 1966 Peanuts Worldwide LLC, Dist. by Universal Uclick
7-19
ALL RIGHT, WHO'S GOT MY BEACH BALL?
www.snoopy.com
SCHULZ

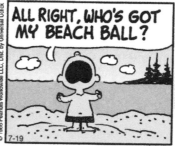

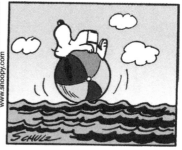

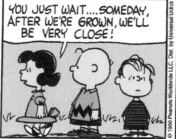

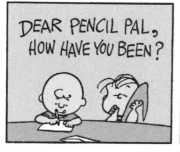

DEAR PENCIL PAL,
HOW HAVE YOU BEEN?
DO YOU THINK I PRINT TOO BIG, LINUS?
© 1966 Peanuts Worldwide LLC, Dist. by Universal Uclick
IN THE SIXTH CHAPTER OF PAUL'S LETTER TO THE GALATIANS, HE SAYS, "SEE WITH WHAT LARGE LETTERS I AM WRITING TO YOU WITH MY OWN HAND"
www.snoopy.com
THANK YOU
7-22
SCHULZ

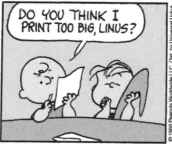

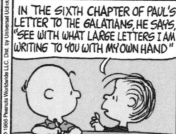

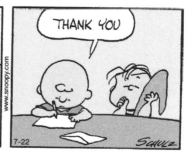

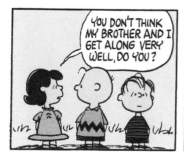

YOU DON'T THINK MY BROTHER AND I GET ALONG VERY WELL, DO YOU?
YOU JUST WAIT....SOMEDAY, AFTER WE'RE GROWN, WE'LL BE VERY CLOSE!
© 1966 Peanuts Worldwide LLC, Dist. by Universal Uclick
WHAT DOES SHE MEAN BY "CLOSE"?
7-27
www.snoopy.com
WE MAY BOTH LIVE ON THE SAME CONTINENT!
SCHULZ

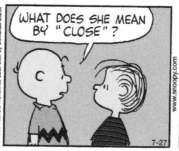

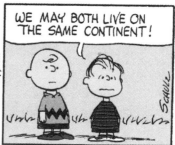

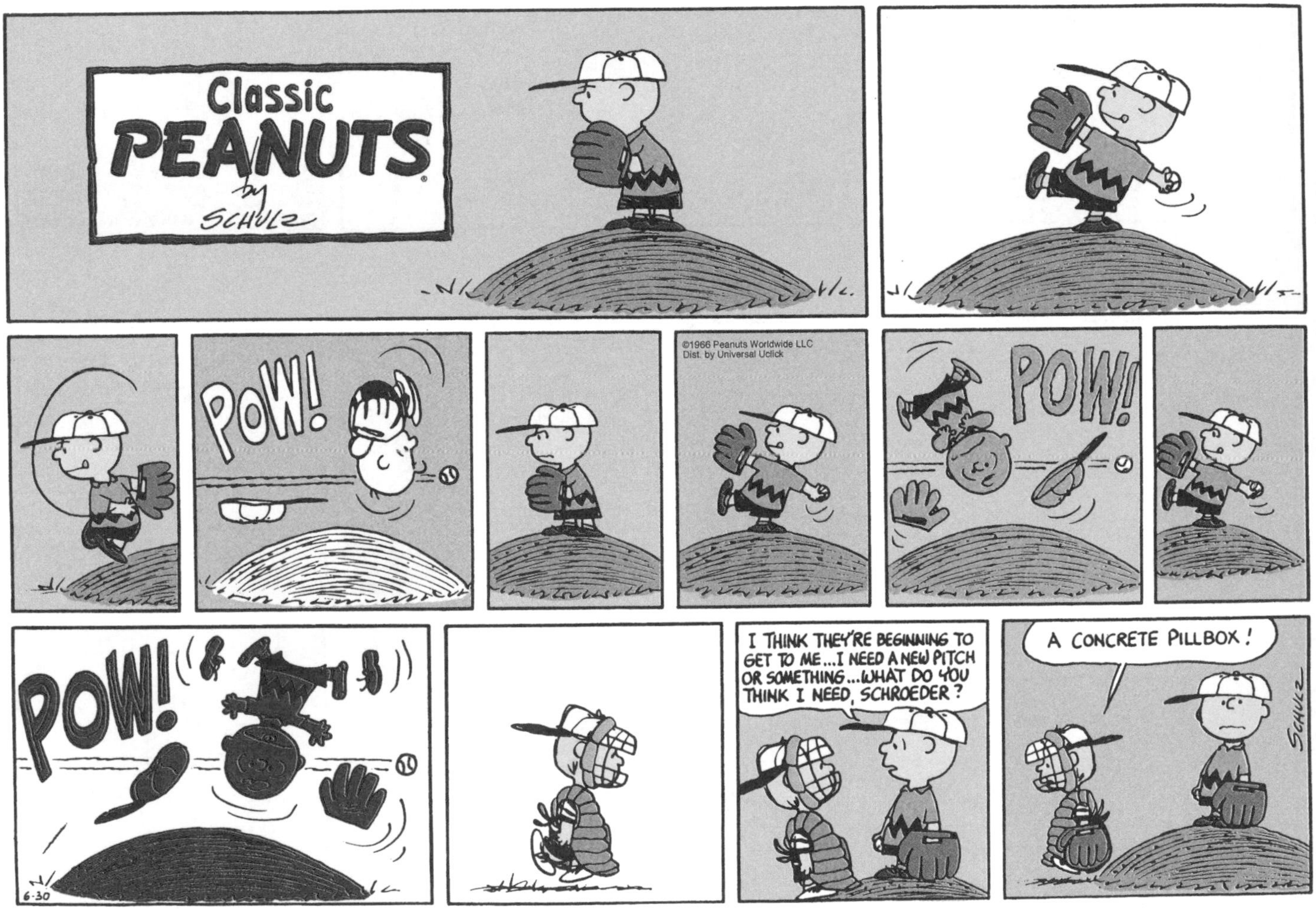
Classic
PEANUTS
by
SCHULZ
©1966 Peanuts Worldwide LLC
Dist. by Universal Uclick
POW!
POW!
POW!
6-30
I THINK THEY'RE BEGINNING TO GET TO ME...I NEED A NEW PITCH OR SOMETHING...WHAT DO YOU THINK I NEED, SCHROEDER?
A CONCRETE PILLBOX!
SCHULZ

DOES IT BOTHER YOU TO THINK THAT THERE MAY BE PEOPLE AROUND WHO DISLIKE YOU?
DISLIKE **ME**? HOW COULD ANYONE POSSIBLY DISLIKE **ME**? THERE'S NOTHING TO DISLIKE!
7-17
© 1966 Peanuts Worldwide LLC. Dist. by Universal Uclick
JEALOUS, MAYBE....YES, I COULD UNDERSTAND THAT...I CAN SEE HOW SOMEONE COULD BE JEALOUS OF ME...BUT DISLIKE? NO, THAT'S JUST NOT POSSIBLE...
www.snoopy.com
SO GETTING BACK TO YOUR ORIGINAL QUESTION...
FORGET IT..
SCHULZ

NYAAH!
NYAAH NYAAH NYAAH!
7-30
© 1965 Peanuts Worldwide LLC. Dist. by Universal Uclick
AND **NYAAH** TO YOU, TOO!
www.snoopy.com
THIS IS A TOUGH NEIGHBORHOOD. YOU NEVER KNOW WHEN YOU'RE GOING TO GET HIT WITH A STRAY "NYAAH"!
SCHULZ

8-1
© 1964 Peanuts Worldwide LLC. Dist. by Universal Uclick
PLUNK!
www.snoopy.com
THAT'S WHAT IS KNOWN AS A SPECTACULAR CATCH OF A ROUTINE FLY BALL!
SCHULZ

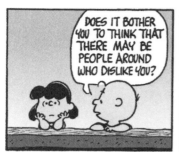

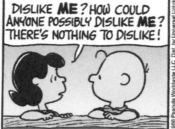

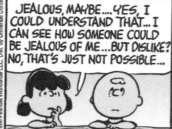

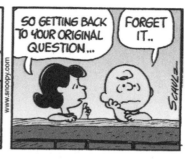

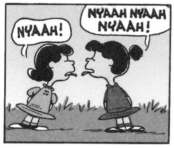

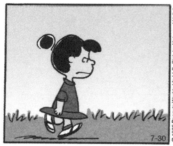

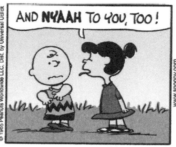

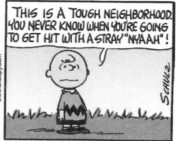

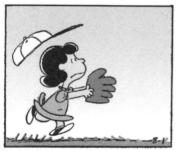

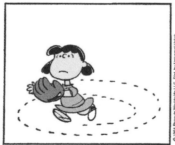

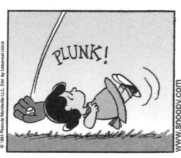

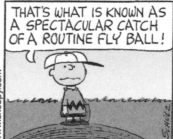

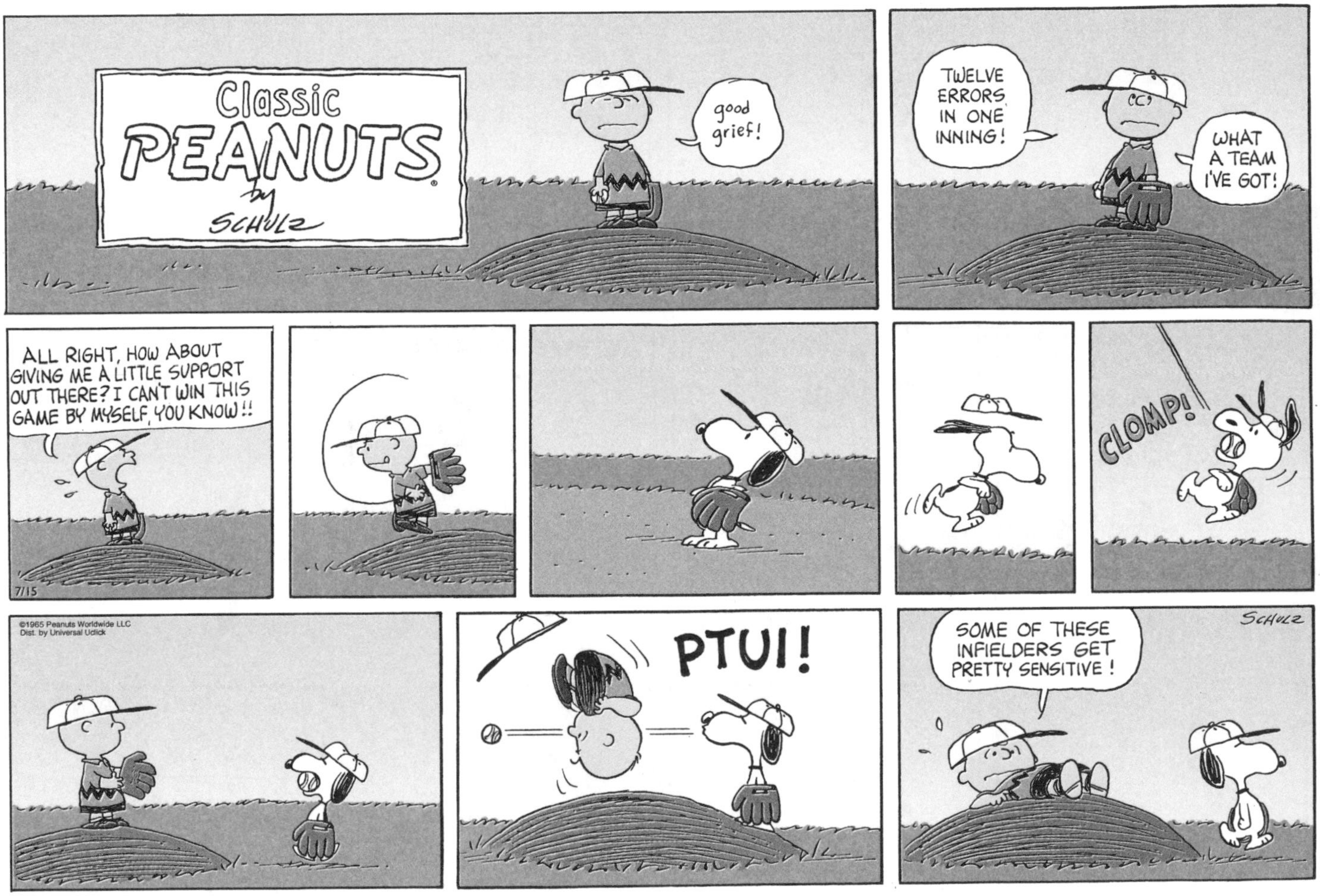
Classic
PEANUTS
by
SCHULZ
good grief!
TWELVE ERRORS IN ONE INNING!
WHAT A TEAM I'VE GOT!
ALL RIGHT, HOW ABOUT GIVING ME A LITTLE SUPPORT OUT THERE? I CAN'T WIN THIS GAME BY MYSELF, YOU KNOW!!
7/15
CLOMP!
©1965 Peanuts Worldwide LLC
Dist. by Universal Uclick
PTUI!
SCHULZ
SOME OF THESE INFIELDERS GET PRETTY SENSITIVE!

BONK
7-30
WHAT HAPPENED?
CHARLIE BROWN GOT HIT WITH A LINE-DRIVE!
© 1966 Peanuts Worldwide LLC, Dist. by Universal Uclick
DOES ANYONE HERE KNOW ANYTHING ABOUT FIRST-AID?
www.snoopy.com
IT'S PROBABLY NOT SERIOUS.. SECOND OR THIRD-AID WILL DO
SCHULZ

CHARLIE BROWN GOT HIT ON THE HEAD WITH THE BALL!
MERCY!
HERE, RUN OVER TO THE DRINKING FOUNTAIN, AND SOAK THIS HANDKERCHIEF IN COLD WATER...
YOU'RE KIDDING!
7-31
© 1966 Peanuts Worldwide LLC, Dist. by Universal Uclick
WITH A HEAD LIKE CHARLIE BROWN'S, YOU'LL NEED A BED SHEET!
www.snoopy.com
I'M DYING, AND ALL I HEAR IS INSULTS!
SCHULZ

WHAT HAPPENED?
YOU GOT HIT ON THE HEAD WITH A LINE-DRIVE, CHARLIE BROWN
I DON'T UNDERSTAND IT...
8-1
© 1966 Peanuts Worldwide LLC, Dist. by Universal Uclick
I USED TO BE ABLE TO DODGE THOSE LINE-DRIVES
www.snoopy.com
WHEN YOU GET OLD, YOUR REFLEXES SLOW DOWN!
SCHULZ

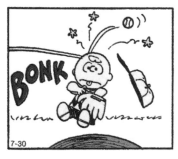

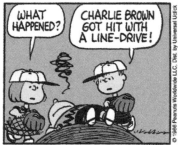

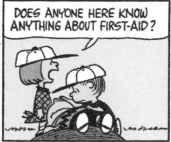

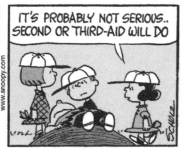

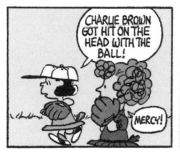

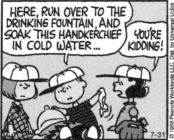

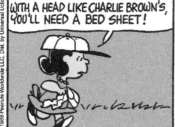

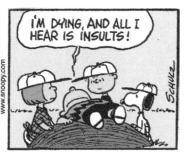

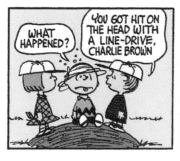

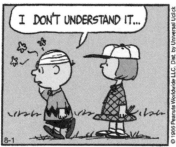

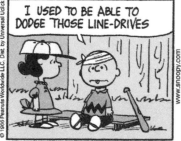

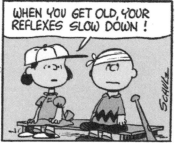

WE WON, CHARLIE BROWN! WE WON THE GAME!

I KNOW

IT'S TOO BAD YOU HAD TO SIT ON THE BENCH THE WHOLE TIME.. MAYBE YOUR HEAD WILL FEEL BETTER TOMORROW......

OF COURSE, WE DID DO VERY WELL WITHOUT...I MEAN...THAT IS...I...WE...WELL....WELL, I MEAN...WELL, WHAT I'M TRYING TO SAY IS....

I KNOW WHAT YOU'RE TRYING TO SAY!!!

DON'T GET HIT WITH ANY MORE LINE-DRIVES, TODAY, CHARLIE BROWN

DON'T WORRY...I FEEL SHARP!

POW!

SEE? I'VE GOT MY OLD REFLEXES BACK!

AAUGH! A SPIDER!!

THERE'S A SPIDER ON THE BALL! WE CAN'T PICK UP THE BALL, CHARLIE BROWN! THERE'S A SPIDER ON IT!

IT WILL BE INTERESTING TO SEE IF THE OFFICIAL SCORER GIVES THE HITTER CREDIT FOR A HOME RUN..

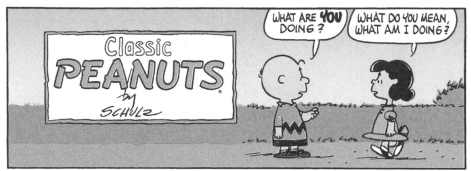

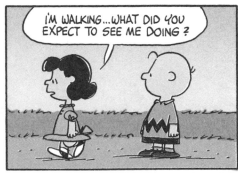

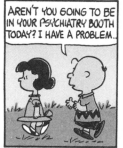

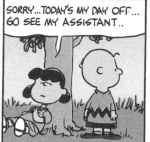

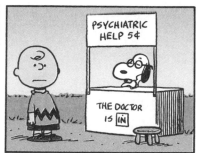

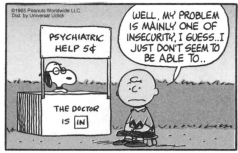

Classic PEANUTS by SCHULZ
WHAT ARE YOU DOING?
WHAT DO YOU MEAN, WHAT AM I DOING?
I'M WALKING...WHAT DID YOU EXPECT TO SEE ME DOING?
AREN'T YOU GOING TO BE IN YOUR PSYCHIATRY BOOTH TODAY? I HAVE A PROBLEM..
SORRY...TODAY'S MY DAY OFF... GO SEE MY ASSISTANT..
PSYCHIATRIC HELP 5¢
THE DOCTOR IS IN
©1965 Peanuts Worldwide LLC
Dist. by Universal Uclick
PSYCHIATRIC HELP 5¢
WELL, MY PROBLEM IS MAINLY ONE OF INSECURITY, I GUESS..I JUST DON'T SEEM TO BE ABLE TO..
THE DOCTOR IS IN
Z
PSYCHIATRIC HELP 5¢
!
THE DOCTOR IS IN
7/22
WHAT IN THE WORLD KIND OF ASSISTANT DO YOU HAVE ANYWAY? HE FELL ASLEEP WHILE I WAS TALKING TO HIM
REALLY? GEE, I'M SORRY. I APOLOGIZE..MAYBE I CAN HELP YOU...WHAT IS YOUR PROBLEM?
WELL, I WAS TELLING HIM ABOUT THIS INSECURE FEELING I HAVE, AND...
Z
SCHULZ

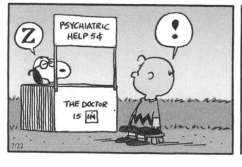

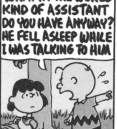

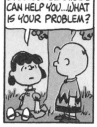

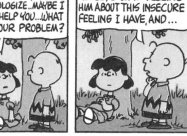

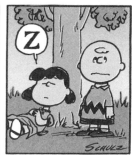

8-5
LIFE IS DIFFICULT, ISN'T IT, CHARLIE BROWN?
YES, IT IS
BUT I'VE DEVELOPED A NEW PHILOSOPHY...
I ONLY DREAD ONE DAY AT A TIME!
www.snoopy.com
SCHULZ

YOU KNOW WHAT YOUR TROUBLE IS, CHARLIE BROWN?
THE WHOLE TROUBLE WITH YOU IS YOU DON'T UNDERSTAND THE MEANING OF LIFE!
8-2
DO **YOU** UNDERSTAND THE MEANING OF LIFE?
WE'RE NOT TALKING ABOUT ME, WE'RE TALKING ABOUT YOU!
www.snoopy.com
SCHULZ

PIG-PEN, YOU ARE A PERPETUAL MESS...
I CAN TELL JUST WHERE YOU'VE BEEN ALL WEEK FROM THE DIRT ON YOUR CLOTHES...YESTERDAY YOU WERE DOWN BY THE TRAIN TRACKS..
8-18
YOU SPENT THE DAY BEFORE DOWN AT THE PLAYGROUND, THE DUMP AND THE WAREHOUSE..
I DON'T HAVE TO LISTEN TO THIS..
www.snoopy.com
AND MONDAY YOU SPENT ALL DAY AT THE BRICK YARD, ISN'T THAT RIGHT?
SCHULZ

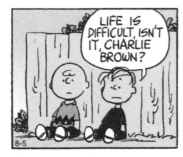

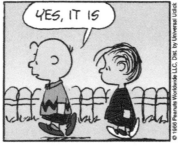

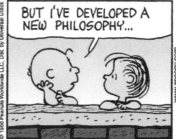

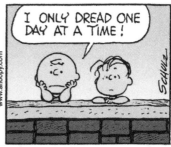

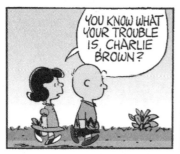

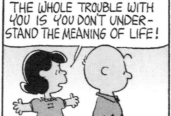

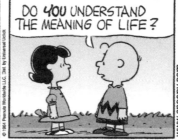

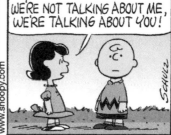

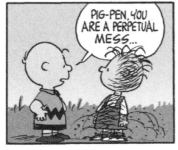

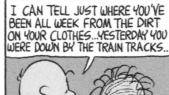

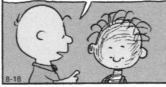

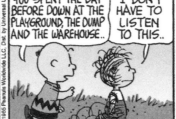

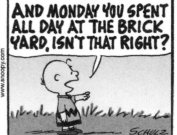

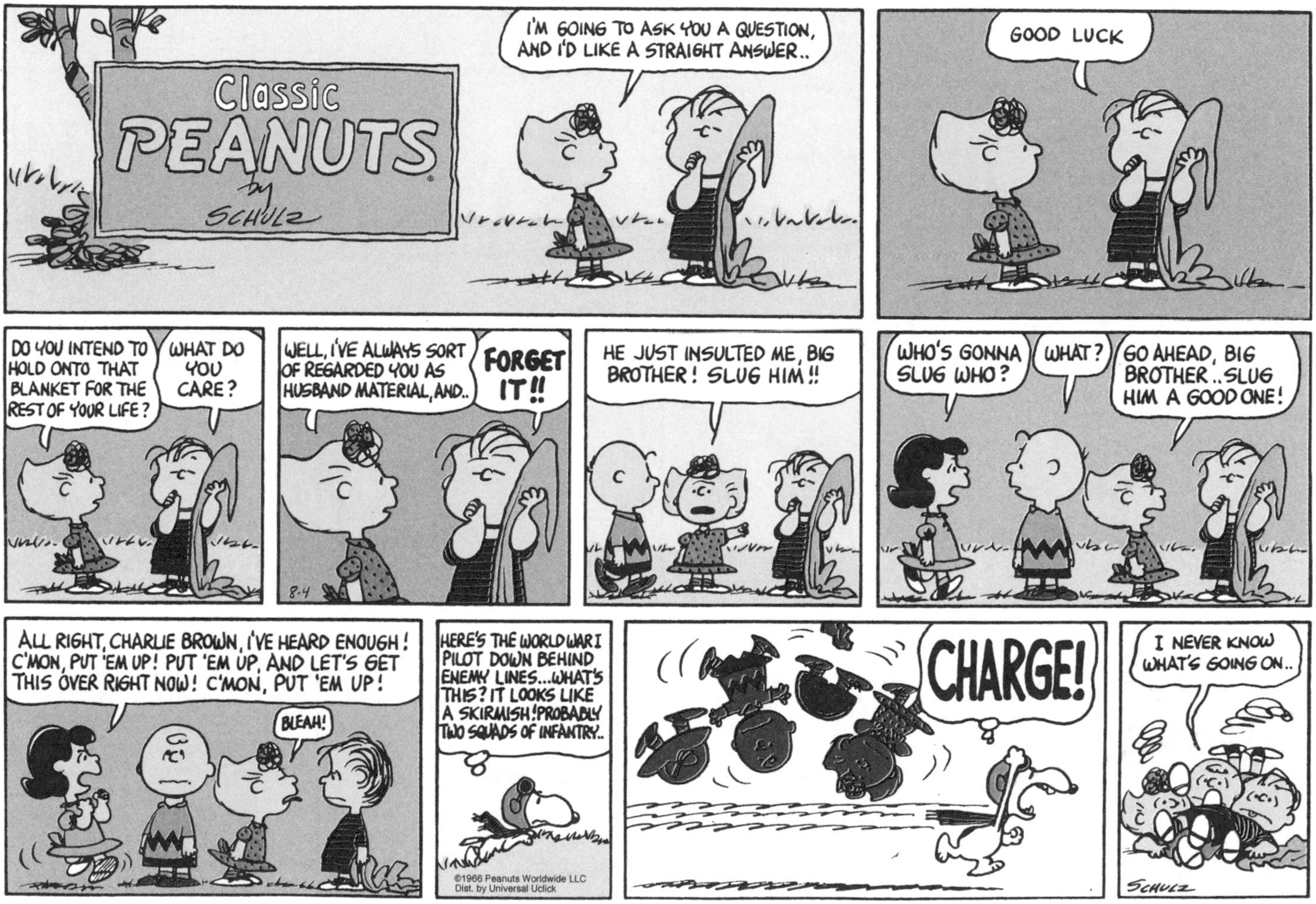

Classic PEANUTS by SCHULZ
I'M GOING TO ASK YOU A QUESTION, AND I'D LIKE A STRAIGHT ANSWER..
GOOD LUCK
DO YOU INTEND TO HOLD ONTO THAT BLANKET FOR THE REST OF YOUR LIFE?
WHAT DO YOU CARE?
WELL, I'VE ALWAYS SORT OF REGARDED YOU AS HUSBAND MATERIAL, AND..
FORGET IT!!
HE JUST INSULTED ME, BIG BROTHER! SLUG HIM!!
WHO'S GONNA SLUG WHO?
WHAT?
GO AHEAD, BIG BROTHER..SLUG HIM A GOOD ONE!
ALL RIGHT, CHARLIE BROWN, I'VE HEARD ENOUGH! C'MON, PUT 'EM UP! PUT 'EM UP, AND LET'S GET THIS OVER RIGHT NOW! C'MON, PUT 'EM UP!
BLEAH!
HERE'S THE WORLD WAR I PILOT DOWN BEHIND ENEMY LINES...WHAT'S THIS? IT LOOKS LIKE A SKIRMISH! PROBABLY TWO SQUADS OF INFANTRY..
©1966 Peanuts Worldwide LLC
Dist. by Universal Uclick
CHARGE!
I NEVER KNOW WHAT'S GOING ON..
SCHULZ

HEY, MANAGER, WAIT! I HAVE A QUESTION..
I'VE BEEN READING ABOUT THIS BASEBALL STADIUM THAT HAS PLASTIC GRASS...HOW COME **WE** DON'T HAVE PLASTIC GRASS?
8-11
© 1965 Peanuts Worldwide LLC, Dist. by Universal Uclick
www.snoopy.com
STANDING OUT HERE IN THE OUTFIELD LIKE THIS, LOTS OF QUESTIONS COME TO YOUR MIND
SCHULZ

WELL, WE LOST AGAIN, BUT WHO CARES?
SURE, IT'S ONLY A GAME...WE LOST, BUT SO WHAT? WHO CARES?
© 1965 Peanuts Worldwide LLC, Dist. by Universal Uclick
www.snoopy.com
JUST WHAT I'VE ALWAYS BEEN AFRAID OF... MY TEAM HAS BUILT UP AN IMMUNITY TO LOSING!
8-13
SCHULZ

I'VE THOUGHT UP SOME STRATEGY FOR YOU, CHARLIE BROWN..
www.snoopy.com
TELL THE OTHER TEAM WE'RE GOING TO PLAY THEM AT A CERTAIN PLACE THAT ISN'T THE REAL PLACE, AND THEN, WHEN THEY DON'T SHOW UP, WE'LL WIN BY FORFEIT!
8-15
ISN'T THAT GOOD STRATEGY?
© 1965 Peanuts Worldwide LLC, Dist. by Universal Uclick
I DON'T UNDERSTAND THESE MANAGERS WHO REFUSE TO USE GOOD STRATEGY!
SCHULZ

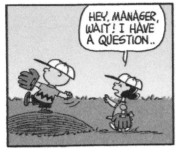

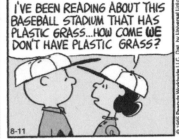

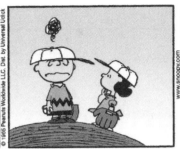

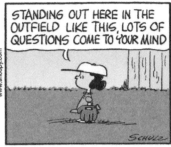

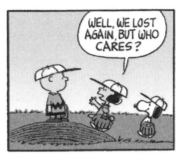

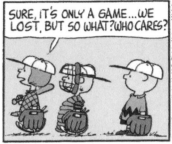

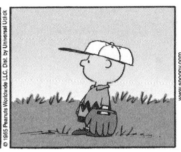

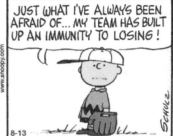

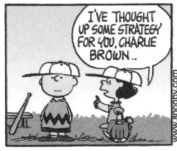

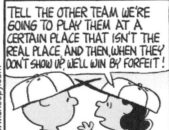

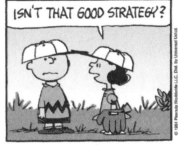

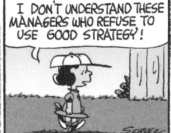

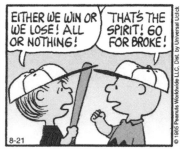

I'M GOING TO TRY FOR A HOME RUN, CHARLIE BROWN!
EITHER WE WIN OR WE LOSE! ALL OR NOTHING!
THAT'S THE SPIRIT! GO FOR BROKE!
8-21
© 1965 Peanuts Worldwide LLC. Dist. by Universal Uclick
SYDNEY OR THE BUSH!
www.snoopy.com
SCHULZ
"SYDNEY OR THE BUSH"?

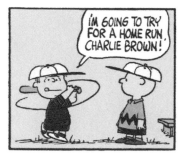

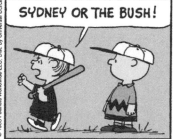

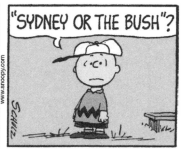

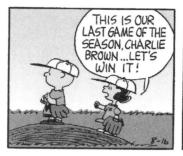

THIS IS OUR LAST GAME OF THE SEASON, CHARLIE BROWN...LET'S WIN IT!
8-16
OKAY, GET OUT THERE AND PLAY YOUR BEST...
www.snoopy.com
© 1964 Peanuts Worldwide LLC. Dist. by Universal Uclick
YOU ALWAYS HAVE TO SAY SOMETHING SARCASTIC, DON'T YOU?
SCHULZ

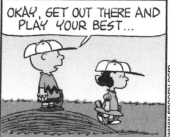

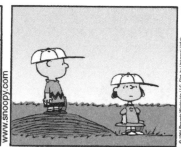

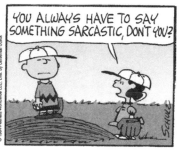

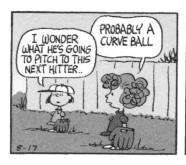

I WONDER WHAT HE'S GOING TO PITCH TO THIS NEXT HITTER..
PROBABLY A CURVE BALL
8-17
PSST, CHARLIE BROWN....WE OUTFIELDERS HAVE BEEN WONDERING WHAT YOU'RE GOING TO PITCH TO THIS GUY..
© 1964 Peanuts Worldwide LLC. Dist. by Universal Uclick
A CURVE BALL
REALLY?
www.snoopy.com
YOU WERE RIGHT! HE'S GONNA THROW HIM THE CURVE BALL!
SCHULZ

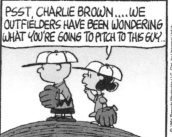

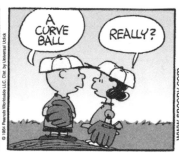

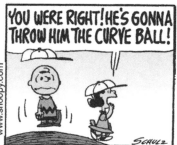

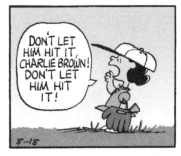

DON'T LET HIM HIT IT, CHARLIE BROWN! DON'T LET HIM HIT IT!
8-18
POW!
© 1984 Peanuts Worldwide LLC. Dist. by Universal Uclick
www.snoopy.com
YOU LET HIM HIT IT!
SCHULZ

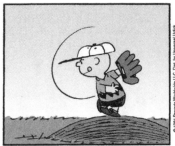

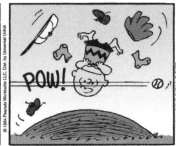

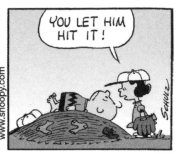

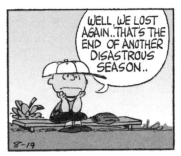

WELL, WE LOST AGAIN.. THAT'S THE END OF ANOTHER DISASTROUS SEASON..
8-19
I GUESS IT'S TIME TO HANG UP THE OL' GLOVE FOR ANOTHER YEAR
© 1984 Peanuts Worldwide LLC. Dist. by Universal Uclick
IT'S TIME TO TAKE THE OL' GLOVE, AND...
www.snoopy.com
THROW IT AS FAR AS I CAN THROW IT!
SCHULZ

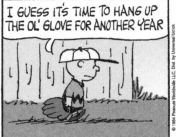

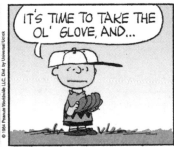

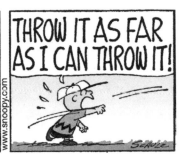

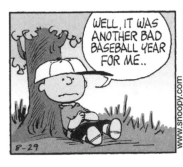

WELL, IT WAS ANOTHER BAD BASEBALL YEAR FOR ME..
8-29
www.snoopy.com
MAYBE MY HERO, JOE SHLABOTNIK, IS HAVING A BETTER TIME... I'LL SEE HOW HE'S DOING...
"JOE SHLABOTNIK STRUCK OUT LAST NIGHT IN THE BOTTOM OF THE NINTH AS STUMPTOWN OF THE GREEN GRASS LEAGUE SANK DEEPER INTO THE CELLAR."
© 1984 Peanuts Worldwide LLC. Dist. by Universal Uclick
DEAR JOE, DON'T BE DISCOURAGED. SOMEONE UNDERSTANDS.
SCHULZ

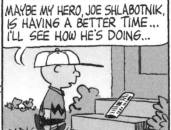

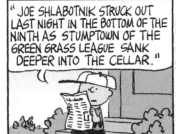

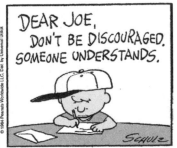

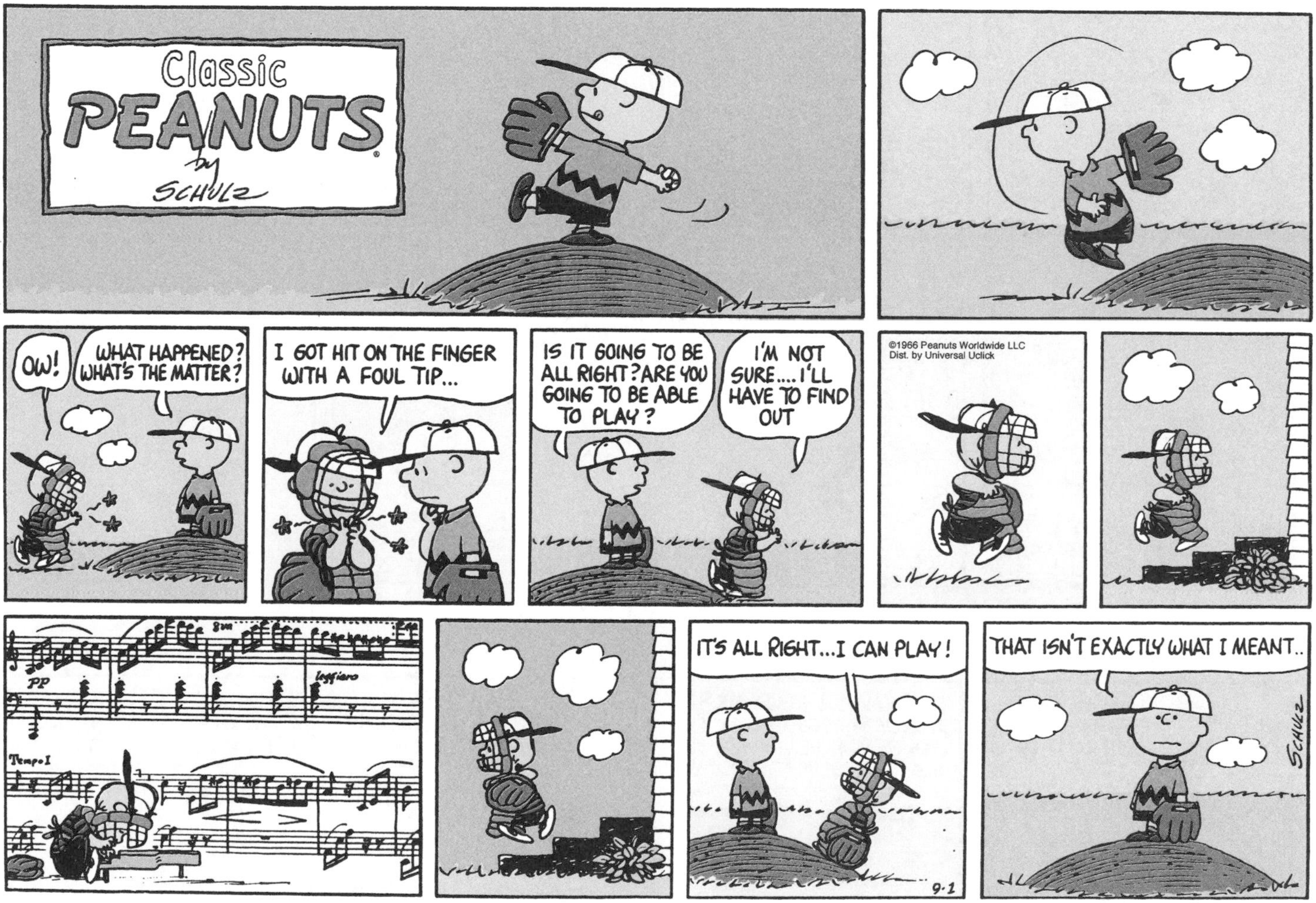
Classic
PEANUTS
by
SCHULZ
OW!
WHAT HAPPENED? WHAT'S THE MATTER?
I GOT HIT ON THE FINGER WITH A FOUL TIP...
IS IT GOING TO BE ALL RIGHT? ARE YOU GOING TO BE ABLE TO PLAY?
I'M NOT SURE.... I'LL HAVE TO FIND OUT
©1966 Peanuts Worldwide LLC
Dist. by Universal Uclick
IT'S ALL RIGHT...I CAN PLAY!
9-1
THAT ISN'T EXACTLY WHAT I MEANT..
SCHULZ

I LIKE BEETHOVEN, BUT BRAHMS MAKES ME GLAD I'M ALIVE..
I THINK I'LL GO HOME, AND LISTEN TO BRAHMS' FOURTH...
© 1965 Peanuts Worldwide LLC, Dist. by Universal Uclick
I FEEL THE NEED TO HAVE THE FEELING THAT IT'S GOOD TO BE ALIVE..
I KNOW WHAT YOU MEAN...
8-14
www.snoopy.com
THAT'S A TERRIBLE FEELING TO HAVE THE NEED OF HAVING THE FEELING OF HAVING...
SCHULZ

DON'T TALK TO ME!
I DON'T WANT ANYONE TO TALK TO ME TODAY! JUST DON'T SAY ANYTHING! DON'T TALK!
8-20
© 1965 Peanuts Worldwide LLC, Dist. by Universal Uclick
!
www.snoopy.com
I DIDN'T SAY ANYTHING ABOUT NOT **LISTENING**!
SCHULZ

I HAVE NEVER SEEN THE SKY AS BLUE AS IT IS TODAY..
OH, I HAVE... I REMEMBER BACK ON JULY 14, 1959, THE SKY WAS REAL BLUE...OH, YES, IT WAS MUCH BLUER THAT DAY...
© 1965 Peanuts Worldwide LLC, Dist. by Universal Uclick
AND THEN I ALSO REMEMBER ON SEPTEMBER 2, 1961, THE SKY WAS A VERY DEEP BLUE...
8-22
www.snoopy.com
AND ON JUNE 1ST OF THE VERY NEXT YEAR THE SKY WAS..
I CAN'T STAND IT...
SCHULZ

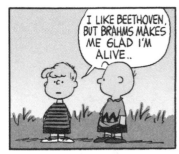

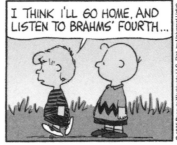

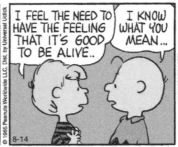

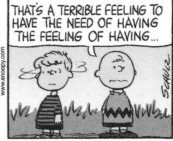

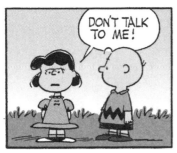

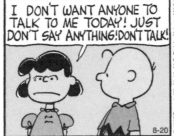

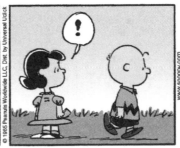

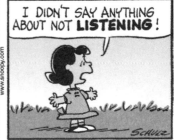

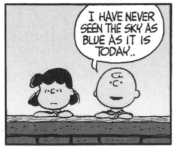

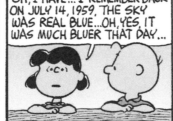

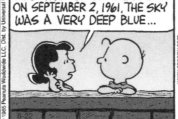

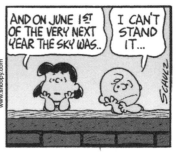

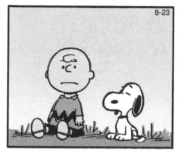

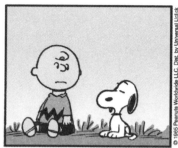

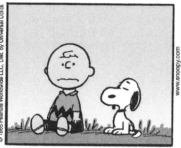

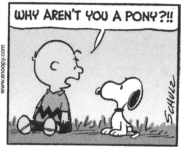

8-23
© 1965 Peanuts Worldwide LLC, Dist. by Universal Uclick
www.snoopy.com
WHY AREN'T YOU A PONY?!!
SCHULZ

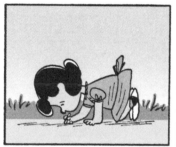

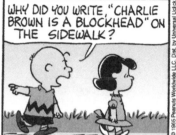

WHY DID YOU WRITE, "CHARLIE BROWN IS A BLOCKHEAD" ON THE SIDEWALK?
© 1965 Peanuts Worldwide LLC, Dist. by Universal Uclick
8-24
BECAUSE I SINCERELY BELIEVE YOU **ARE** A BLOCKHEAD! I HAVE TO WRITE WHAT I BELIEVE IS TRUE.. IT'S MY MORAL RESPONSIBILITY!
www.snoopy.com
DEEP DOWN I ADMIRE HER INTEGRITY..
SCHULZ

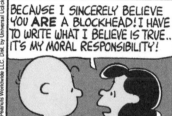

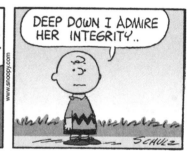

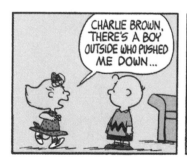

CHARLIE BROWN, THERE'S A BOY OUTSIDE WHO PUSHED ME DOWN...
I TOLD HIM I'D GET MY BIG BROTHER AFTER HIM SO I WANT YOU TO GO OUT THERE, AND SLUG HIM
© 1965 Peanuts Worldwide LLC, Dist. by Universal Uclick
8-27
YOU MEAN YOU WANT ME TO GO OUTSIDE, AND FIND OUT WHAT HIS PURPOSE WAS IN PUSHING YOU DOWN, AND ASK HIM NOT TO DO IT AGAIN..
www.snoopy.com
NO, I WANT YOU TO GO OUT THERE, AND **SLUG** HIM!
THAT'S WHAT I WAS AFRAID OF...
SCHULZ

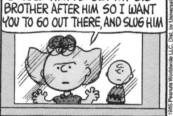

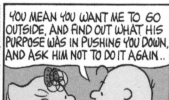

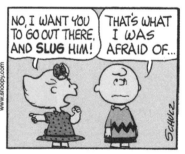

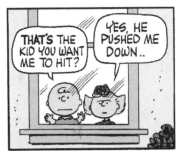

THAT'S THE KID YOU WANT ME TO HIT?
YES, HE PUSHED ME DOWN..
YOU CAN TAKE HIM, CHARLIE BROWN...HE'S REAL FAT..
© 1965 Peanuts Worldwide LLC, Dist. by Universal Uclick
HE'S NOT FAT...HE'S HUSKY!
8-28
www.snoopy.com
MY BROTHER IS A COWARD!
OH, GOOD GRIEF!
SCHULZ

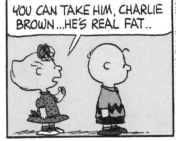

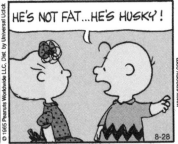

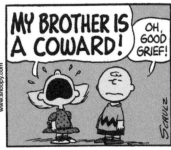

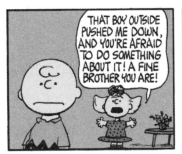

THAT BOY OUTSIDE PUSHED ME DOWN, AND YOU'RE AFRAID TO DO SOMETHING ABOUT IT! A FINE BROTHER YOU ARE!
ALL RIGHT! I'LL GO OUT THERE! I'LL EITHER TEACH HIM A LESSON, OR GET MYSELF KILLED!
© 1965 Peanuts Worldwide LLC, Dist. by Universal Uclick
THAT'S THE SPIRIT!! "SYDNEY OR THE BUSH"!
8-29
www.snoopy.com
"SYDNEY OR THE BUSH"?
SCHULZ

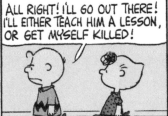

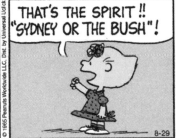

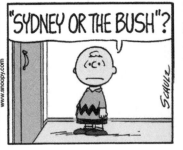

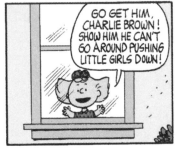

GO GET HIM, CHARLIE BROWN! SHOW HIM HE CAN'T GO AROUND PUSHING LITTLE GIRLS DOWN!
OH, MY! WOW! OOPS!
© 1965 Peanuts Worldwide LLC, Dist. by Universal Uclick
GOOD GRIEF! OOO! WOW!
www.snoopy.com
WHAT HAVE I DONE?
8-30
SCHULZ

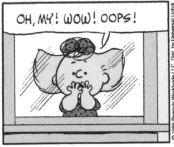

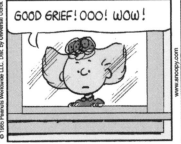

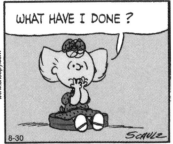

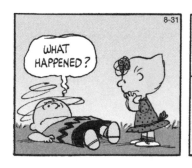

8-31
WHAT HAPPENED?
WELL, FIRST YOU GOT HIT WITH A LEFT, THEN A RIGHT...THEN A JUDO CHOP AND THEN SOME MORE LEFTS...LOTS MORE!
© 1965 Peanuts Worldwide LLC, Dist. by Universal Uclick
THEN YOU GOT HIT WITH A REAL HARD RIGHT, TWO MORE LEFTS, ANOTHER RIGHT, A LEFT, AND A RIGHT, AND A LEFT, AND A..
www.snoopy.com
ALL RIGHT!
SCHULZ

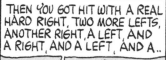

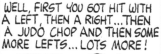

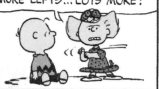

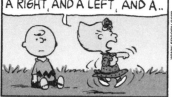

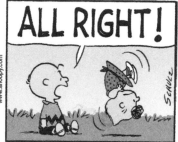

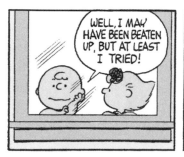

WELL, I MAY HAVE BEEN BEATEN UP, BUT AT LEAST I TRIED!
AT LEAST I WENT OUT THERE, AND FACED THAT BIG KID WHO PUSHED YOU DOWN! AT LEAST I KNOW I TRIED!
9-1
© 1965 Peanuts Worldwide LLC, Dist. by Universal Uclick
HE MAY HAVE BEEN BIGGER THAN THAN I, BUT I FACED UP TO HIM!
www.snoopy.com
THAT WASN'T HIM WHO BEAT YOU UP...IT WAS HIS SISTER!
SCHULZ

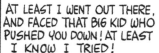

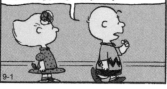

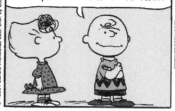

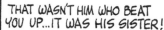

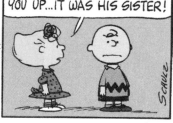

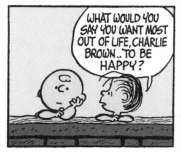

WHAT WOULD YOU SAY YOU WANT MOST OUT OF LIFE, CHARLIE BROWN..TO BE HAPPY?
9-6
OH, NO..
© 1966 Peanuts Worldwide LLC, Dist. by Universal Uclick
I DON'T EXPECT THAT... I REALLY DON'T
www.snoopy.com
I JUST DON'T WANT TO BE UNHAPPY!
SCHULZ

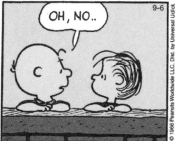

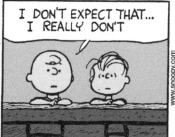

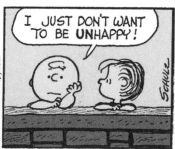

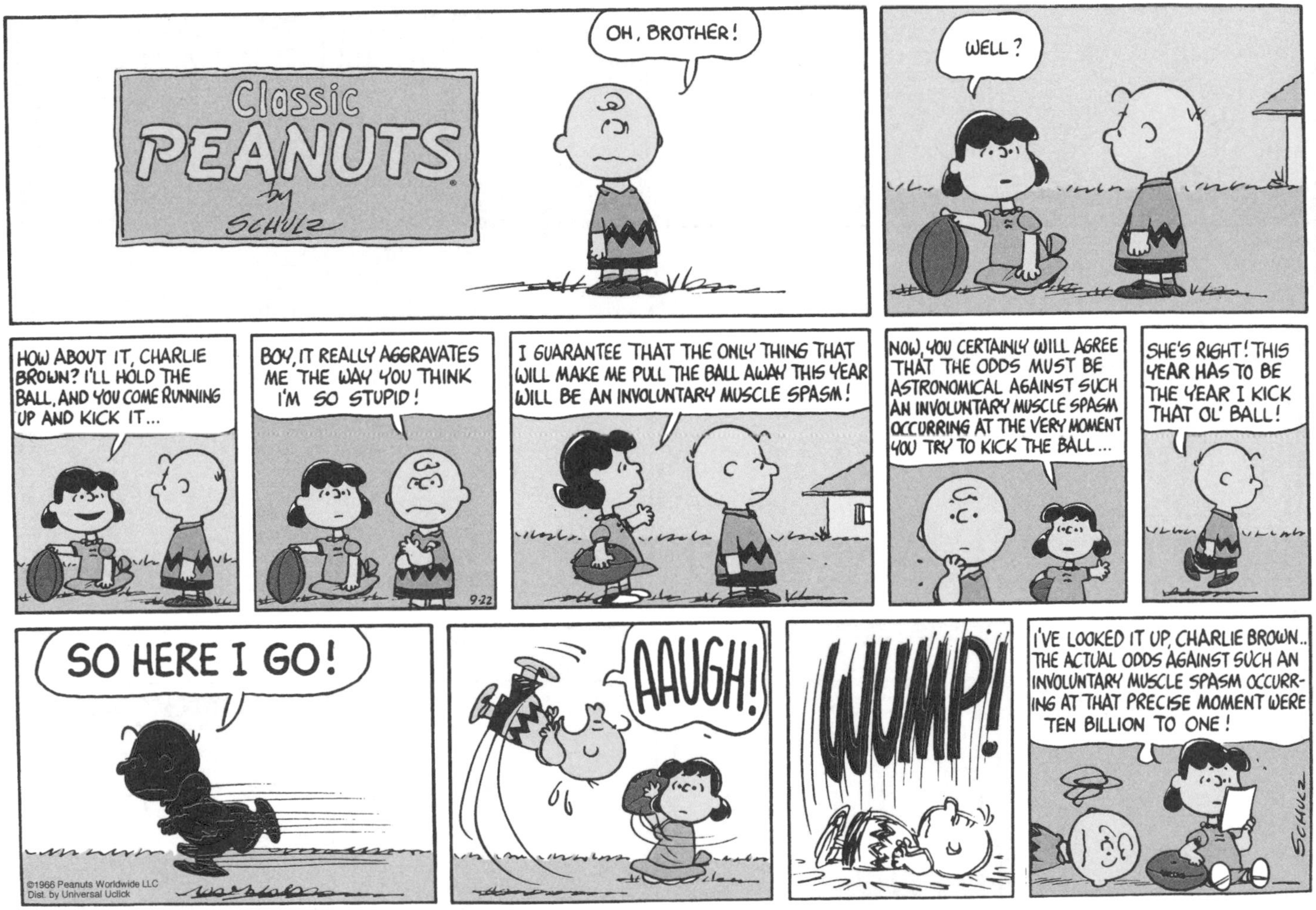
Classic PEANUTS by SCHULZ
OH, BROTHER!
WELL?
HOW ABOUT IT, CHARLIE BROWN? I'LL HOLD THE BALL, AND YOU COME RUNNING UP AND KICK IT...
BOY, IT REALLY AGGRAVATES ME THE WAY YOU THINK I'M SO STUPID!
I GUARANTEE THAT THE ONLY THING THAT WILL MAKE ME PULL THE BALL AWAY THIS YEAR WILL BE AN INVOLUNTARY MUSCLE SPASM!
NOW, YOU CERTAINLY WILL AGREE THAT THE ODDS MUST BE ASTRONOMICAL AGAINST SUCH AN INVOLUNTARY MUSCLE SPASM OCCURRING AT THE VERY MOMENT YOU TRY TO KICK THE BALL...
SHE'S RIGHT! THIS YEAR HAS TO BE THE YEAR I KICK THAT OL' BALL!
SO HERE I GO!
AAUGH!
WUMP!
I'VE LOOKED IT UP, CHARLIE BROWN.. THE ACTUAL ODDS AGAINST SUCH AN INVOLUNTARY MUSCLE SPASM OCCURRING AT THAT PRECISE MOMENT WERE TEN BILLION TO ONE!
SCHULZ
©1966 Peanuts Worldwide LLC
Dist. by Universal Uclick

WHAT'S THIS?
I HAVE HEARD THAT IT IS BETTER TO LIGHT A SINGLE CANDLE THAN TO CURSE THE DARKNESS
THAT'S TRUE..ALTHOUGH THERE WILL ALWAYS BE THOSE WHO WILL DISAGREE WITH YOU....
YOU STUPID DARKNESS!
© 1965 Peanuts Worldwide LLC. Dist. by Universal Uclick
www.snoopy.com
9-6
SCHULZ

DEAR PENCIL-PAL, HAVE YOU HAD A NICE SUMMER?
9-8
I LIKE TO READ, DO YOU? I AM VERY FOND OF BOOKS.
I CAN ALWAYS ENJOY A GOOD BOOK. I HAVE ALWAYS BEEN THE SORT OF PERSON WHO ENJOYS READING.
WHEN I HAVE NOTHING ELSE TO DO, I READ.
© 1965 Peanuts Worldwide LLC. Dist. by Universal Uclick
www.snoopy.com
SCHULZ

YOU KNOW WHAT I THINK MY BEST QUALITY IS?
I THINK I'M NICE TO HAVE AROUND
9-9
I'D HATE IT IF I WEREN'T AROUND!
© 1966 Peanuts Worldwide LLC. Dist. by Universal Uclick
www.snoopy.com
SCHULZ

HOMEWORK ALREADY! WRITE A THOUSAND-WORD ESSAY ON WHAT WE DID DURING THE SUMMER!
9-10
NOBODY CAN WRITE A THOUSAND-WORD ESSAY ON WHAT HE DID DURING THE SUMMER! IT'S RIDICULOUS!
© 1965 Peanuts Worldwide LLC, Dist. by Universal Uclick
WHEN ARE YOU GOING TO TRY TO WRITE YOURS... THIS EVENING?
MINE'S ALREADY FINISHED..I WROTE IT DURING STUDY PERIOD!
www.snoopy.com
YOU DRIVE ME CRAZY!!!
SCHULZ

DO YOU KNOW WHY ENGLISH TEACHERS GO TO COLLEGE FOR FOUR YEARS?
NO, I DON'T KNOW WHY ENGLISH TEACHERS GO TO COLLEGE FOR FOUR YEARS..
9-11
© 1965 Peanuts Worldwide LLC, Dist. by Universal Uclick
WELL, THEN I'LL TELL YOU WHY ENGLISH TEACHERS GO TO COLLEGE FOR FOUR YEARS....
www.snoopy.com
SO THEY CAN MAKE STUPID LITTLE KIDS WRITE STUPID ESSAYS ON WHAT THEY DID ALL STUPID SUMMER!!
SCHULZ

English Essay
"What I Did This Summer"
9-12
I played ball, and I went to camp.
© 1965 Peanuts Worldwide LLC, Dist. by Universal Uclick
ONE, TWO, THREE, FOUR, FIVE, SIX, SEVEN, EIGHT....
www.snoopy.com
NINE HUNDRED AND NINETY-TWO WORDS TO GO!

MY ESSAY? YES, MA'AM... I HAVE IT RIGHT HERE..
BUT I COULDN'T WRITE A THOUSAND WORDS.... I ONLY WROTE EIGHT..
DETAIL? WELL, YES, I SUPPOSE I COULD HAVE GONE INTO MORE DETAIL...
BUT WITH THE KIND OF SUMMERS I HAVE, IT'S BEST TO TRY TO FORGET THE DETAILS
9-13
© 1965 Peanuts Worldwide LLC. Dist. by Universal Uclick
www.snoopy.com
SCHULZ

YOU WANT ME TO READ MY ESSAY IN FRONT OF THE CLASS? YES, MA'AM...
"WHAT I DID THIS SUMMER... I WENT TO CAMP, AND I PLAYED BALL.........THE END"
HAHAHAHA
I LOVE SCHOOL...IT'S SUCH A SATISFYING EXPERIENCE!
9-14
© 1965 Peanuts Worldwide LLC. Dist. by Universal Uclick
www.snoopy.com
SCHULZ

WHEN I GET BIG, I'D LIKE TO BE A PROPHET
THAT'S A FINE AMBITION..THE WORLD CAN ALWAYS USE A FEW GOOD PROPHETS...
THE ONLY TROUBLE IS THAT MOST OF THEM TURN OUT TO BE FALSE PROPHETS
MAYBE I COULD BE A SINCERE FALSE PROPHET
9-12
www.snoopy.com
SCHULZ

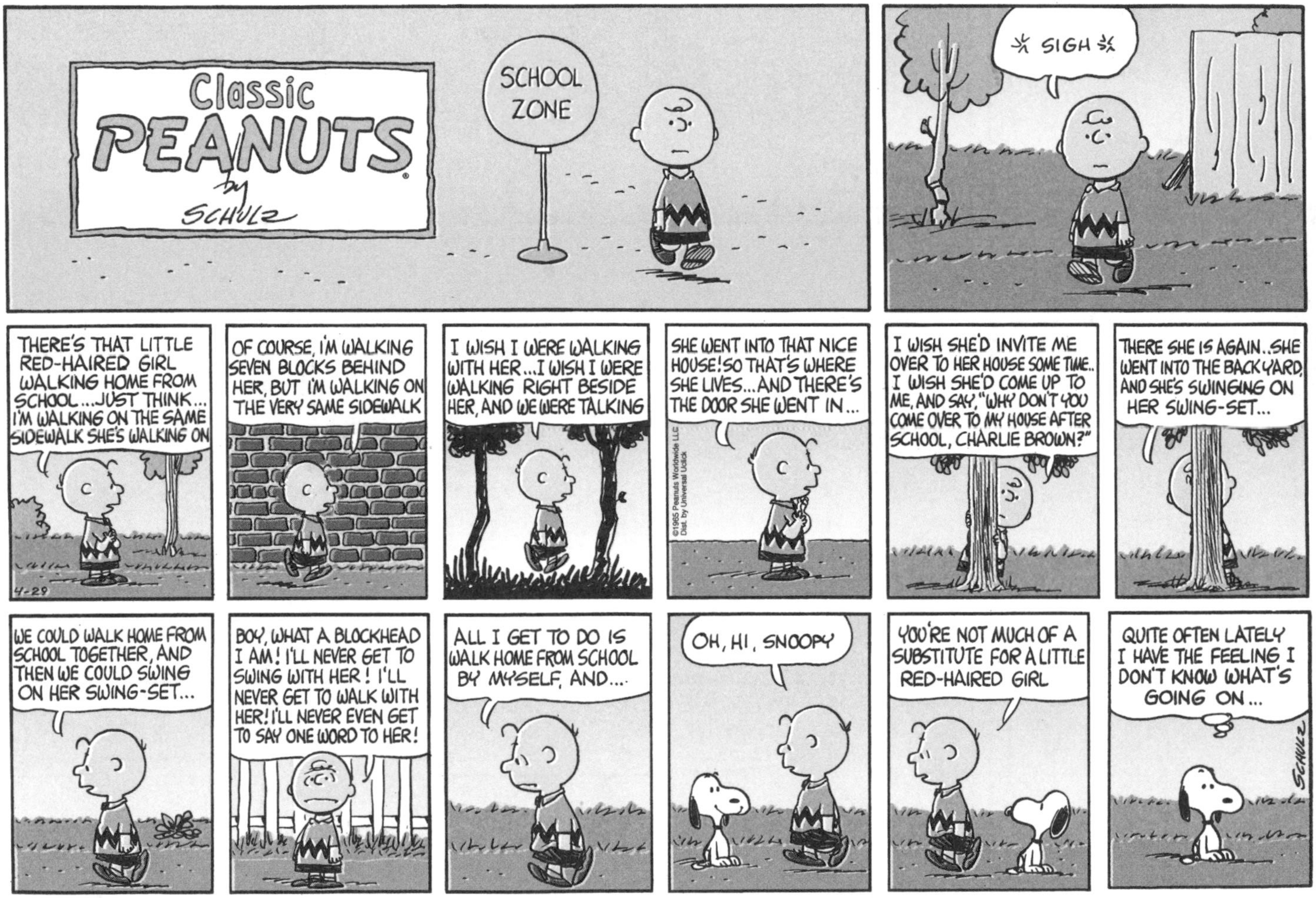
Classic PEANUTS by SCHULZ
SCHOOL ZONE
SIGH
THERE'S THAT LITTLE RED-HAIRED GIRL WALKING HOME FROM SCHOOL...JUST THINK... I'M WALKING ON THE SAME SIDEWALK SHE'S WALKING ON
4-29
OF COURSE, I'M WALKING SEVEN BLOCKS BEHIND HER, BUT I'M WALKING ON THE VERY SAME SIDEWALK
I WISH I WERE WALKING WITH HER...I WISH I WERE WALKING RIGHT BESIDE HER, AND WE WERE TALKING
SHE WENT INTO THAT NICE HOUSE! SO THAT'S WHERE SHE LIVES...AND THERE'S THE DOOR SHE WENT IN...
©1965 Peanuts Worldwide LLC Dist. by Universal Uclick
I WISH SHE'D INVITE ME OVER TO HER HOUSE SOME TIME.. I WISH SHE'D COME UP TO ME, AND SAY, "WHY DON'T YOU COME OVER TO MY HOUSE AFTER SCHOOL, CHARLIE BROWN?"
THERE SHE IS AGAIN..SHE WENT INTO THE BACK YARD, AND SHE'S SWINGING ON HER SWING-SET...
WE COULD WALK HOME FROM SCHOOL TOGETHER, AND THEN WE COULD SWING ON HER SWING-SET...
BOY, WHAT A BLOCKHEAD I AM! I'LL NEVER GET TO SWING WITH HER! I'LL NEVER GET TO WALK WITH HER! I'LL NEVER EVEN GET TO SAY ONE WORD TO HER!
ALL I GET TO DO IS WALK HOME FROM SCHOOL BY MYSELF, AND....
OH, HI, SNOOPY
YOU'RE NOT MUCH OF A SUBSTITUTE FOR A LITTLE RED-HAIRED GIRL
QUITE OFTEN LATELY I HAVE THE FEELING I DON'T KNOW WHAT'S GOING ON...
SCHULZ

MAKING A MAP FOR SCHOOL?
YES, I ENJOY IT... I LIKE MAKING ALL THOSE MERIDIANS AND LATITUDES
9-14
STAND BACK NOW...I'M GOING TO PUT IN A DESERT
www.snoopy.com
SCHOOL WORK CAN BE FUN!
SCHULZ

DID THE TEACHER LIKE YOUR MAP?
9-15
I GUESS NOT...SHE GAVE ME A "C" ON IT...
www.snoopy.com
ONLY A "C"? HOW COME?
I MERIDIANED WHERE I SHOULD HAVE LATITUDED!
SCHULZ

THIS TIME I'M GOING TO DRAW A REAL DETAILED MAP...
9-16
I'M GOING TO PUT IN ALL THE NOOKS AND CRANNIES
www.snoopy.com
IS HUDSON BAY A NOOK OR A CRANNY?
SCHULZ

I GOT ANOTHER "C" ON MY MAP..
9-17
MY TEACHER SAID I PUT IN TOO MUCH DETAIL
www.snoopy.com
SHE SAID I PUT IN COUNTRIES SHE'S NEVER EVEN HEARD OF, BUT WHAT'S WRONG WITH THAT?
I LIKE TO THINK OF MY MAP AS BEING FIFTY YEARS AHEAD OF ITS TIME!
SCHULZ

PSYCHIATRI HELP 5¢
EVERYTHING SEEMS HOPELESS...
THE DOCTOR IS IN
9-24
I'M COMPLETELY DEPRESSED..
THE DOCTOR IS IN
GO HOME, AND EAT A JELLY-BREAD SANDWICH FOLDED OVER...FIVE CENTS, PLEASE
THE DOCTOR IS IN
www.snoopy.com
THERE ARE SOME CURES YOU DON'T LEARN IN MEDICAL SCHOOL
THE DOCTOR IS IN
SCHULZ

WHY DON'T YOU TRY IT?
OKAY, I WILL
WHAT'S HE GOING TO TRY?
www.snoopy.com
I TOLD HIM THAT WHEN THE PACE OF LIFE GETS TO BE TOO MUCH, HE SHOULD GO OUT, AND JUST LIE AND LISTEN TO THE GRASS GROW...
9-24
HE'S THE KIND WHO WILL REALLY HEAR IT!
SCHULZ

Classic **PEANUTS** by SCHULZ

GOOD MORNING, CHARLIE BROWN..

GOOD MORNING..

DO YOU MIND IF I ASK YOU A QUESTION?

WHAT IN THE WORLD IS THAT?

THIS IS A "YOKE".. I'M GOING TO USE IT FOR A SPECIAL SCHOOL REPORT

I'M GOING TO TELL HOW THE YOKE IS A SYMBOL OF SUBJECTION OF ONE INDIVIDUAL TO ANOTHER, AS ESAU TO JACOB (GENESIS 27:40)

THEN I'LL TELL HOW THE YOKE WAS SOMETIMES PLACED LITERALLY ON THE NECK OF A PERSON REDUCED TO SUBMISSION ...MY REFERENCE WILL BE JEREMIAH 28:10

THEN I'LL TELL OF THE YOKE PLACED ON ISRAEL BY SOLOMON AND REHOBOAM (I KINGS 12:9) AND WIND UP BY TALKING ABOUT THE YOKE OF SIN SUGGESTED IN LAMENTATIONS 1:14 AND THE "EASY" YOKE OF MATTHEW 11:29

10/2

I THINK THAT WILL COVER THE SUBJECT PRETTY WELL..

© 1964 Peanuts Worldwide LLC
Dist. by Universal Uclick

WHAT ABOUT THE "YOKE OF INFERIORITY" YOU'VE GIVEN **ME**?!

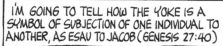

113

9-30

DEAR AGNES, I LIKE YOUR ADVICE COLUMN IN THE PAPER.

I FEEL THAT I COULD USE SOME OF YOUR ADVICE MYSELF.

I DON'T KNOW, HOWEVER, EXACTLY WHAT IT IS THAT I WANT TO ASK YOU.

JUST SEND ME SOME ADVICE.

PSYCHIATRIC HELP 5¢

THE DOCTOR IS [IN]

I'M WORRIED ABOUT MY DAD...

10-1

EVERY NIGHT HE SITS IN THE KITCHEN EATING COLD CEREAL AND LOOKING AT THE PICTURES IN HIS OLD HIGH SCHOOL YEAR BOOK

THE DOCTOR IS [IN]

HOW OLD IS YOUR FATHER?

I THINK HE JUST TURNED FORTY...

NOTHING TO WORRY ABOUT... HE'S RIGHT ON SCHEDULE! FIVE CENTS, PLEASE...

THE DOCTOR

10-3

HELLO, HARDWARE STORE? DO YOU HAVE ANY MINI-BIKES?

HOW MUCH MONEY IS A MINI-BIKE? I SEE... WELL, DO YOU HAVE MANY MINI-BIKES?

HOW MANY MINI-BIKES DO YOU HAVE? YOU DON'T HAVE MANY MINI-BIKES? HOW MANY?

THANK YOU FOR THE INFORMATION ON YOUR MINI-BIKES... NO, I DON'T THINK SO... I DON'T HAVE ANY MONEY FOR A MINI-BIKE...

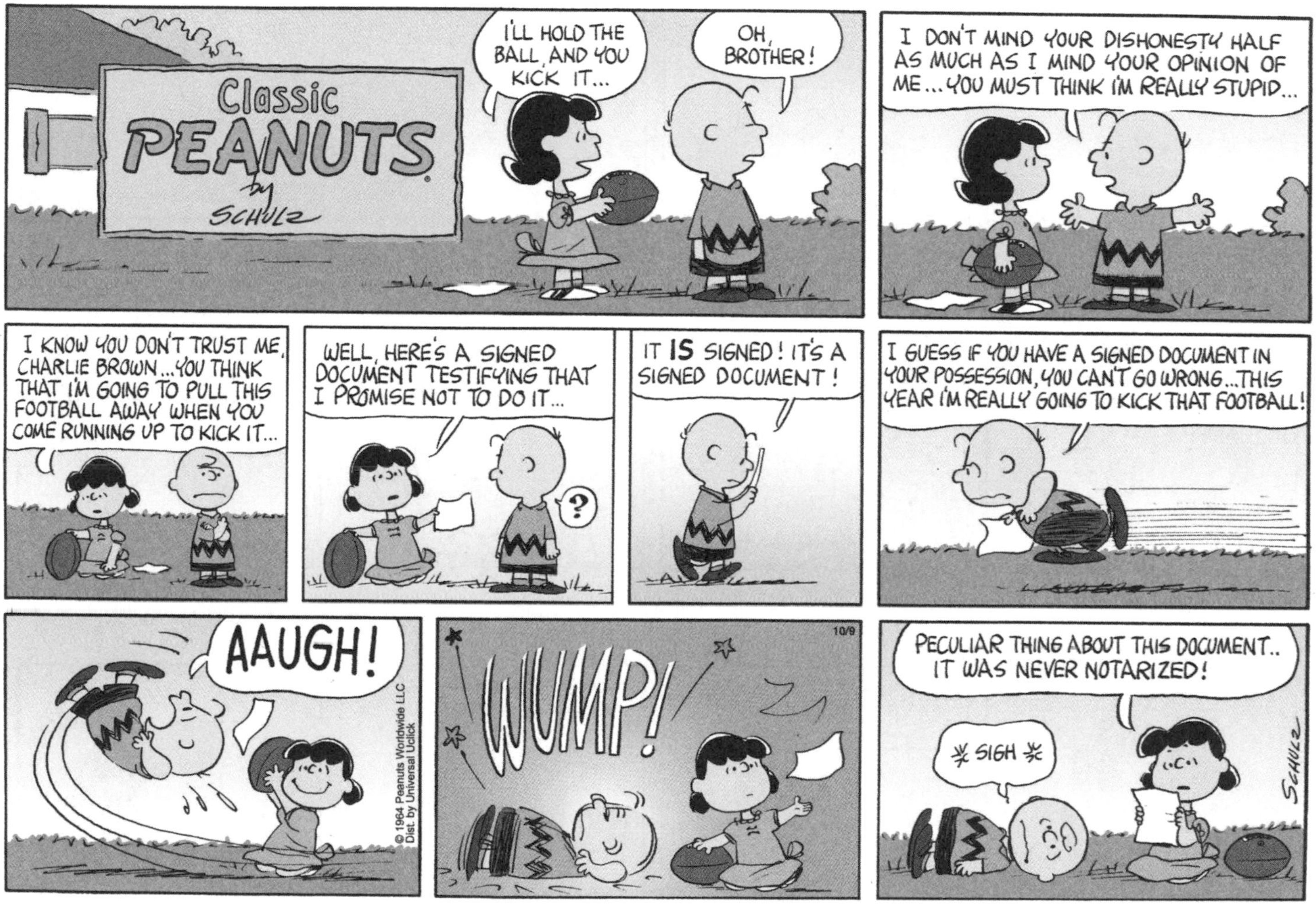
Classic PEANUTS by SCHULZ
I'LL HOLD THE BALL, AND YOU KICK IT...
OH, BROTHER!
I DON'T MIND YOUR DISHONESTY HALF AS MUCH AS I MIND YOUR OPINION OF ME... YOU MUST THINK I'M REALLY STUPID...
I KNOW YOU DON'T TRUST ME, CHARLIE BROWN... YOU THINK THAT I'M GOING TO PULL THIS FOOTBALL AWAY WHEN YOU COME RUNNING UP TO KICK IT...
WELL, HERE'S A SIGNED DOCUMENT TESTIFYING THAT I PROMISE NOT TO DO IT...
?
IT IS SIGNED! IT'S A SIGNED DOCUMENT!
I GUESS IF YOU HAVE A SIGNED DOCUMENT IN YOUR POSSESSION, YOU CAN'T GO WRONG... THIS YEAR I'M REALLY GOING TO KICK THAT FOOTBALL!
AAUGH!
© 1964 Peanuts Worldwide LLC
Dist. by Universal Uclick
10/9
WUMP!
PECULIAR THING ABOUT THIS DOCUMENT.. IT WAS NEVER NOTARIZED!
SIGH
SCHULZ

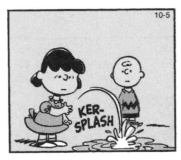

10-5
KER-SPLASH
KER-LEAF!
"KER-LEAF"?!!
SCHULZ
© 1966 Peanuts Worldwide LLC, Dist. by Universal Uclick
www.snoopy.com

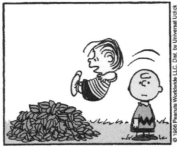

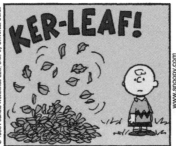

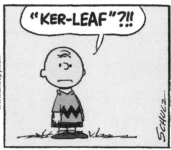

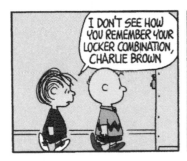

I DON'T SEE HOW YOU REMEMBER YOUR LOCKER COMBINATION, CHARLIE BROWN
IT'S EASY... 3-24-7....SEE?
BUT HOW IN THE WORLD DO YOU REMEMBER IT?
BABE RUTH WAS NUMBER 3, WILLIE MAYS IS NUMBER 24 AND MICKEY MANTLE IS NUMBER 7!
10-8
SCHULZ
© 1966 Peanuts Worldwide LLC, Dist. by Universal Uclick
www.snoopy.com

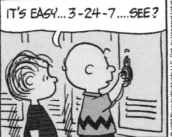

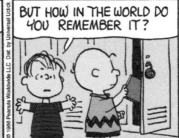

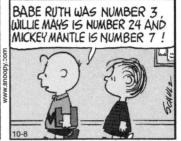

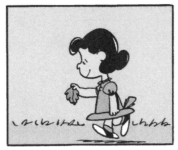

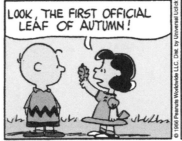

LOOK, THE FIRST OFFICIAL LEAF OF AUTUMN!
LEAVES HAVE BEEN FALLING FOR WEEKS... WHAT MAKES THAT ONE SO OFFICIAL?
10-10
I HAD IT NOTARIZED!
SCHULZ
© 1966 Peanuts Worldwide LLC, Dist. by Universal Uclick
www.snoopy.com

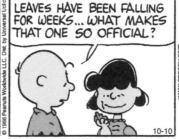

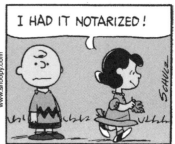

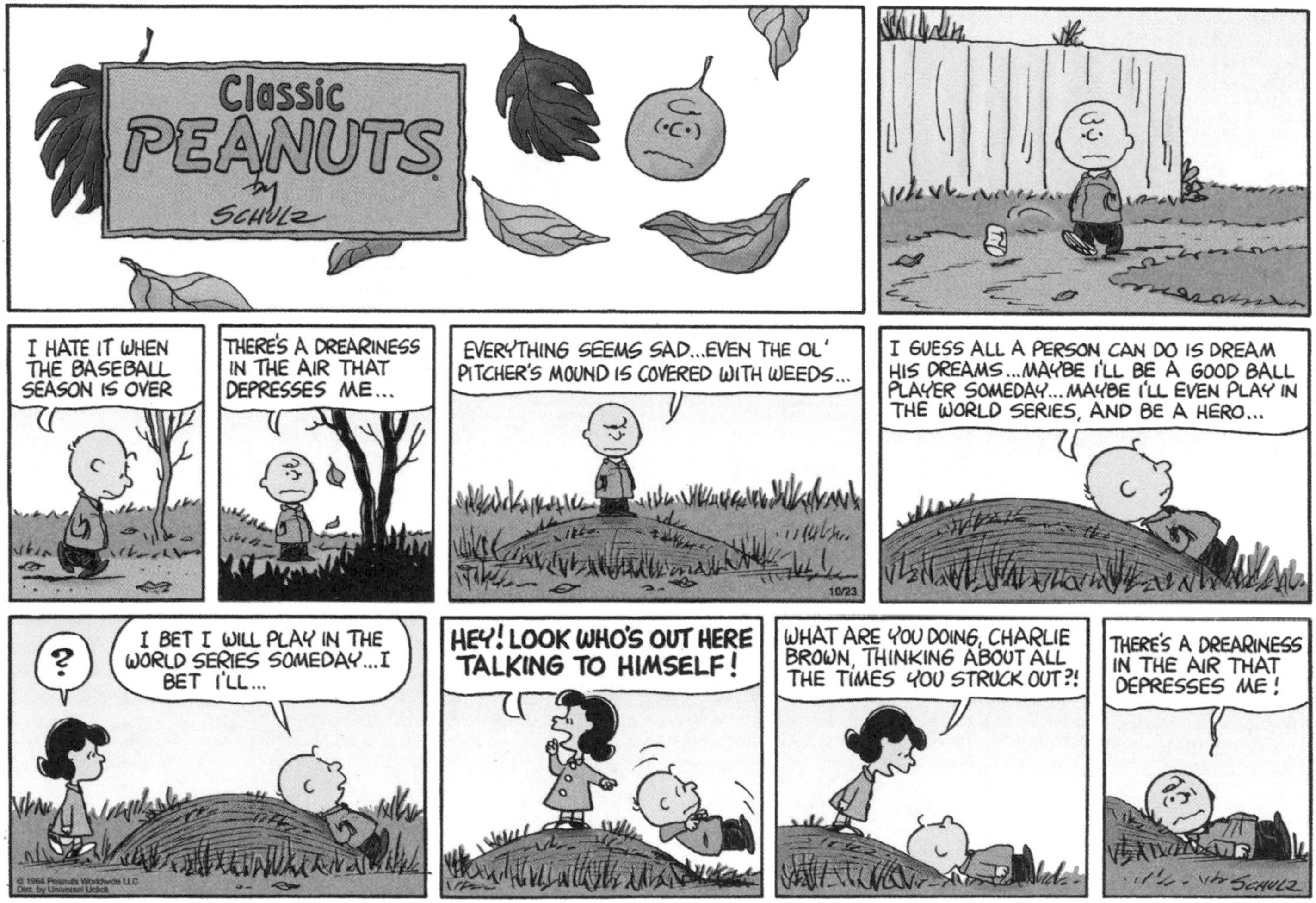
Classic
PEANUTS
by
SCHULZ
I HATE IT WHEN THE BASEBALL SEASON IS OVER
THERE'S A DREARINESS IN THE AIR THAT DEPRESSES ME...
EVERYTHING SEEMS SAD...EVEN THE OL' PITCHER'S MOUND IS COVERED WITH WEEDS...
10/23
I GUESS ALL A PERSON CAN DO IS DREAM HIS DREAMS...MAYBE I'LL BE A GOOD BALL PLAYER SOMEDAY...MAYBE I'LL EVEN PLAY IN THE WORLD SERIES, AND BE A HERO...
?
I BET I WILL PLAY IN THE WORLD SERIES SOMEDAY...I BET I'LL...
© 1964 Peanuts Worldwide LLC
Dist. by Universal Uclick
HEY! LOOK WHO'S OUT HERE TALKING TO HIMSELF!
WHAT ARE YOU DOING, CHARLIE BROWN, THINKING ABOUT ALL THE TIMES YOU STRUCK OUT?!
THERE'S A DREARINESS IN THE AIR THAT DEPRESSES ME!
SCHULZ

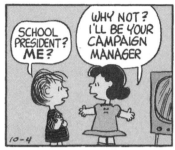

SCHOOL PRESIDENT? ME?
WHY NOT? I'LL BE YOUR CAMPAIGN MANAGER
BUT I COULD NEVER BE SCHOOL PRESIDENT.. THINK OF THE WORK.. THINK OF THE RESPONSIBILITY..
THINK OF THE POWER
I'LL DO IT!!
10-4
© 1964 Peanuts Worldwide LLC, Dist. by Universal Uclick
www.snoopy.com
SCHULZ

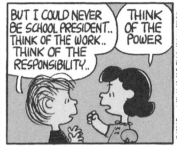

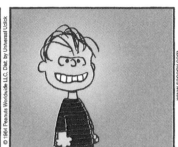

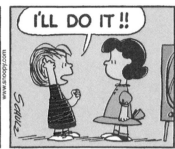

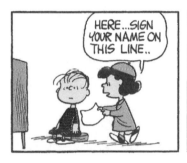

HERE...SIGN YOUR NAME ON THIS LINE..
WHEN WE GET TO SCHOOL, I'LL TAKE THIS INTO THE PRINCIPAL'S OFFICE, AND YOU WILL THEN BE OFFICIALLY ENTERED IN THE RACE FOR SCHOOL PRESIDENT!
GOOD...WE'RE ON OUR WAY!
I HOPE I WON'T BE EXPECTED TO DO SOMETHING RIGHT AWAY ABOUT TEACHERS' SALARIES...
10-5
© 1964 Peanuts Worldwide LLC, Dist. by Universal Uclick
www.snoopy.com
SCHULZ

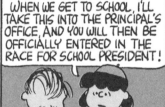

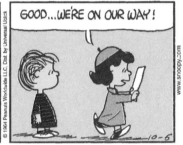

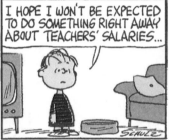

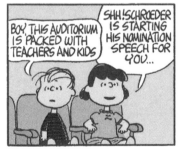

BOY, THIS AUDITORIUM IS PACKED WITH TEACHERS AND KIDS
SHH! SCHROEDER IS STARTING HIS NOMINATION SPEECH FOR YOU...
I AM HERE THIS MORNING TO NOMINATE FOR THE OFFICE OF SCHOOL PRESIDENT, A GREAT YOUNG MAN
BUT FIRST, I'D LIKE TO SAY A FEW WORDS ABOUT BEETHOVEN!
OH, GOOD GRIEF!
10-6
© 1964 Peanuts Worldwide LLC, Dist. by Universal Uclick
www.snoopy.com
SCHULZ

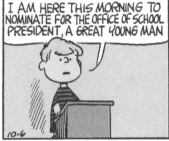

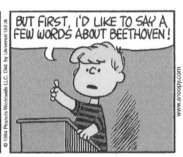

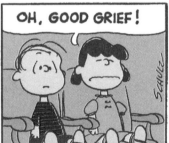

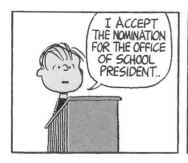

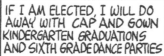

I ACCEPT THE NOMINATION FOR THE OFFICE OF SCHOOL PRESIDENT..
IF I AM ELECTED, I WILL DO AWAY WITH CAP AND GOWN KINDERGARTEN GRADUATIONS AND SIXTH GRADE DANCE PARTIES
© 1964 Peanuts Worldwide LLC, Dist. by Universal Uclick
IN MY ADMINISTRATION CHILDREN WILL BE CHILDREN AND ADULTS WILL BE ADULTS!!
www.snoopy.com
10-7
I MAY EVEN DO AWAY WITH STUPID ELECTIONS LIKE THIS....THANK YOU..
SCHULZ

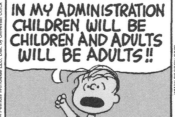

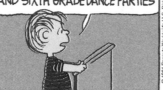

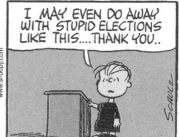

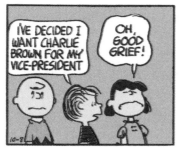

I'VE DECIDED I WANT CHARLIE BROWN FOR MY VICE-PRESIDENT
OH, GOOD GRIEF!
WELL, WHAT'S WRONG WITH HIM? I THINK HE'D MAKE A GOOD VICE-PRESIDENT
© 1964 Peanuts Worldwide LLC, Dist. by Universal Uclick
MAYBE YOU'RE RIGHT..HE MIGHT EVEN HELP US WIN THE ELECTION
www.snoopy.com
HE'LL PROBABLY BRING IN THE WISHY-WASHY VOTE!
SCHULZ

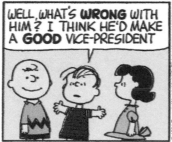

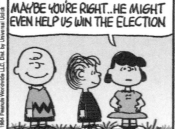

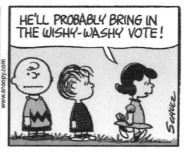

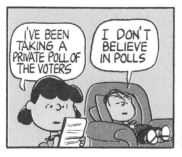

I'VE BEEN TAKING A PRIVATE POLL OF THE VOTERS
I DON'T BELIEVE IN POLLS
THE WAY I SEE IT, YOU HAVE THE BACKLASH VOTE, THE FRONTLASH VOTE, THE WHIPLASH VOTE, THE EYELASH VOTE AND THE TONGUE LASH VOTE...
© 1964 Peanuts Worldwide LLC, Dist. by Universal Uclick
THIS WOULD GIVE YOU 73% AND YOUR OPPONENTS 22% WITH ONLY 5% UNDECIDED...
www.snoopy.com
10-10
I BELIEVE IN POLLS!
SCHULZ

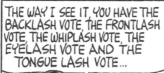

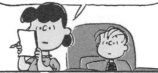

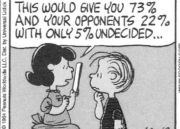

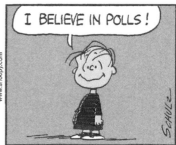

I'M A REPORTER FROM OUR SCHOOL PAPER, LINUS...
WOULD YOU CARE TO TELL US WHAT YOU INTEND TO DO IF YOU'RE ELECTED SCHOOL PRESIDENT?
I INTEND TO STRAIGHTEN THINGS OUT!
10-11
WE ARE IN THE MIDST OF A MORAL DECLINE!! WE ARE...
I'LL JUST PUT DOWN THAT YOU'RE VERY HONORED, AND WILL DO YOUR BEST IF ELECTED..
THE PRESS IS AGAINST ME!
© 1964 Peanuts Worldwide LLC. Dist. by Universal Uclick
www.snoopy.com
SCHULZ

I'M A REPORTER FROM OUR SCHOOL PAPER, CHARLIE BROWN...
WOULD YOU CARE TO TELL US WHAT YOU INTEND TO DO IF YOU'RE ELECTED VICE-PRESIDENT?
CERTAINLY... I INTEND TO WORK FOR NEW AND...
10-12
I'LL JUST PUT DOWN THAT YOU'RE VERY HONORED, AND WILL DO YOUR BEST IF ELECTED...
SHE HAS ALL THE MAKINGS OF A GOOD POLITICAL COLUMNIST!
© 1964 Peanuts Worldwide LLC. Dist. by Universal Uclick
www.snoopy.com
SCHULZ

IF I AM ELECTED SCHOOL PRESIDENT, I WILL PURGE THE KINGDOM!
MY ADMINISTRATION WILL RELEASE US FROM OUR SPIRITUAL BABYLON!
10-13
MY ADMINISTRATION WILL BRING DOWN THE FALSE IDOLS IN HIGH PLACES! MY ADMINISTRATION WILL..
I WONDER WHY THE PRINCIPAL LOOKS SO PALE....
© 1964 Peanuts Worldwide LLC. Dist. by Universal Uclick
www.snoopy.com
SCHULZ

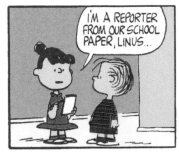

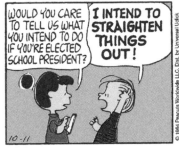

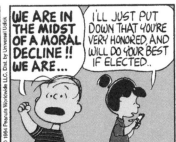

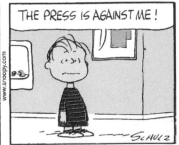

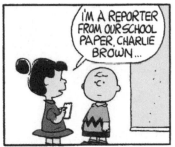

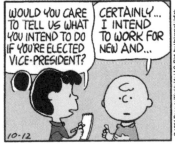

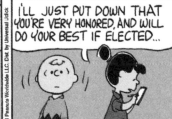

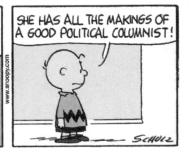

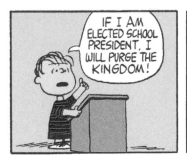

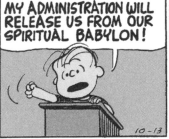

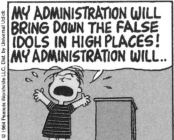

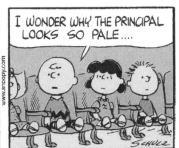

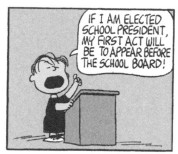

IF I AM ELECTED SCHOOL PRESIDENT, MY FIRST ACT WILL BE TO APPEAR BEFORE THE SCHOOL BOARD!
PSST! PSSSPPSSTTSSPT!
© 1964 Peanuts Worldwide LLC, Dist. by Universal Uclick
HMM....
www.snoopy.com
I'M SORRY...I WILL NOT BE ABLE TO APPEAR BEFORE THE SCHOOL BOARD... THEY MEET AT EIGHT O'CLOCK, AND I GO TO BED AT SEVEN THIRTY...
10-15
SCHULZ

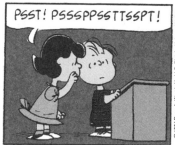

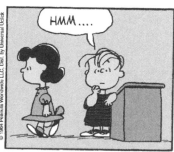

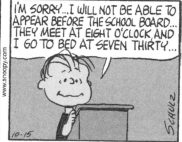

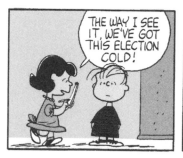

THE WAY I SEE IT, WE'VE GOT THIS ELECTION COLD!
MY PERSONAL POLL NOW SHOWS YOU LEADING WITH 92% OF THE VOTE TO YOUR OPPONENTS' 7%! 1% IS STILL UNDECIDED...
© 1964 Peanuts Worldwide LLC, Dist. by Universal Uclick
UNDECIDED?!
www.snoopy.com
IT'S DEPRESSING TO THINK THAT SOMEWHERE IN THIS SCHOOL THERE ARE STUDENTS WHO STILL CAN'T DECIDE TO VOTE FOR A NICE GUY LIKE ME!
10-19
SCHULZ

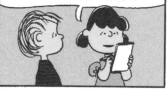

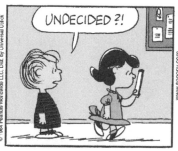

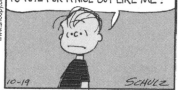

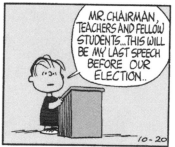

MR. CHAIRMAN, TEACHERS AND FELLOW STUDENTS...THIS WILL BE MY LAST SPEECH BEFORE OUR ELECTION..
10-20
WE'VE GOT IT COLD, CHARLIE BROWN...IF HE DOESN'T SAY ANY-THING STUPID, WE CAN'T LOSE!
JUST THINK... I'LL BE VICE-PRESIDENT
© 1964 Peanuts Worldwide LLC, Dist. by Universal Uclick
I WANT TO TALK TO YOU THIS MORNING ABOUT THE "GREAT PUMPKIN"....
www.snoopy.com
AAAUGHH!!
SCHULZ

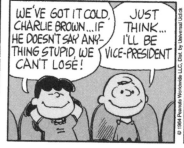

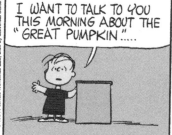

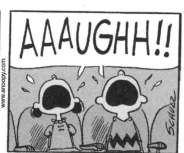

HALLOWEEN WILL SOON BE WITH US...

ON HALLOWEEN NIGHT THE "GREAT PUMPKIN" RISES OUT OF THE PUMPKIN PATCH, AND BRINGS TOYS TO ALL THE GOOD LITTLE CHILDREN..

10-21

HA HA HA HA
HA   HAHA
HAHAHA HAHA

© 1964 Peanuts Worldwide LLC. Dist. by Universal Uclick

www.snoopy.com

HAHAHAHA

I'VE BLOWN THE ELECTION!

SCHULZ

ALL RIGHT, SAY IT! GO AHEAD, AND SAY IT!

I KNOW YOU WANT TO SAY IT! I TALKED TOO MUCH, AND I BLEW THE ELECTION; SO GO AHEAD, AND SAY IT! JUST GO RIGHT AHEAD, AND SAY IT!

10-22

OH, YOU BLOCKHEAD!

© 1964 Peanuts Worldwide LLC. Dist. by Universal Uclick

www.snoopy.com

SHE SAID IT!

SCHULZ

BUT WHY DID YOU HAVE TO BRING UP THE "GREAT PUMPKIN"?

IT WAS MY DUTY, CHARLIE BROWN! HALLOWEEN WILL BE HERE IN A WEEK, AND EVERYONE SHOULD BE TOLD ABOUT THE "GREAT PUMPKIN"

OH, GOOD GRIEF!

10-24

© 1964 Peanuts Worldwide LLC. Dist. by Universal Uclick

HE RISES OUT OF THE PUMPKIN PATCH WITH HIS BAG OF TOYS, AND FLIES THROUGH THE AIR BRINGING JOY TO ALL THE CHILDREN OF THE WORLD!

www.snoopy.com

YOU'RE LOOKING AT ME LIKE I'M CRAZY..

I'M LOOKING AT YOU LIKE I COULD HAVE BEEN VICE-PRESIDENT!

SCHULZ

122

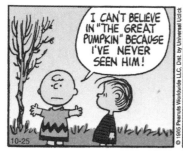

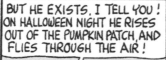

I CAN'T BELIEVE IN "THE GREAT PUMPKIN" BECAUSE I'VE NEVER SEEN HIM!
10-25
© 1965 Peanuts Worldwide LLC. Dist. by Universal Uclick
BUT HE EXISTS, I TELL YOU! ON HALLOWEEN NIGHT HE RISES OUT OF THE PUMPKIN PATCH, AND FLIES THROUGH THE AIR!
www.snoopy.com
I THINK YOU HAVE HIM CONFUSED WITH SANTA CLAUS
WOULD I CONFUSE THE SUN AND THE MOON?
WOULD I CONFUSE NBC WITH CBS? WOULD I CONFUSE THE AMERICAN LEAGUE WITH THE NATIONAL LEAGUE? WOULD I?
I CAN'T STAND IT..
SCHULZ

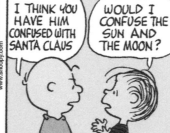

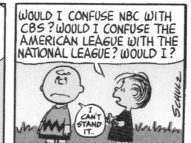

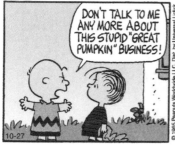

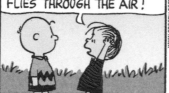

DON'T TALK TO ME ANY MORE ABOUT THIS STUPID "GREAT PUMPKIN" BUSINESS!
10-27
© 1965 Peanuts Worldwide LLC. Dist. by Universal Uclick
STUPID, IS IT? THAT'S AN INSULT! I OUGHTA HIT YOU, CHARLIE BROWN!
JUST TRY IT! KNOCK THIS CHIP OFF MY SHOULDER!
ALL RIGHT, I WILL!!!
WHACK!
SCHULZ

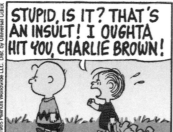

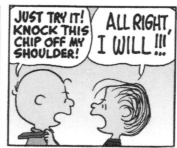

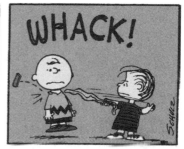

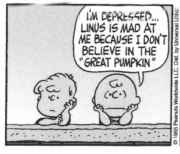

I'M DEPRESSED... LINUS IS MAD AT ME BECAUSE I DON'T BELIEVE IN THE "GREAT PUMPKIN"
© 1965 Peanuts Worldwide LLC. Dist. by Universal Uclick
DON'T BE TOO DEPRESSED, CHARLIE BROWN...BEETHOVEN ALSO HAD PROBLEMS...
10-30
www.snoopy.com
WHAT'S THAT GOT TO DO WITH IT?
NOTHING, I GUESS.. IT JUST CAME TO MY MIND..
OH, GOOD GRIEF!
SCHULZ

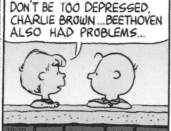

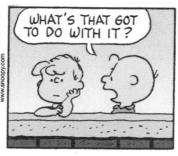

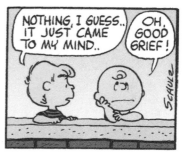

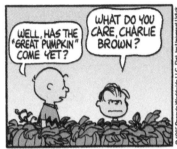

WELL, HAS THE "GREAT PUMPKIN" COME YET?
WHAT DO YOU CARE, CHARLIE BROWN?
© 1965 Peanuts Worldwide LLC, Dist. by Universal Uclick
I'M SORRY I INSULTED YOUR BELIEF...I DON'T THINK ANY POINT OF DOCTRINE IS WORTH SPLITTING UP A FRIENDSHIP...I APOLOGIZE...
10-31
www.snoopy.com
I APOLOGIZE, TOO, CHARLIE BROWN... SIT DOWN, AND WE'LL WAIT FOR THE "GREAT PUMPKIN" TOGETHER...
THERE IS NO "GREAT PUMPKIN"!
THERE IS TOO!!!
SCHULZ

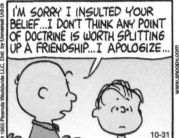

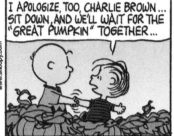

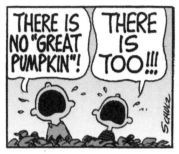

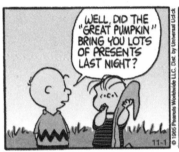

WELL, DID THE "GREAT PUMPKIN" BRING YOU LOTS OF PRESENTS LAST NIGHT?
11-1
© 1965 Peanuts Worldwide LLC, Dist. by Universal Uclick
www.snoopy.com
PERHAPS YOU DIDN'T HEAR ME, LINUS......I SAID,...
I HEARD WHAT YOU SAID!!
SCHULZ

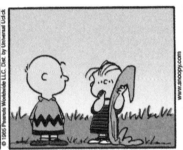

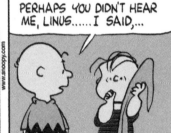

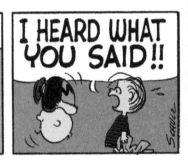

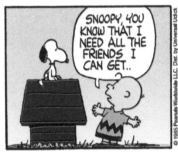

SNOOPY, YOU KNOW THAT I NEED ALL THE FRIENDS I CAN GET..
© 1965 Peanuts Worldwide LLC, Dist. by Universal Uclick
THEN WHY DID I DELIBERATELY GO OUT OF MY WAY TO BUG LINUS ABOUT THE "GREAT PUMPKIN"?
11-2
www.snoopy.com
LINUS IS REALLY A WONDERFUL LITTLE GUY, AND I SHOULDN'T INSULT HIS BELIEFS...WHY DO I DO THINGS LIKE THAT?
YOU'RE RIGHT...IT'S BECAUSE I'M STUPID!
SCHULZ

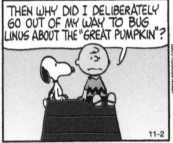

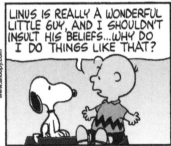

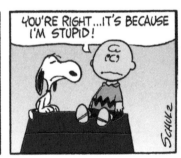

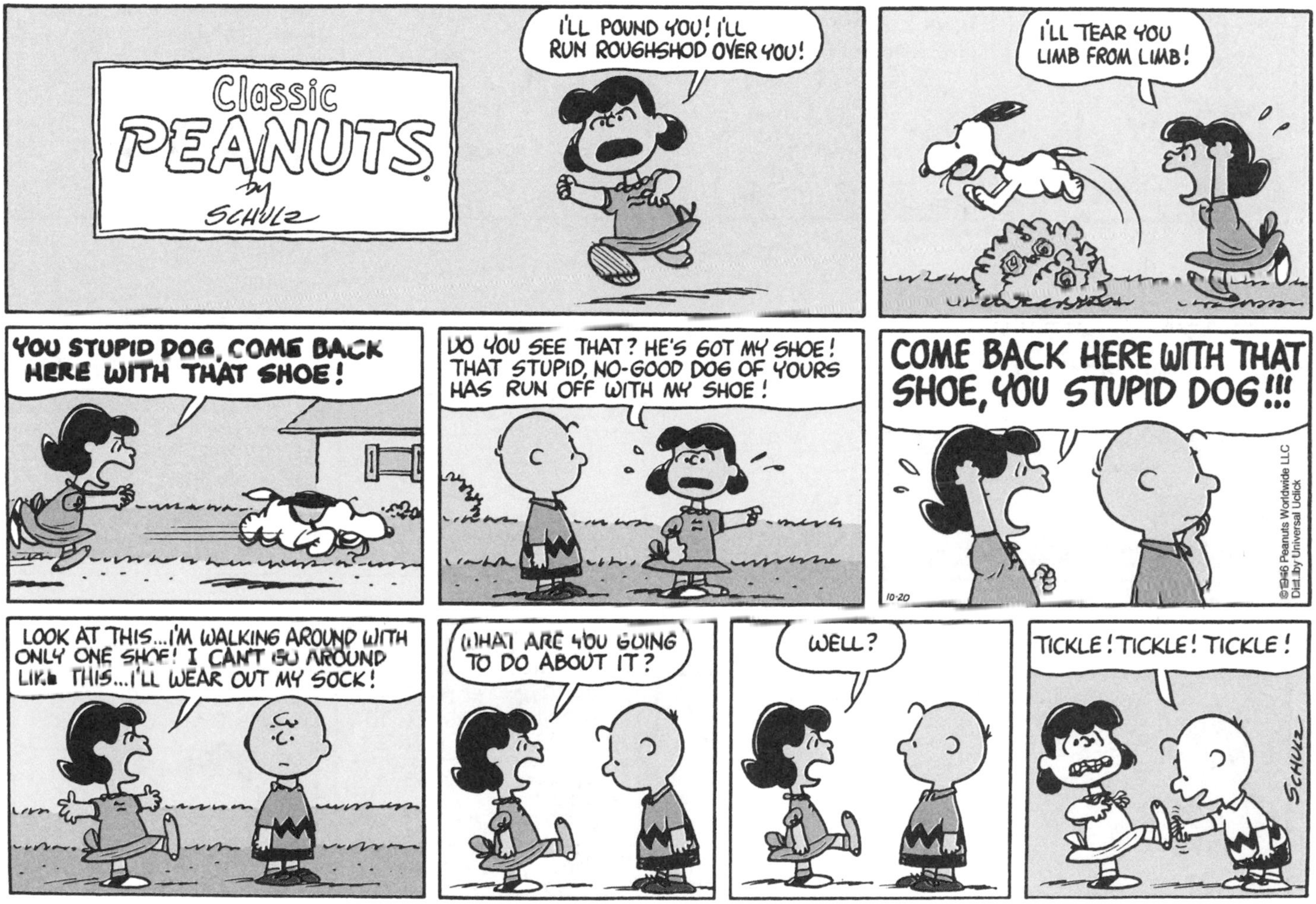
Classic PEANUTS by SCHULZ
I'LL POUND YOU! I'LL RUN ROUGHSHOD OVER YOU!
I'LL TEAR YOU LIMB FROM LIMB!
YOU STUPID DOG, COME BACK HERE WITH THAT SHOE!
DO YOU SEE THAT? HE'S GOT MY SHOE! THAT STUPID, NO-GOOD DOG OF YOURS HAS RUN OFF WITH MY SHOE!
COME BACK HERE WITH THAT SHOE, YOU STUPID DOG!!!
Peanuts Worldwide LLC Dist. by Universal Uclick
10-20
LOOK AT THIS...I'M WALKING AROUND WITH ONLY ONE SHOE! I CAN'T GO AROUND LIKE THIS...I'LL WEAR OUT MY SOCK!
WHAT ARE YOU GOING TO DO ABOUT IT?
WELL?
TICKLE! TICKLE! TICKLE!
SCHULZ

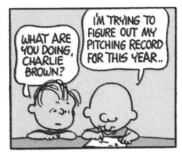

WHAT ARE YOU DOING, CHARLIE BROWN?
I'M TRYING TO FIGURE OUT MY PITCHING RECORD FOR THIS YEAR..
YOU TAKE THE NUMBER OF EARNED RUNS, AND MULTIPLY BY NINE AND THEN DIVIDE BY THE NUMBER OF INNINGS PITCHED
WHAT DID YOU GET?
A FIGURE MUCH TOO EMBARRASSING TO MENTION!
10-12
www.snoopy.com
SCHULZ

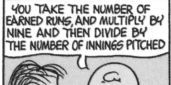

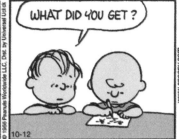

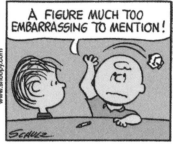

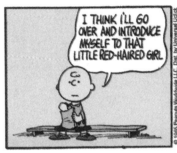

I THINK I'LL GO OVER AND INTRODUCE MYSELF TO THAT LITTLE RED-HAIRED GIRL
I THINK I'LL INTRODUCE MYSELF, AND THEN ASK HER TO COME OVER AND SIT NEXT TO ME
I THINK I'LL ASK HER TO SIT NEXT TO ME HERE, AND THEN I THINK I'LL TELL HER HOW MUCH I'VE ALWAYS ADMIRED HER...
I THINK I'LL FLAP MY ARMS, AND FLY TO THE MOON
10-18
www.snoopy.com
SCHULZ

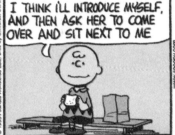

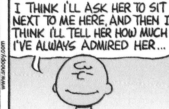

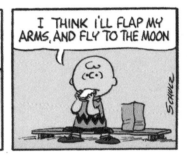

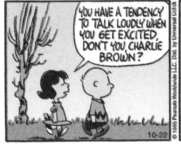

YOU HAVE A TENDENCY TO TALK LOUDLY WHEN YOU GET EXCITED, DON'T YOU, CHARLIE BROWN?
WHY DO YOU SUPPOSE YOU DO THIS?
I DON'T KNOW...NO ONE HAS EVER BEEN RUDE ENOUGH TO TELL ME ABOUT IT BEFORE!
WE CRITICAL PEOPLE ARE ALWAYS BEING CRITICIZED!
10-22
www.snoopy.com
SCHULZ

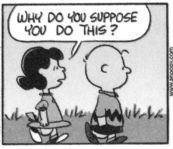

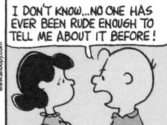

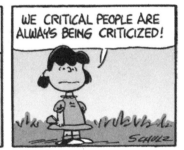

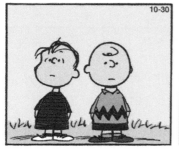

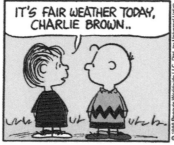

10-30
IT'S FAIR WEATHER TODAY, CHARLIE BROWN..
© 1966 Peanuts Worldwide LLC, Dist. by Universal Uclick
www.snoopy.com
SO WHERE ARE ALL MY FRIENDS?
SCHULZ

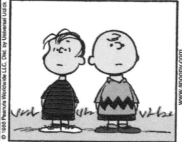

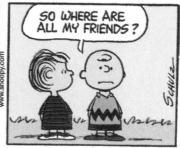

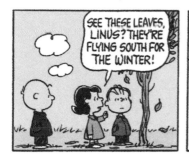

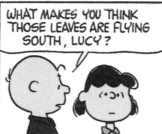

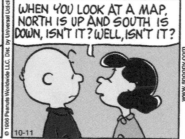

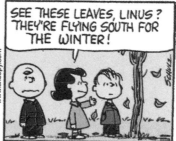

SEE THESE LEAVES, LINUS? THEY'RE FLYING SOUTH FOR THE WINTER!
WHAT MAKES YOU THINK THOSE LEAVES ARE FLYING SOUTH, LUCY?
© 1966 Peanuts Worldwide LLC, Dist. by Universal Uclick
WHEN YOU LOOK AT A MAP, NORTH IS UP AND SOUTH IS DOWN, ISN'T IT? WELL, ISN'T IT?
10-11
www.snoopy.com
SEE THESE LEAVES, LINUS? THEY'RE FLYING SOUTH FOR THE WINTER!
SCHULZ

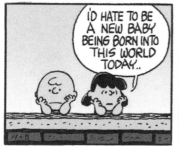

I'D HATE TO BE A NEW BABY BEING BORN INTO THIS WORLD TODAY..
THERE SEEMS TO BE SO MUCH TROUBLE EVERYWHERE
© 1964 Peanuts Worldwide LLC, Dist. by Universal Uclick
IF I WERE A NEW BABY, I DON'T THINK I COULD STAND KNOWING WHAT I WAS GOING TO HAVE TO GO THROUGH...
www.snoopy.com
THAT'S WHY THEY DON'T SHOW THEM ANY NEWSPAPERS FOR THE FIRST TWO YEARS!
SCHULZ

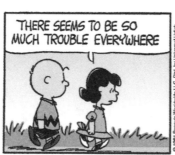

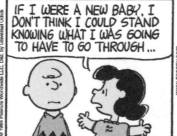

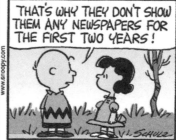

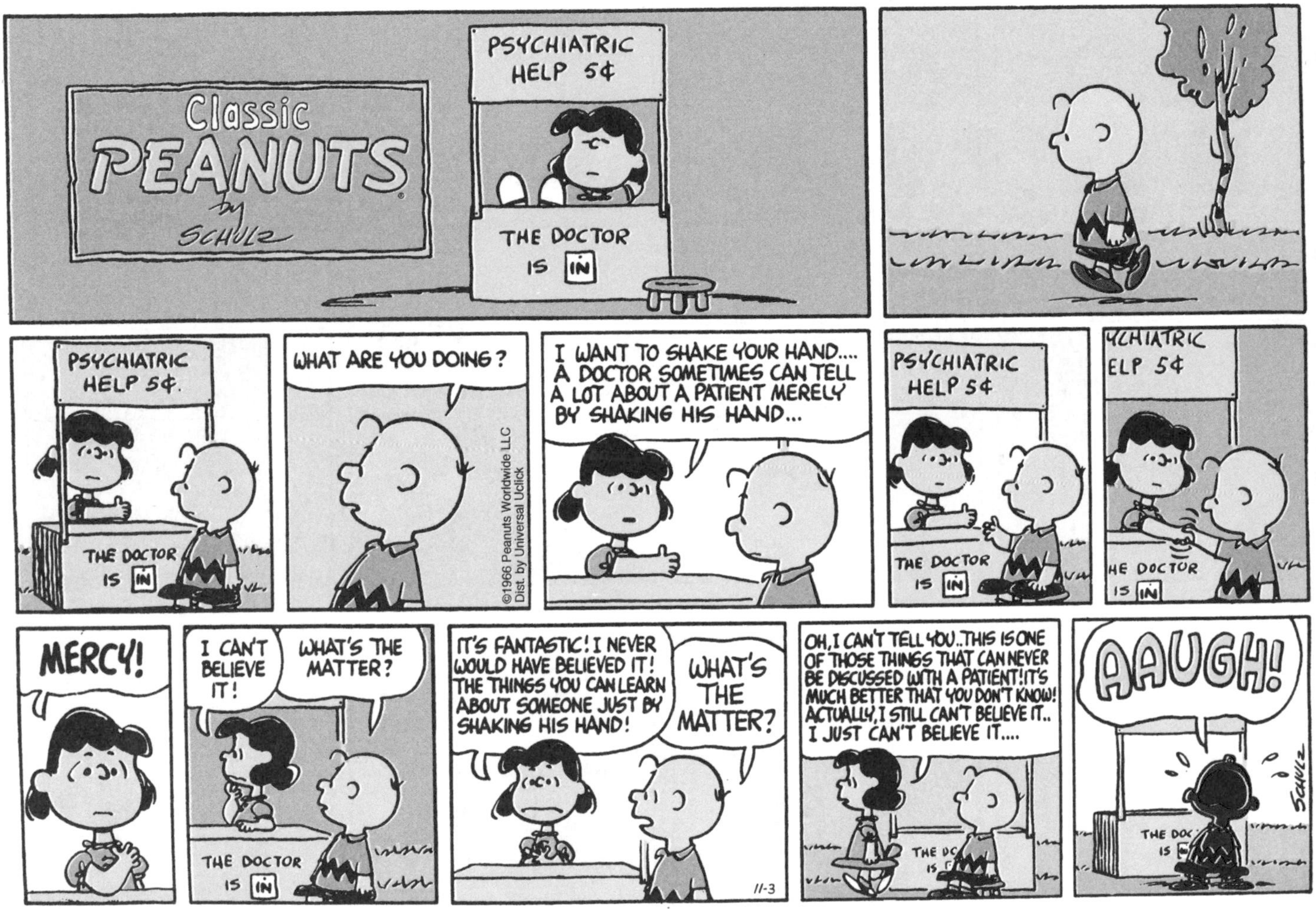
Classic PEANUTS by SCHULZ
PSYCHIATRIC HELP 5¢
THE DOCTOR IS IN
PSYCHIATRIC HELP 5¢.
THE DOCTOR IS IN
WHAT ARE YOU DOING?
©1966 Peanuts Worldwide LLC Dist. by Universal Uclick
I WANT TO SHAKE YOUR HAND.... A DOCTOR SOMETIMES CAN TELL A LOT ABOUT A PATIENT MERELY BY SHAKING HIS HAND...
PSYCHIATRIC HELP 5¢
THE DOCTOR IS IN
YCHIATRIC ELP 5¢
HE DOCTOR IS IN
MERCY!
I CAN'T BELIEVE IT!
WHAT'S THE MATTER?
THE DOCTOR IS IN
IT'S FANTASTIC! I NEVER WOULD HAVE BELIEVED IT! THE THINGS YOU CAN LEARN ABOUT SOMEONE JUST BY SHAKING HIS HAND!
WHAT'S THE MATTER?
11-3
OH, I CAN'T TELL YOU..THIS IS ONE OF THOSE THINGS THAT CAN NEVER BE DISCUSSED WITH A PATIENT! IT'S MUCH BETTER THAT YOU DON'T KNOW! ACTUALLY, I STILL CAN'T BELIEVE IT.. I JUST CAN'T BELIEVE IT....
AAUGH!
SCHULZ

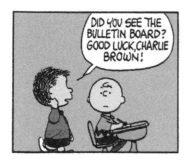

DID YOU SEE THE BULLETIN BOARD? GOOD LUCK, CHARLIE BROWN!
"THE FOLLOWING STUDENTS WILL BE PARTNERS IN THIS SEMESTER'S SCIENCE PROJECTS...STUDENTS WHO DO NOT DO A PROJECT WILL RECEIVE A FAILING GRADE."
© 1966 Peanuts Worldwide LLC, Dist. by Universal Uclick
GOOD GRIEF! I'VE BEEN PAIRED WITH THAT PRETTY, LITTLE RED-HAIRED GIRL! HOW CAN I BE HER PARTNER? I CAN'T EVEN TALK TO HER!
www.snoopy.com
SUDDENLY I HAVE THE FEELING OF IMPENDING DOOM!
SCHULZ
11-4

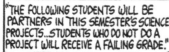

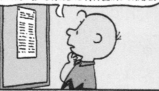

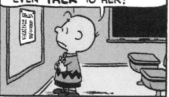

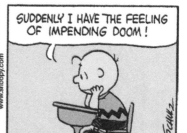

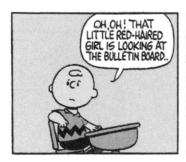

OH, OH! THAT LITTLE RED-HAIRED GIRL IS LOOKING AT THE BULLETIN BOARD..
NOW SHE KNOWS THAT THE TEACHER HAS MADE US PARTNERS IN THE SCIENCE PROJECT! MAYBE SHE'LL COME OVER HERE AND SAY, "HI, CHARLIE BROWN..I SEE YOU AND I ARE PARTNERS!"
© 1966 Peanuts Worldwide LLC, Dist. by Universal Uclick
MAYBE SHE'LL EVEN OFFER TO SHAKE HANDS...I'LL BET HER HANDS ARE SMOOTH AND COOL...
www.snoopy.com
11-5
MY HEAD IS HOT AND STUPID!
SCHULZ

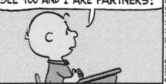

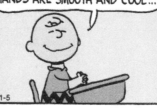

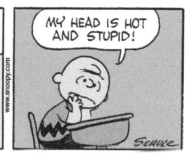

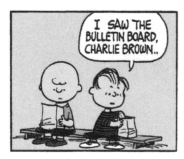

I SAW THE BULLETIN BOARD, CHARLIE BROWN..
YOU AND THAT LITTLE RED-HAIRED GIRL ARE SUPPOSED TO BE PARTNERS IN A SCIENCE PROJECT...ANYONE NOT DOING A SCIENCE PROJECT WILL GET A FAILING GRADE..THAT'S WHAT IT SAID!
© 1966 Peanuts Worldwide LLC, Dist. by Universal Uclick
WELL, I GUESS THAT MEANS I JUST HAVE TO GO OVER AND INTRODUCE MYSELF TO HER...I'LL GO OVER AND SAY, "HI, PARTNER"... I'LL... I'LL.....
www.snoopy.com
I'LL TAKE THE FAILING GRADE!
SCHULZ
11-6

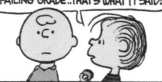

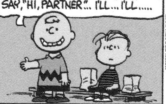

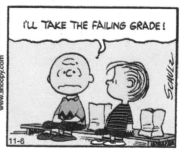

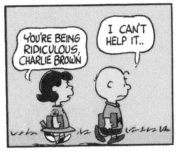

YOU'RE BEING RIDICULOUS, CHARLIE BROWN
I CAN'T HELP IT..
I CAN'T JUST GO UP TO THAT LITTLE RED-HAIRED GIRL AND TALK TO HER.. SHE HAS A PRETTY FACE, AND PRETTY FACES MAKE ME NERVOUS...
© 1966 Peanuts Worldwide LLC, Dist. by Universal Uclick
HOW COME MY FACE DOESN'T MAKE YOU NERVOUS? HUH?!
11-7
www.snoopy.com
I NOTICE YOU CAN TALK TO ME! I HAVE A PRETTY FACE! HOW COME YOU CAN TALK TO ME?!
SCHULZ

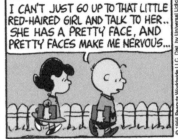

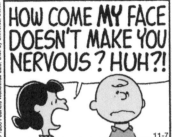

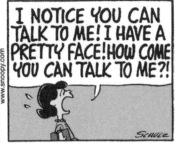

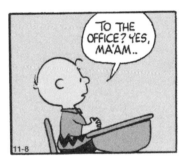

TO THE OFFICE? YES, MA'AM..
11-8
I'VE BEEN CALLED TO THE OFFICE! WHY SHOULD I BE CALLED TO THE OFFICE? I HAVEN'T DONE ANYTHING WRONG! IT CAN'T BE ABOUT OUR SCIENCE PROJECT.. THAT ISN'T DUE FOR A WEEK
© 1966 Peanuts Worldwide LLC, Dist. by Universal Uclick
MAYBE SOMETHING HAPPENED AT HOME! MAYBE SOMEONE IS SICK...I USUALLY NEVER GET CALLED TO THE OFFICE... WHY SHOULD THEY CALL ME? WHY ME? I HAVEN'T DONE ANYTHING...
www.snoopy.com
OFFICE, WHY DO YOU PERSECUTE ME?
OFFICE

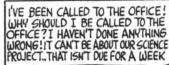

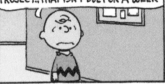

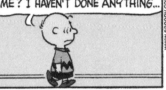

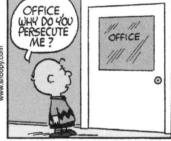

CHARLIE BROWN GOT SENT TO THE OFFICE..
HE DIDN'T GET "SENT."... HE WAS CALLED! THERE'S A BIG DIFFERENCE, YOU KNOW!
© 1966 Peanuts Worldwide LLC, Dist. by Universal Uclick
SHH! LOOK, HE'S COMING BACK.. CHARLIE BROWN IS COMING BACK FROM THE PRINCIPAL'S OFFICE...
www.snoopy.com
SCHULZ
MERCY!
?
WELL, I'LL BE!!
11-9

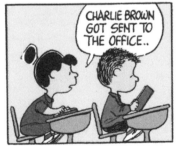

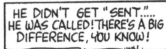

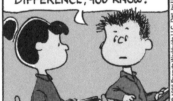

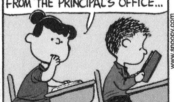

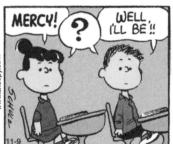

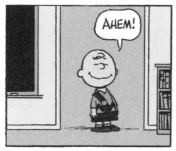

AHEM!
WELL, WILL YOU LOOK AT THAT? CHARLIE BROWN HAS BEEN PUT ON SAFETY PATROL! HOW ABOUT THAT?
OH, BOY! EVERYONE IS LOOKING AT ME! IF THIS DOESN'T IMPRESS THAT LITTLE RED-HAIRED GIRL, NOTHING WILL!
WHEN I GOT CALLED TO THE OFFICE, I WAS A NOBODY...NOW, I'M A MAN WITH A BADGE!
© 1956 Peanuts Worldwide LLC, Dist. by Universal Uclick
www.snoopy.com
11-11
SCHULZ

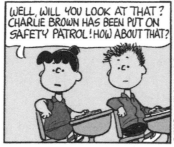

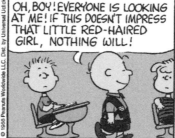

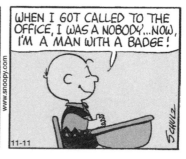

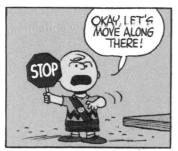

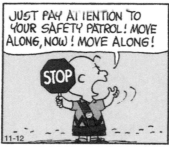

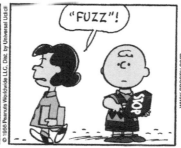

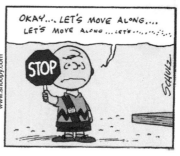

OKAY, LET'S MOVE ALONG THERE!
STOP
JUST PAY ATTENTION TO YOUR SAFETY PATROL! MOVE ALONG, NOW! MOVE ALONG!
STOP
11-12
© 1956 Peanuts Worldwide LLC, Dist. by Universal Uclick
"FUZZ"!
STOP
www.snoopy.com
OKAY.... LET'S MOVE ALONG.... LET'S MOVE ALONG ... LET'S
STOP
SCHULZ

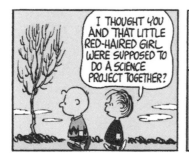

I THOUGHT YOU AND THAT LITTLE RED-HAIRED GIRL WERE SUPPOSED TO DO A SCIENCE PROJECT TOGETHER?
WE ARE...DON'T RUSH ME...I HAVE TO TALK TO HER ABOUT IT FIRST...I FIGURE NOW THAT I'M ON SAFETY PATROL SHE'LL BE REAL ANXIOUS TO MEET ME
11-13
© 1956 Peanuts Worldwide LLC, Dist. by Universal Uclick
IF YOU DON'T DO THAT SCIENCE PROJECT, CHARLIE BROWN, YOU'LL GET A FAILING GRADE...AND IF YOU GET A FAILING GRADE, THEY'LL TAKE YOU OFF THE SCHOOL SAFETY PATROL!
www.snoopy.com
THANK YOU, VOICE OF DOOM!
SCHULZ

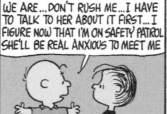

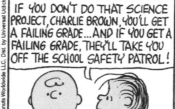

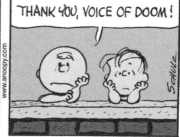

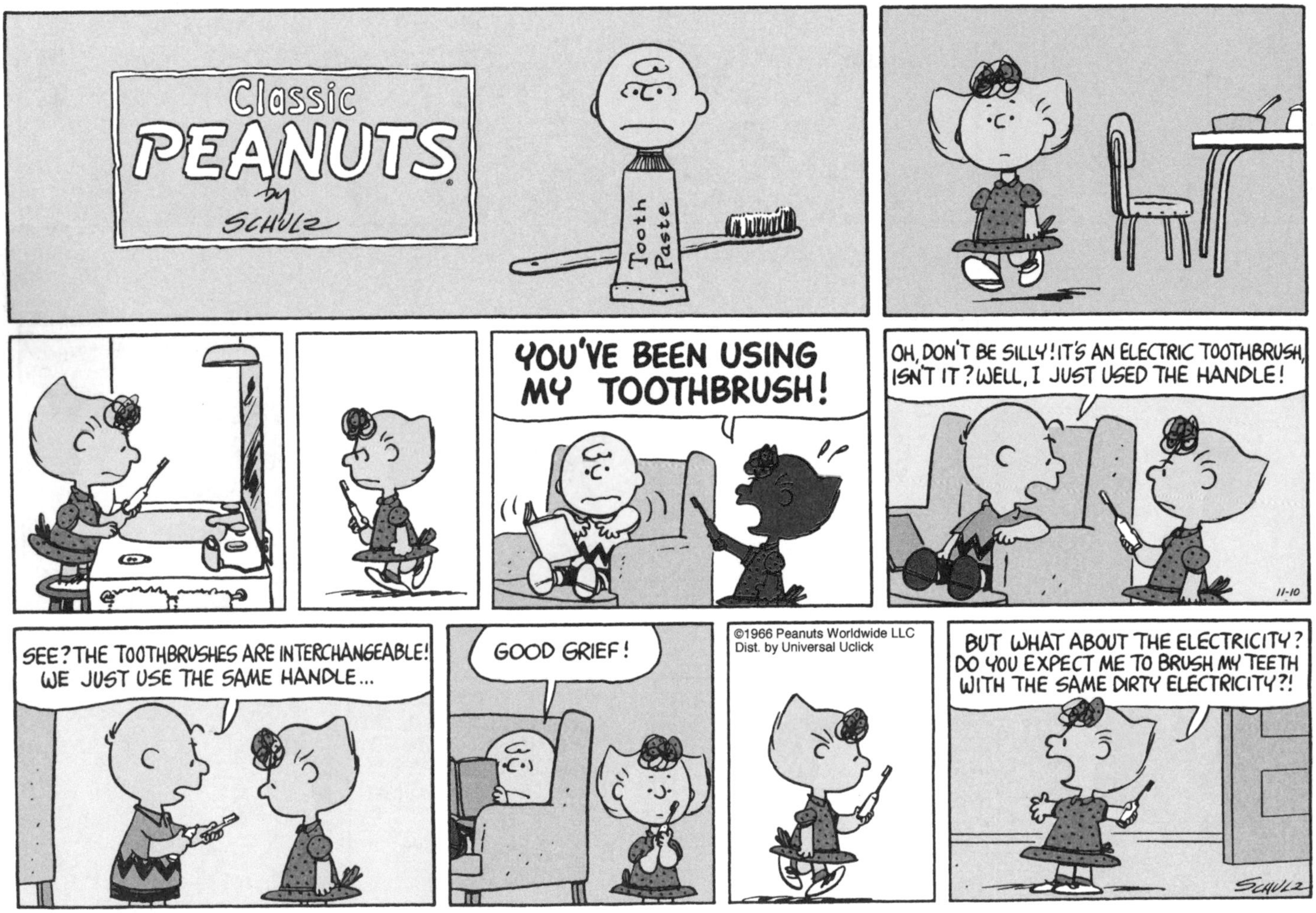
Classic PEANUTS by SCHULZ
Tooth Paste
YOU'VE BEEN USING MY TOOTHBRUSH!
OH, DON'T BE SILLY! IT'S AN ELECTRIC TOOTHBRUSH, ISN'T IT? WELL, I JUST USED THE HANDLE!
11-10
SEE? THE TOOTHBRUSHES ARE INTERCHANGEABLE! WE JUST USE THE SAME HANDLE...
GOOD GRIEF!
©1966 Peanuts Worldwide LLC
Dist. by Universal Uclick
BUT WHAT ABOUT THE ELECTRICITY? DO YOU EXPECT ME TO BRUSH MY TEETH WITH THE SAME DIRTY ELECTRICITY?!
SCHULZ

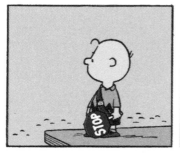

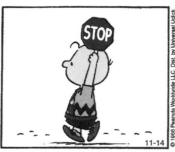

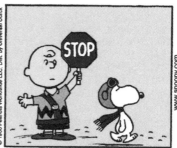

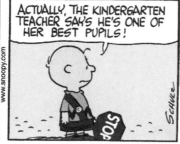

STOP
STOP
11-14
© 1966 Peanuts Worldwide LLC, Dist. by Universal Uclick
STOP
www.snoopy.com
ACTUALLY, THE KINDERGARTEN TEACHER SAYS HE'S ONE OF HER BEST PUPILS!
STOP
SCHULZ

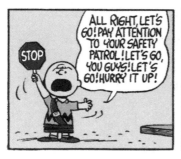

ALL RIGHT, LET'S GO! PAY ATTENTION TO YOUR SAFETY PATROL! LET'S GO, YOU GUYS! LET'S GO! HURRY IT UP!
STOP
HAVE YOU EVER NOTICED HOW OBNOXIOUS SOME PEOPLE GET IF YOU GIVE THEM A BADGE, OR A UNIFORM, OR A HAT, OR A CLUB, OR A SIGN, OR SOMETHING?
STOP
C'MON, GIRLS, HURRY IT UP!
© 1966 Peanuts Worldwide LLC, Dist. by Universal Uclick
11-15
BLEAH!
STOP
www.snoopy.com
YOU CAN'T FOOL ME! THAT WAS A JEALOUS BLEAH!
STOP
SCHULZ

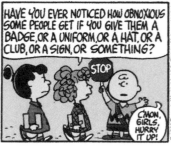

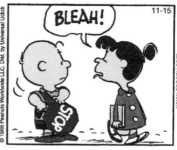

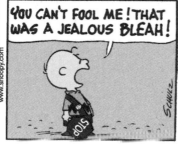

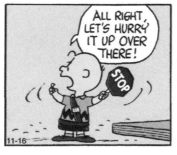

ALL RIGHT, LET'S HURRY IT UP OVER THERE!
STOP
11-16
C'MON, LET'S GO! PAY ATTENTION TO YOUR SAFETY PATROL... C'MON, LET'S GO!
STOP
© 1966 Peanuts Worldwide LLC, Dist. by Universal Uclick
TODAY IS SATURDAY, YOU BLOCKHEAD!
STOP
www.snoopy.com
I WAS WONDERING WHERE EVERYONE WAS....
SCHULZ

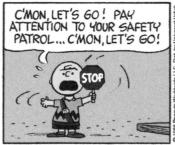

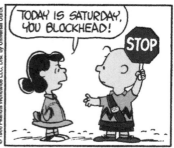

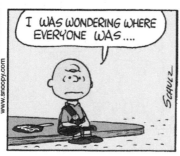

I HEARD SOMETHING ABOUT THAT LITTLE RED-HAIRED GIRL, CHARLIE BROWN..
GOOD GRIEF!
SHE'S GOING TO DO YOUR SCIENCE PROJECT WITH SOME OTHER KIDS... THAT MEANS YOU'LL GET A FAILING GRADE AND LOSE YOUR BADGE.. YOU'LL BE OFF THE SAFETY PATROL...
I DON'T KNOW WHAT ELSE CAN HAPPEN TO YOU, CHARLIE BROWN..
I DO....THE ANTS GOT INTO MY LUNCH!
11-18
© 1966 Peanuts Worldwide LLC, Dist. by Universal Uclick
www.snoopy.com
SCHULZ

ALL RIGHT, LET'S GO! HURRY IT UP, OVER THERE! LET'S GO!
11-19
AS SOON AS OUR TEACHER FINDS I DIDN'T DO A SCIENCE PROJECT, SHE'LL GIVE ME A FAILING GRADE, AND THEN THEY'LL TAKE ME OFF SAFETY PATROL..
STOP
THIS IS THE FIRST TIME I'VE EVER REALLY FELT LIKE I WAS SOMEBODY..I LIKE DOING THIS...I DON'T WANT TO LOSE MY BADGE..I..
WUMP
GOOD GRIEF!
STOP
© 1966 Peanuts Worldwide LLC, Dist. by Universal Uclick
www.snoopy.com

WHAT HAPPENED?
YOU GOT BUMPED BY A CAR, DEAR BROTHER!
YOU MEAN WHILE I WAS ON SAFETY PATROL? I WAS INJURED IN THE LINE OF DUTY?
ME?!
WOW!
11-20
© 1966 Peanuts Worldwide LLC, Dist. by Universal Uclick
www.snoopy.com
SCHULZ

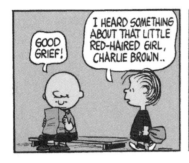

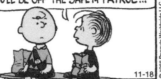

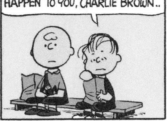

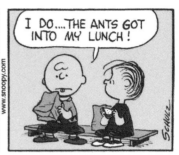

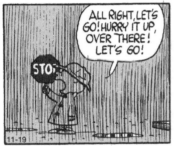

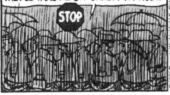

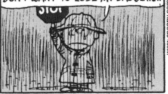

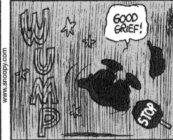

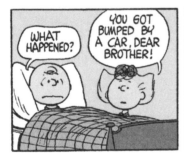

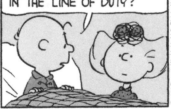

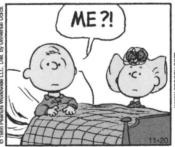

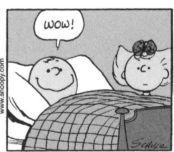

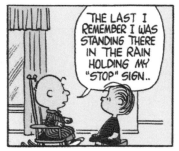

THE LAST I REMEMBER I WAS STANDING THERE IN THE RAIN HOLDING MY "STOP" SIGN..
WELL, THEY SAY THE CAR ONLY BUMPED YOU, CHARLIE BROWN, BUT IT WAS A VERY CLOSE CALL...
11-22
© 1956 Peanuts Worldwide LLC, Dist. by Universal Uclick
ACTUALLY, I FEEL FINE.. I DON'T HAVE A SINGLE PAIN..
I ASKED THAT LITTLE RED-HAIRED GIRL IF SHE WANTED ME TO GIVE YOU ANY MESSAGE...
www.snoopy.com
SHE SAID SHE DIDN'T EVEN REMEMBER WHAT YOU LOOK LIKE!
I HURT ALL OVER!
SCHULZ

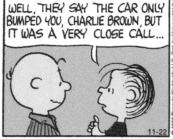

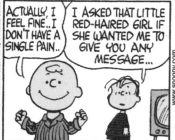

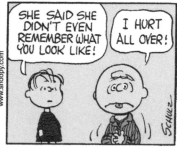

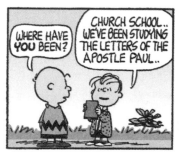

WHERE HAVE **YOU** BEEN?
CHURCH SCHOOL.. WE'VE BEEN STUDYING THE LETTERS OF THE APOSTLE PAUL..
THAT SHOULD BE INTERESTING
IT IS..
11-4
© 1954 Peanuts Worldwide LLC, Dist. by Universal Uclick
ALTHOUGH I MUST ADMIT IT MAKES ME FEEL A LITTLE GUILTY...
www.snoopy.com
I ALWAYS FEEL LIKE I'M READING SOMEONE ELSE'S MAIL!
SCHULZ

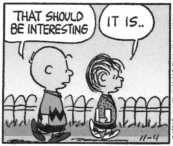

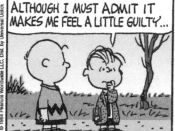

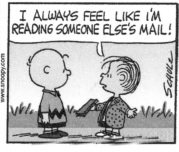

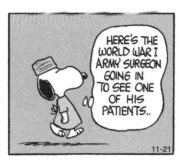

HERE'S THE WORLD WAR I ARMY SURGEON GOING IN TO SEE ONE OF HIS PATIENTS..
11-21
"IT'S A LONG WAY TO TIPPERARY.."
© 1966 Peanuts Worldwide LLC, Dist. by Universal Uclick
SMAK!
www.snoopy.com
I WONDER WHERE HE TOOK HIS RESIDENCY?
SCHULZ

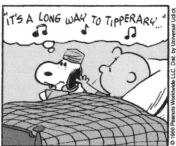

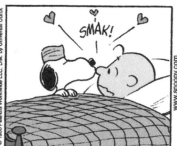

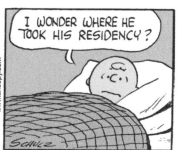

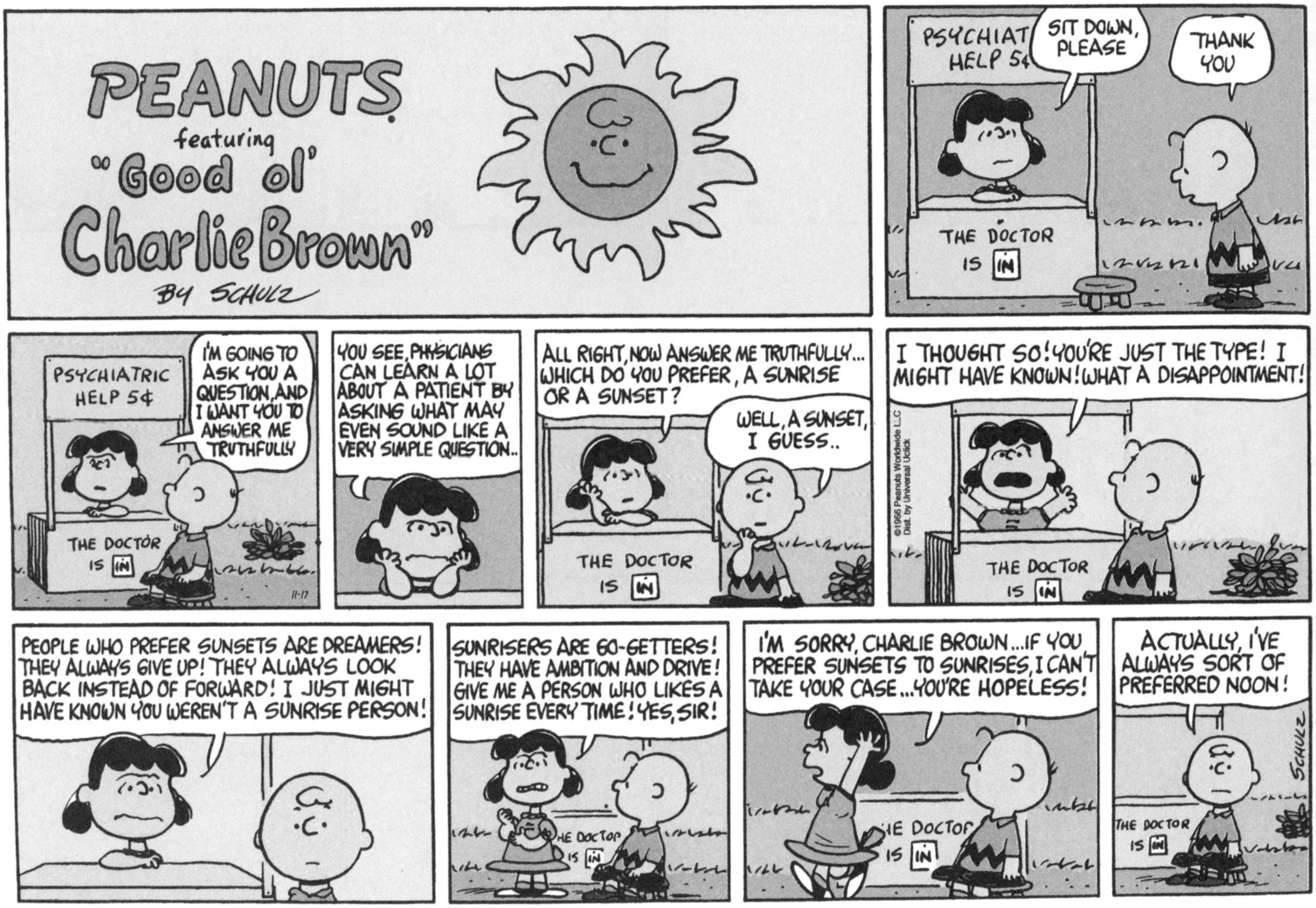
PEANUTS
featuring
"Good ol' Charlie Brown"
BY SCHULZ
PSYCHIATRIC HELP 5¢
SIT DOWN, PLEASE
THANK YOU
THE DOCTOR IS IN
PSYCHIATRIC HELP 5¢
I'M GOING TO ASK YOU A QUESTION, AND I WANT YOU TO ANSWER ME TRUTHFULLY
THE DOCTOR IS IN
YOU SEE, PHYSICIANS CAN LEARN A LOT ABOUT A PATIENT BY ASKING WHAT MAY EVEN SOUND LIKE A VERY SIMPLE QUESTION..
ALL RIGHT, NOW ANSWER ME TRUTHFULLY... WHICH DO YOU PREFER, A SUNRISE OR A SUNSET?
WELL, A SUNSET, I GUESS..
THE DOCTOR IS IN
I THOUGHT SO! YOU'RE JUST THE TYPE! I MIGHT HAVE KNOWN! WHAT A DISAPPOINTMENT!
©1956 Peanuts Worldwide LLC
Dist. by Universal Uclick
THE DOCTOR IS IN
PEOPLE WHO PREFER SUNSETS ARE DREAMERS! THEY ALWAYS GIVE UP! THEY ALWAYS LOOK BACK INSTEAD OF FORWARD! I JUST MIGHT HAVE KNOWN YOU WEREN'T A SUNRISE PERSON!
SUNRISERS ARE GO-GETTERS! THEY HAVE AMBITION AND DRIVE! GIVE ME A PERSON WHO LIKES A SUNRISE EVERY TIME! YES, SIR!
I'M SORRY, CHARLIE BROWN...IF YOU PREFER SUNSETS TO SUNRISES, I CAN'T TAKE YOUR CASE...YOU'RE HOPELESS!
ACTUALLY, I'VE ALWAYS SORT OF PREFERRED NOON!
THE DOCTOR IS IN
SCHULZ

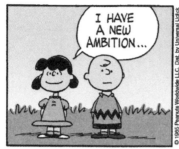

I HAVE A NEW AMBITION...
WHEN I GET BIG, I'D LIKE TO BE A BASEBALL UMPIRE..
WHAT IN THE WORLD MAKES YOU THINK YOU COULD BE A GOOD BASEBALL UMPIRE?
BECAUSE I'M ALWAYS RIGHT!
© 1965 Peanuts Worldwide LLC, Dist. by Universal Uclick
www.snoopy.com
11-23
SCHULZ

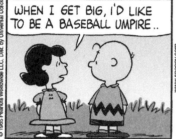

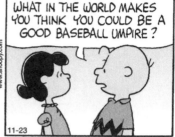

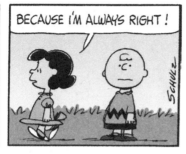

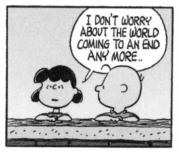

I DON'T WORRY ABOUT THE WORLD COMING TO AN END ANY MORE..
THE WAY I FIGURE IT, THE WORLD CAN'T COME TO AN END TODAY BECAUSE IT IS ALREADY TOMORROW IN SOME OTHER PART OF THE WORLD!
ISN'T THAT A COMFORTING THEORY?
I'VE NEVER FELT SO COMFORTED IN ALL MY LIFE!
www.snoopy.com
11-23
SCHULZ

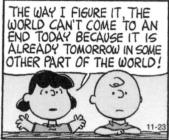

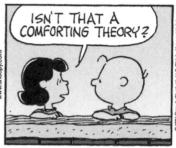

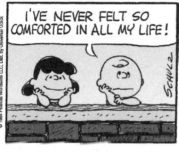

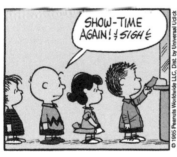

SHOW-TIME AGAIN! SIGH
EVERY SATURDAY AFTERNOON I GO TO THE SHOW...IT'S SURPRISING HOW QUICKLY THE WEEKS GO BY WHEN YOU DO THE SAME THING EVERY SATURDAY
I SHOULD DO SOMETHING DIFFERENT
IT'S MAKING MY LIFE GO BY TOO FAST!
© 1965 Peanuts Worldwide LLC, Dist. by Universal Uclick
www.snoopy.com
11-24
SCHULZ

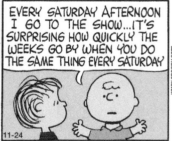

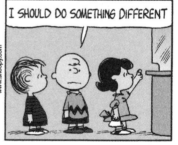

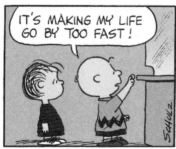

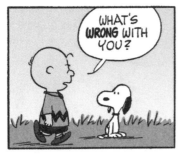

WHAT'S **WRONG** WITH YOU?
OTHER DOGS JUMP UP AND DOWN WHEN THEIR MASTERS COME HOME FROM SCHOOL...
www.snoopy.com
11-25
THAT'S THE MOST SARCASTIC JUMPING UP AND DOWN I'VE EVER SEEN
© 1964 Peanuts Worldwide LLC. Dist. by Universal Uclick
SCHULZ

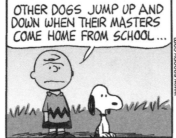

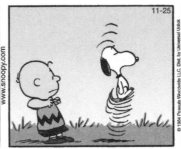

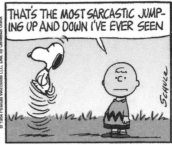

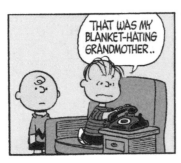

THAT WAS MY BLANKET-HATING GRANDMOTHER..
I WAS TRYING TO EXPLAIN WHY I NEED MY SECURITY BLANKET, BUT I JUST COULDN'T GET THROUGH TO HER..
12-2
© 1966 Peanuts Worldwide LLC. Dist. by Universal Uclick
WAS IT A BAD CONNECTION?
YES
SCHULZ
www.snoopy.com
IT'S ALWAYS DIFFICULT TO TALK FROM ONE GENERATION TO ANOTHER

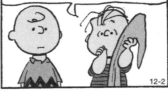

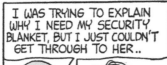

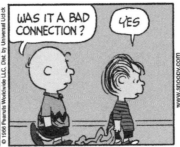

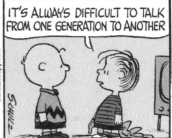

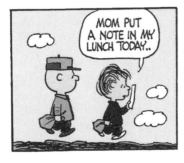

MOM PUT A NOTE IN MY LUNCH TODAY..
"DEAR SON, I HOPE YOU ENJOY THE LUNCH I MADE FOR YOU TODAY.. STUDY HARD...IT IS IMPORTANT TO BE A GOOD STUDENT..."
12-4
© 1966 Peanuts Worldwide LLC. Dist. by Universal Uclick
"HOWEVER, DO NOT NEGLECT YOUR PEER-GROUP RATING"
www.snoopy.com
WHEN SHE WAS YOUNG, MOM NEVER FELT SHE HAD A VERY GOOD PEER-GROUP RATING...
SCHULZ

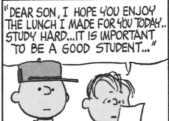

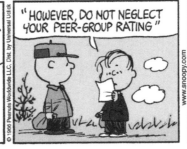

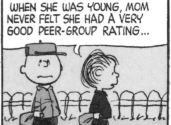

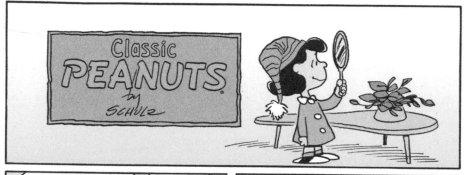

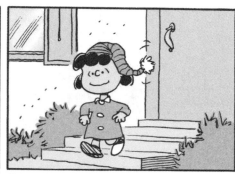

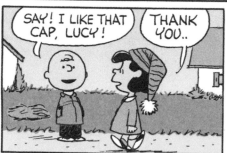

Classic
PEANUTS
by
SCHULZ
SAY! I LIKE THAT CAP, LUCY!
THANK YOU..
YOU'RE ALL SET FOR COLD WEATHER, AREN'T YOU?
YES, I GUESS I AM..
YOU KNOW WHAT IT'S LIKE TO BE COLD AND UNCOMFORTABLE, DON'T YOU?
OH, YES...I KNOW THAT FEELING...
YOU LIKE ANIMALS, DON'T YOU? I MEAN, YOU'VE ALWAYS BEEN SORT OF AN ANIMAL LOVER, HAVEN'T YOU?
OF COURSE!
DOGS, TOO? ESPECIALLY DOGS WHO SLEEP OUTSIDE, AND SHIVER AND SHAKE ALL NIGHT?
SIGH
11/20
© 1964 Peanuts Worldwide LLC
Dist. by Universal Uclick
SCHULZ

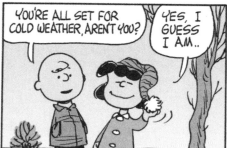

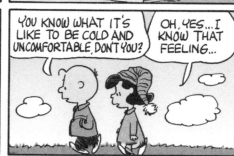

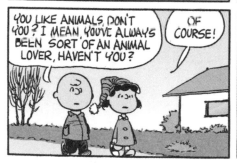

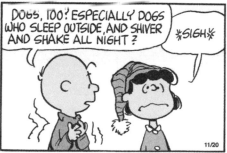

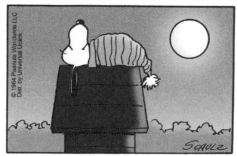

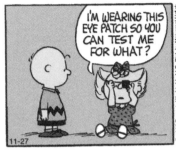

I'M WEARING THIS EYE PATCH SO YOU CAN TEST ME FOR WHAT?
11-27
© 1965 Peanuts Worldwide LLC, Dist. by Universal Uclick
FOR "AMBLYOPIA EX ANOPSIA" OR WHAT IS CALLED "LAZY EYE"
www.snoopy.com
"AMBLYOPIA" REFERS TO DIMNESS OF VISION, AND "EX ANOPSIA" TO THE LACK OF USE WHICH IS RESPONSIBLE FOR THE DIMNESS OF VISION
ARE YOU SURE THIS DOESN'T HAVE SOMETHING TO DO WITH THE "NEW MATH"?
OH, GOOD GRIEF!
SCHULZ

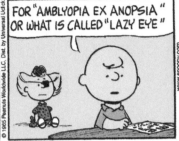

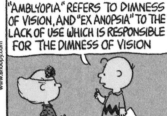

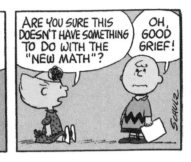

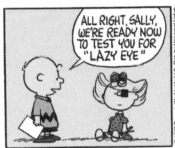

ALL RIGHT, SALLY, WE'RE READY NOW TO TEST YOU FOR "LAZY EYE"
© 1965 Peanuts Worldwide LLC, Dist. by Universal Uclick
I'M GOING TO HOLD UP THIS MODIFIED ILLITERATE "E" CHART, AND I WANT YOU TO..
11-28
www.snoopy.com
ILLITERATE?! I'M NOT ILLITERATE! I'M JUST AS AS GOOD AS ANYONE! I WAS BORN IN THIS COUNTRY!
I EVEN HAVE MY OWN I.Q.! I DIDN'T COME HERE TO BE INSULTED!
SIGH
SCHULZ

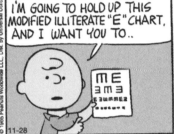

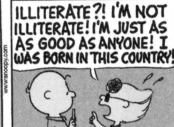

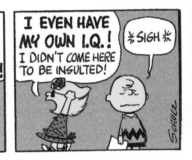

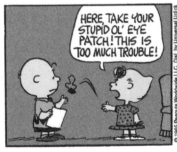

HERE, TAKE YOUR STUPID OL' EYE PATCH! THIS IS TOO MUCH TROUBLE!
© 1965 Peanuts Worldwide LLC, Dist. by Universal Uclick
BUT I HAVE TO TEST YOU FOR AMBLYOPIA EX ANOPSIA...
www.snoopy.com
I DON'T WANT TO BE TESTED FOR AMBLYOPIA EX ANOPSIA OR OOPSY DOOPSY EX FOOPSIA OR ANYTHING ELSE!
OOPSY DOOPSY EX FOOPSIA?!
11-29
SCHULZ

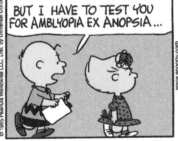

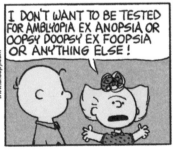

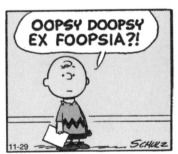

LOOK, LET'S DO THIS EYE TEST WITHOUT THE PATCH.. JUST HOLD YOUR HAND OVER ONE EYE...
© 1965 Peanuts Worldwide LLC, Dist. by Universal Uclick
11-30
NOW, LOOK AT THIS CHART, AND TELL ME WHICH WAY THE "E" IS POINTING.. HOW ABOUT THIS "E"? THIS ONE? NOW, THIS ONE...
www.snoopy.com
ALL RIGHT, NOW COVER THE OTHER EYE, AND TELL ME WHICH WAY THIS "E" IS POINTING...THIS ONE?
HELLO, DOCTOR? I'D LIKE TO MAKE AN APPOINTMENT FOR YOU TO SEE SALLY...
THE WORLD HAS COME TO AN END!
SCHULZ

WELL, I HOPE YOU'RE SATISFIED! I HAVE TO GO SEE AN OPHTHALMOLOGIST!
© 1965 Peanuts Worldwide LLC, Dist. by Universal Uclick
12-1
BUT JUST BECAUSE YOU FAILED OUR HOME EYE TEST, IT DOESN'T MEAN SOMETHING IS DEFINITELY WRONG WITH YOUR EYES...YOU'RE LUCKY YOU'RE GETTING THEM CHECKED...
www.snoopy.com
I SUPPOSE SO, BUT I CAN TELL YOU ONE THING...
I'M NOT GONNA WEAR BIFOCALS!

YOU DID HAVE A "LAZY EYE" DIDN'T YOU?
YES, MY OPHTHALMOLOGIST SAID I HAVE TO WEAR THIS PATCH FOR SIX MONTHS..
© 1965 Peanuts Worldwide LLC, Dist. by Universal Uclick
12-3
BUT JUST THINK...AFTER THAT MY EYE WILL BE ALL RIGHT...HE PUT THE PATCH ON MY GOOD EYE SO THE WEAK ONE WILL WORK HARDER
www.snoopy.com
HOW DO I LOOK WITH AN EYE PATCH?
YOU LOOK FINE...YOU REALLY DO...
I FEEL LIKE AN AD FOR MEN'S SHIRTS!
SCHULZ

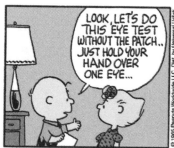

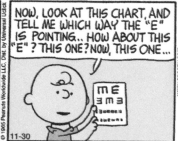

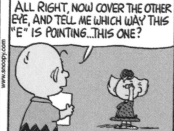

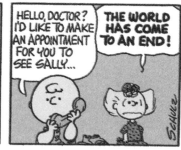

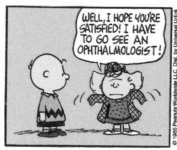

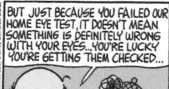

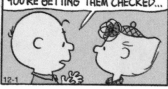

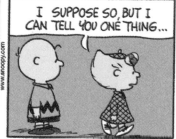

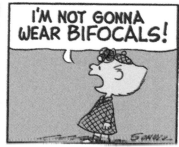

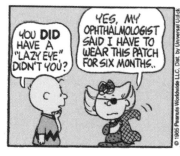

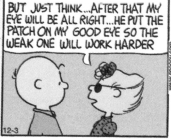

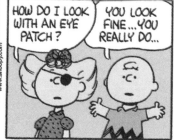

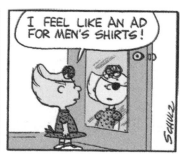

WAAH!
GOOD GRIEF! WHAT'S THE MATTER, SALLY? WHY ARE YOU CRYING?
© 1985 Peanuts Worldwide LLC. Dist. by Universal Uclick
SOME STUPID KID AT SCHOOL WAS TEASING ME ABOUT MY EYE PATCH! HE SAID I LOOKED LIKE "LONG JOHN SILVER"!
12-5
www.snoopy.com
WELL, DON'T LET THAT BOTHER YOU... THIS IS JUST ONE OF THOSE THINGS YOU HAVE TO LEARN TO GET USED TO...
IT ISN'T THAT....I HURT MY HAND GIVING HIM A JUDO CHOP!
SCHULZ

SOME STUPID KID IN SCHOOL TODAY ASKED ME WHY I'M WEARING THIS EYE PATCH..
12-11
© 1985 Peanuts Worldwide LLC. Dist. by Universal Uclick
I SAID TO HIM, "YOU STUPID KID, I'VE BEEN WEARING IT FOR A WEEK, AND YOU'RE JUST NOTICING IT NOW?!" THEN I KNOCKED HIM DOWN!
www.snoopy.com
IT'S STRANGE, THOUGH...
I'M NOT AS SENSITIVE ABOUT THIS EYE PATCH AS I THOUGHT I WAS GOING TO BE!
SCHULZ

Z
BEAGLES ON THE GRASS, ALAS
© 1960 Peanuts Worldwide LLC. Dist. by Universal Uclick
www.snoopy.com
SCHULZ
12-5
I AIN'T NO STUPID BEAGLE!

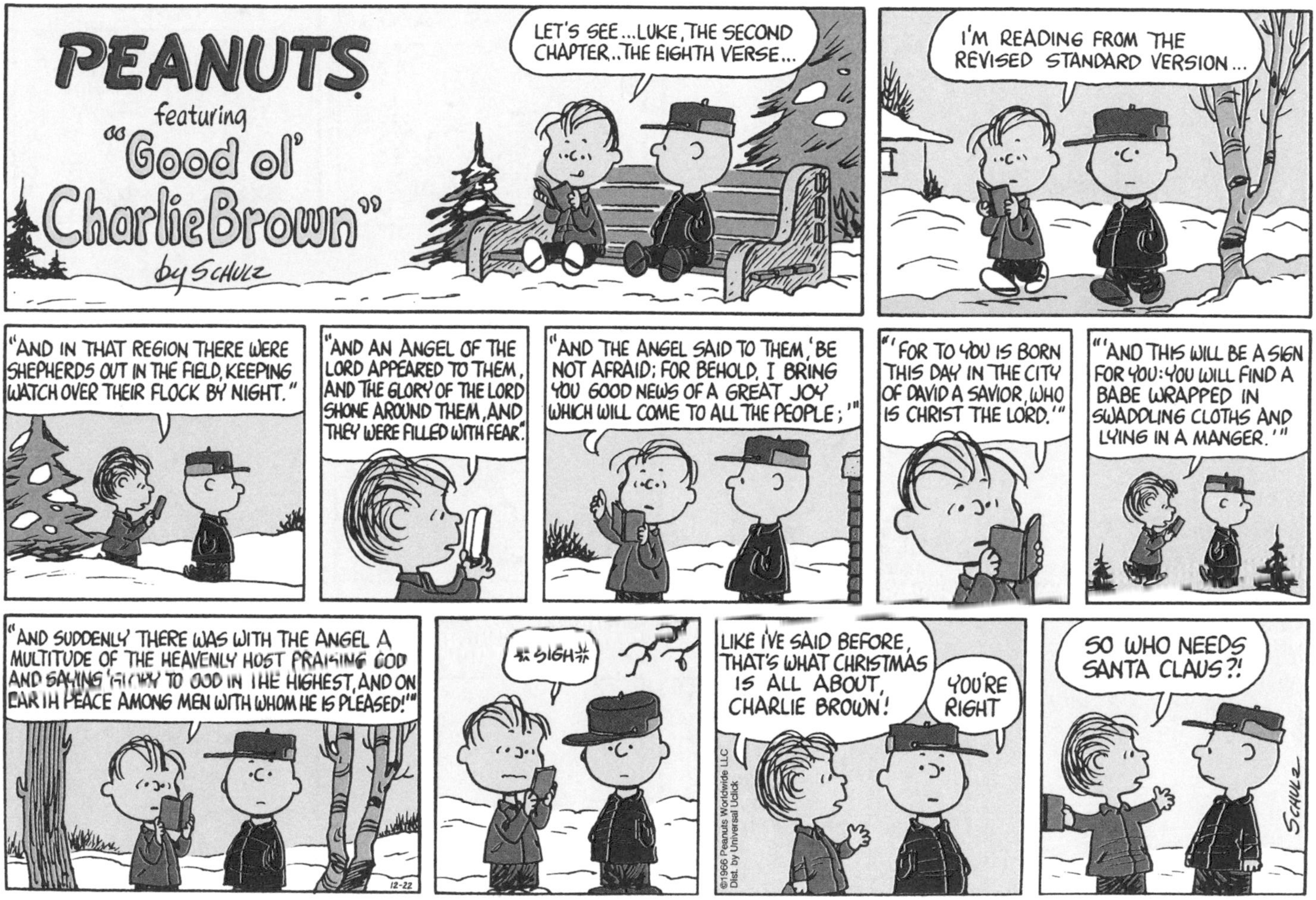
PEANUTS
featuring
"Good ol' Charlie Brown"
by SCHULZ
LET'S SEE...LUKE, THE SECOND CHAPTER..THE EIGHTH VERSE...
I'M READING FROM THE REVISED STANDARD VERSION...
"AND IN THAT REGION THERE WERE SHEPHERDS OUT IN THE FIELD, KEEPING WATCH OVER THEIR FLOCK BY NIGHT."
"AND AN ANGEL OF THE LORD APPEARED TO THEM, AND THE GLORY OF THE LORD SHONE AROUND THEM, AND THEY WERE FILLED WITH FEAR."
"AND THE ANGEL SAID TO THEM, 'BE NOT AFRAID; FOR BEHOLD, I BRING YOU GOOD NEWS OF A GREAT JOY WHICH WILL COME TO ALL THE PEOPLE;'"
"'FOR TO YOU IS BORN THIS DAY IN THE CITY OF DAVID A SAVIOR, WHO IS CHRIST THE LORD.'"
"'AND THIS WILL BE A SIGN FOR YOU: YOU WILL FIND A BABE WRAPPED IN SWADDLING CLOTHS AND LYING IN A MANGER.'"
"AND SUDDENLY THERE WAS WITH THE ANGEL A MULTITUDE OF THE HEAVENLY HOST PRAISING GOD AND SAYING 'GLORY TO GOD IN THE HIGHEST, AND ON EARTH PEACE AMONG MEN WITH WHOM HE IS PLEASED!'"
12-22
SIGH
©1966 Peanuts Worldwide LLC
Dist. by Universal Uclick
LIKE I'VE SAID BEFORE, THAT'S WHAT CHRISTMAS IS ALL ABOUT, CHARLIE BROWN!
YOU'RE RIGHT
SO WHO NEEDS SANTA CLAUS?!
SCHULZ

MY STOMACH HURTS
SPEAKING OF STOMACHS...AREN'T YOU GAINING A LITTLE WEIGHT?
12-6
© 1966 Peanuts Worldwide LLC. Dist. by Universal Uclick
YES, I GUESS I AM... MAYBE THAT'S MY TROUBLE...
www.snoopy.com
MAYBE I'M HAVING **FAT** PAINS!
SCHULZ

12-10
© 1965 Peanuts Worldwide LLC. Dist. by Universal Uclick
ONLY 6 DAYS UNTIL BEETHOVEN'S BIRTHDAY
ELEVEN DAYS TO THE FIRST DAY OF WINTER
ONLY 12 SHOPPING DAYS UNTIL CHRISTMAS
www.snoopy.com
IT'S UNUSUAL FOR ONE AGENCY TO HAVE ALL THREE ACCOUNTS!
SCHULZ

12-14
ONLY TWO MORE DAYS UNTIL BEETHOVEN'S BIRTHDAY!
© 1966 Peanuts Worldwide LLC. Dist. by Universal Uclick
www.snoopy.com
THIS ANNOUNCEMENT VOID WHERE PROHIBITED BY LAW
SCHULZ

THAT LITTLE RED-HAIRED GIRL IS SURE CUTE..
I'D GIVE ANYTHING IN THE WORLD TO BE SITTING THERE NEXT TO HER EATING LUNCH..
www.snoopy.com
12-13
BLEAH!
© 1964 Peanuts Worldwide LLC, Dist. by Universal Uclick
NOTHING TAKES THE TASTE OUT OF PEANUT BUTTER LIKE UNREQUITED LOVE!
SCHULZ

WHY DON'T I GO OVER AND TALK TO THAT LITTLE RED-HAIRED GIRL?
I CAN'T... I JUST CAN'T...
www.snoopy.com
I HATE MYSELF FOR NOT HAVING ENOUGH NERVE TO TALK TO HER!
12-14
© 1964 Peanuts Worldwide LLC, Dist. by Universal Uclick
WELL, THAT ISN'T EXACTLY TRUE...I HATE MYSELF FOR A LOT OF OTHER REASONS, TOO...
SCHULZ

IF I WERE YOU, CHARLIE BROWN, I'D FORGET THAT LITTLE RED-HAIRED GIRL..YOU'RE NOT HER KIND..
WHO'S KIND AM I?
NOW, THAT'S A GOOD QUESTION! YES, SIR, THAT'S A VERY GOOD QUESTION!
12-15
www.snoopy.com
BOY, YOU'VE SURE GOT ME THERE.. WHO'S KIND ARE YOU? WOW! THAT'S A REAL STICKLER!
© 1964 Peanuts Worldwide LLC, Dist. by Universal Uclick
THAT'S A PUZZLER IF I EVER HEARD ONE! YES, SIR! THAT'S A ROUGH ONE! THAT'S A POSER! THAT'S A..
OH, GOOD GRIEF!
SCHULZ

I FEEL GUILTY ABOUT THE WAY I FEED SNOOPY...HIS MEALS ARE SO DRAB...
12-17
© 1966 Peanuts Worldwide LLC, Dist. by Universal Uclick
I SHOULD DO SOMETHING TO MAKE HIS MEALS MORE INTERESTING..
Dog Food
www.snoopy.com
SCHULZ

READY?
12-17
© 1965 Peanuts Worldwide LLC, Dist. by Universal Uclick
READY?
READY?
www.snoopy.com
READY
SCHULZ

12-19
SHOVEL YOUR WALK?
© 1966 Peanuts Worldwide LLC, Dist. by Universal Uclick
YOU?
www.snoopy.com
I NEVER KNOW HOW TO ANSWER THOSE ONE-WORD QUESTIONS...
SCHULZ

GOOD GRIEF! I JUST REMEMBERED SOMETHING!
WE'RE SUPPOSED TO READ "GULLIVER'S TRAVELS" DURING CHRISTMAS VACATION, AND WRITE A REPORT ON IT! HAVE YOU STARTED YET?
www.snoopy.com
STARTED? I DID MINE RIGHT AWAY SO I WOULDN'T HAVE TO WORRY ABOUT IT DURING VACATION
12-23
© 1964 Peanuts Worldwide LLC, Dist. by Universal Uclick
I HATE YOUR KIND!
SCHULZ

PSYCHIATF HELP
THE WHOLE TROUBLE WITH YOU IS THAT YOU'RE WISHY-WASHY
THE DOCTOR IS IN
WHAT'S THE DIFFERENCE BETWEEN BEING WISHY-WASHY AND BEING HUMBLE?
© 1966 Peanuts Worldwide LLC, Dist. by Universal Uclick
YOU ARE WISHY-WASHY....
THE DOCTOR IS IN
12-26
www.snoopy.com
I AM HUMBLE!
THE DOCTOR IS IN
SCHULZ

YOU KNOW WHAT WE OUGHT TO DO, SNOOPY?
© 1965 Peanuts Worldwide LLC, Dist. by Universal Uclick
WE OUGHT TO GET A HARNESS FOR YOU SO WE COULD HITCH YOU TO MY SLED, AND GO RACING ACROSS THE FIELDS OF SNOW!
12-27
www.snoopy.com
HA!
I THOUGHT IT WAS A PRETTY GOOD IDEA..
SCHULZ

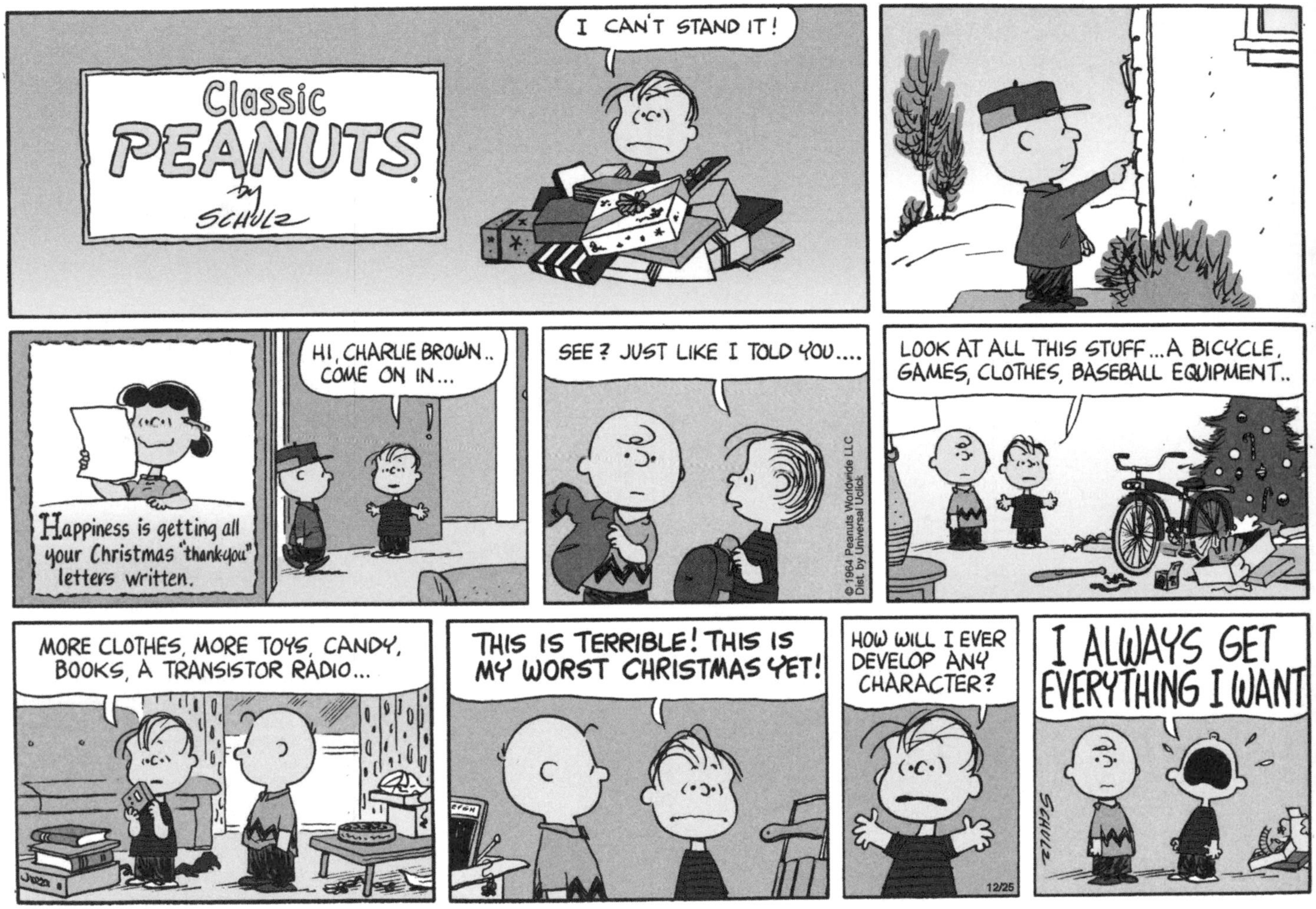
Classic PEANUTS by SCHULZ
I CAN'T STAND IT!
Happiness is getting all your Christmas "thank-you" letters written.
HI, CHARLIE BROWN.. COME ON IN...
!
SEE? JUST LIKE I TOLD YOU....
© 1964 Peanuts Worldwide LLC
Dist. by Universal Uclick
LOOK AT ALL THIS STUFF...A BICYCLE, GAMES, CLOTHES, BASEBALL EQUIPMENT..
MORE CLOTHES, MORE TOYS, CANDY, BOOKS, A TRANSISTOR RADIO...
THIS IS TERRIBLE! THIS IS MY WORST CHRISTMAS YET!
HOW WILL I EVER DEVELOP ANY CHARACTER?
12/25
I ALWAYS GET EVERYTHING I WANT
SCHULZ

"ON THE FIRST DAY OF CHRISTMAS..
..MY TRUE LOVE GAVE TO ME....
A PARTRIDGE IN A PEAR TREEEEEEE..."
Merry Christmas!
SCHULZ
12-24
www.snoopy.com
© 1964 Peanuts Worldwide LLC. Dist. by Universal Uclick

MERRY CHRISTMAS, CHARLIE BROWN!
AT THIS TIME OF YEAR I THINK WE SHOULD PUT ASIDE ALL OUR DIFFERENCES, AND TRY TO BE KIND
WHY DOES IT HAVE TO BE FOR JUST THIS TIME OF YEAR? WHY CAN'T IT BE ALL YEAR 'ROUND?
WHAT ARE YOU, SOME KIND OF FANATIC OR SOMETHING?
SCHULZ
12-25
www.snoopy.com
© 1965 Peanuts Worldwide LLC. Dist. by Universal Uclick

WELL, LINUS, WHAT DID YOU GET FOR CHRISTMAS?
OH, LOTS OF THINGS..
I GOT A NEW BICYCLE, A RECORD PLAYER, AN ELECTRIC TRAIN, SOME MONEY, SOME MITTENS, A SCOUT KNIFE, A SKI JACKET, A MYSTERY GAME, SOME PUZZLES, FOUR SPORT SHIRTS AND A RACING CAR...
AND YOU KNOW WHAT ELSE I GOT?
GUILT FEELINGS, THAT'S WHAT I GOT!!
SCHULZ
12-26
www.snoopy.com
© 1965 Peanuts Worldwide LLC. Dist. by Universal Uclick

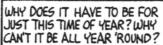

NEXT YEAR I'M GOING TO BE A CHANGED PERSON!
THAT'S A LAUGH, CHARLIE BROWN
© 1965 Peanuts Worldwide LLC. Dist. by Universal Uclick
12-28
I MEAN IT! I'M GOING TO BE STRONG AND FIRM..
FORGET IT..YOU'LL ALWAYS BE WISHY-WASHY!
www.snoopy.com
WHY CAN'T I CHANGE JUST A LITTLE BIT?
I'LL BE WISHY ONE DAY AND WASHY THE NEXT!
SCHULZ

CHRISTMAS VACATION IS ALMOST OVER..
I STILL HAVEN'T WRITTEN MY BOOK REPORT ON "GULLIVER'S TRAVELS"... I HAVEN'T EVEN STARTED TO READ IT YET!
12-27
www.snoopy.com
WHY DON'T I GET STARTED? WHY DO I PUT THINGS OFF?
© 1964 Peanuts Worldwide LLC. Dist. by Universal Uclick
WHAT'S WRONG WITH ME?
SCHULZ

"GULLIVER'S TRAVELS...PART ONE...CHAPTER ONE..."
"MY FATHER HAD A SMALL ESTATE IN NOTTINGHAMSHIRE; I WAS THE THIRD OF FIVE SONS. HE SENT ME TO..."
12-28
www.snoopy.com
GOOD GRIEF! THIS BOOK HAS TWO HUNDRED AND FIFTY-FOUR PAGES
© 1964 Peanuts Worldwide LLC. Dist. by Universal Uclick
SCHULZ
I'LL START READING IT TOMORROW...

12-29
I SHOULDN'T BE OUTSIDE PLAYING LIKE THIS...
I SHOULD BE INSIDE READING "GULLIVER'S TRAVELS" AND WRITING A BOOK REPORT...
www.snoopy.com
IT'S GOOD FOR YOU TO BE OUTSIDE, THOUGH...YOU NEED THE FRESH AIR..
YOU'RE RIGHT.. I DO!
© 1964 Peanuts Worldwide LLC, Dist. by Universal Uclick
GOOD OL' WISHY-WASHY CHARLIE BROWN..
SCHULZ

12-30
YOU SHOULDN'T BE WATCHING TV! YOU SHOULD BE READING "GULLIVER'S TRAVELS"
EVEN MY LITTLE SISTER BUGS ME
BUT VACATION'S ALMOST OVER! SCHOOL-TIME WILL SOON BE ROLLING AROUND
www.snoopy.com
SCHOOL-TIME DOESN'T "ROLL AROUND"...
© 1965 Peanuts Worldwide LLC, Dist. by Universal Uclick
IT LEAPS RIGHT OUT AT YOU!
SCHULZ

"GULLIVER'S TRAVELS.... PART ONE... CHAPTER ONE.."
RATS! I CAN'T READ A BOOK ON A SATURDAY....I STILL HAVE TOMORROW TO READ IT.. WHY DON'T I WAIT UNTIL TOMORROW?
www.snoopy.com
12-31
I CAN READ IT TOMORROW AFTERNOON, AND WRITE THE REPORT TOMORROW EVENING.. WHY WASTE A GOOD DAY LIKE TODAY?
© 1965 Peanuts Worldwide LLC, Dist. by Universal Uclick
I WAS GOING TO SAY SOMETHING, BUT I CHANGED MY MIND!
SCHULZ

YOU KNOW WHAT?
WHAT?
ANOTHER YEAR HAS COME AND GONE
AAUGH!
ACTUALLY, I SUPPOSE THAT'S A PRETTY NORMAL REACTION..